T0339034

WEAPON OF CHOICE

WEAPON OF CHOICE

**FIGHTING
GUN VIOLENCE
WHILE RESPECTING
GUN RIGHTS**

IAN AYRES & FREDRICK E. VARS

Harvard University Press
Cambridge, Massachusetts
London, England
2020

First printing

Library of Congress Cataloging-in-Publication Data

Names: Ayres, Ian, 1959– author. | Vars, Fredrick E., author.
Title: Weapon of choice : fighting gun violence while respecting gun rights /
    Ian Ayres and Fredrick E. Vars.
Description: Cambridge, Massachusetts : Harvard University Press, 2020. |
    Includes bibliographical references and index.
Identifiers: LCCN 2020013935 | ISBN 9780674241091 (hardcover)
Subjects: LCSH: Gun control—United States. | Firearms ownership—United States. |
    Suicide prevention—United States.
Classification: LCC HV7436 .A96 2020 | DDC 363.330973—dc23
LC record available at https://lccn.loc.gov/2020013935

To Charlotte, Adam, and Caroline
FEV

To Jennifer Gerarda Brown
IA

CONTENTS

Preface: Fred's Story   ix

Introduction   1

Part I: Empowering Self-Restriction   11
1 Donna's Law   13
2 Analogies, Choices, and Constraints   26
3 Laboratories of Democracy   39

Part II: Harnessing Others' Association Preferences   59
4 Emails and the Associational Marketplace   61
5 Libertarian Contracting and Its Limits   72
6 Privatizing Gun-Free Zones   80

Part III: Harnessing Others' Information   101
7 Symptom-Based Gun Removal Orders   103
8 Unlawful Possession Petitions   120
9 Incentivizing Disclosure   153

Appendixes   169
Notes   187
Acknowledgments   233
Index   235

PREFACE: FRED'S STORY

I once escaped from a locked psychiatric ward. My wife, Caroline, was a few minutes late for visiting hours. I lived for her visits. I stood casually near the entrance at the line that patients were not supposed to cross. A group of doctors headed for the staff entrance on the other side of the line. Not pausing to look back at the glass nurses' station, I followed. I caught the door just before it closed and held it cracked open until the noise from the doctors disappeared.

I went down one floor and found the public elevators. I pressed both the up and down buttons. I figured she might be going up, and I might catch her that way. Amazingly, when the doors of the next elevator opened, there was Caroline, who was shocked to see me outside the locked ward. I pleaded to go home with her. She persuaded me to go back upstairs.

It was a hard sell. The euphoric early days of my mania had been replaced by paranoia. I had decided that one of my fellow patients was the devil. I often wandered the ward at night. One time the staff couldn't quiet me, so they called security. The guards tried to convince me to step into the TV room. No doubt they wanted to get the noise out of the hallway. I was sure they were going to sodomize me with nightsticks. But the worst moment by far was when I saw (or thought I saw) the second hand stop on the wall clock in the cafeteria. In my mind, this meant that my wife would never come back, and I would be stuck on the psych ward forever. I'd have rather died.

Eventually, I recovered enough that they let me out, this time through the front door. I sank into a deep depression. It was months before I could go back to work full time. Because I feared hurting myself, I stayed away from the apartment windows and kitchen knives. Since that time, I have been back on the psych ward only once more, with another manic episode, confirming my diagnosis of bipolar disorder.

After that second hospitalization, I've been healthy enough to succeed in my career as a law professor, to sustain my marriage, and to raise two happy children. My relatively stable mental health is partly due to good luck—medications are effective for me—and partly due to excellent psychiatrists, a wise therapist, and, more than anyone else, Caroline, who has been my bedrock. But nothing and no one could keep me healthy if I did not take care of myself: I take the meds, I schedule the appointments, I listen to my doctors, therapist, and wife, I exercise, I keep a routine. I even changed my career.

I still suffer from depressive episodes (including at times while writing this book), sometimes intense, but before being awarded tenure I managed to keep my diagnosis a secret from my dean and colleagues. I might never have disclosed it publicly but for an unlikely hunting trip.

I had been invited to participate in a Second Amendment symposium at the University of Connecticut Law School, and I was casting about for a topic. By chance, I went to hear Justice Elena Kagan speak at my law school at the University of Alabama. Justice Kagan spoke about wanting to better understand other perspectives on gun rights. To that end, she asked the late Justice Antonin Scalia to take her hunting. He did, and they ended up hunting together several times.

Somehow while I was listening to that story, a lightbulb switched on: the government should let people who fear suicide suspend their own ability to buy a gun. I immediately saw the appeal of self-restriction for someone like me who has had moments of suicidality but who has many more moments of lucidity. The idea came from my own personal experiences, but my research confirmed that suicide is often impulsive and that restricting access to firearms works.

But would anyone sign up? To find out, three coauthors and I designed a survey and administered it to two hundred psychiatric patients. I thought a fair number of people like me would be willing to sign up; my coauthors were less optimistic. What we discovered shocked us: nearly half of respondents said they would sign up. That was the moment I realized that if the idea were actually implemented, it could save many lives. Our advocacy work began in earnest.

After some success and more failure in the legislative arena, I finally realized the persuasive power of a personal story. And so I publicly disclosed my diagnosis for the first time in a hot, overcrowded hearing room in the Massachusetts State House:

> House Bill 3611 would allow people who fear suicide to put distance between themselves and firearms.
>
> The greatest virtue of the bill is that it is voluntary. No one is affected who doesn't want to be. It is not gun control; it is self-control.
>
> But a voluntary program is effective only if people volunteer. What if the Commonwealth of Massachusetts passes the bill, but no one signs up?
>
> That's not going to happen. I know this for personal and empirical reasons.
>
> I have bipolar disorder. I've been suicidal. I want to sign up.
>
> Fifteen percent of people with bipolar disorder die by suicide. If I had had easy access to a gun at certain points in my life, I'd already be one of them.
>
> People who have never been severely depressed cannot understand what it's like. You lose joy, you lose hope, and you lose the ability to make rational decisions.

However, like almost all people with mental illness, I have periods of clarity. During these periods, I want to protect myself against future dark days.

Gun policy and mental health look different from the inside. Mental illness is powerful, but people with mental illness are not powerless. Our proposals reflect that perspective and build on the notion that the government can reduce gun deaths by creating new choices for all individuals, with and without mental illness. Empowering people to take care of themselves and each other can save lives and expand liberty at the same time.

—FEV

INTRODUCTION

The problem of gun violence is enormous, but as of 2020 the political pendulum has begun to swing in favor of solutions, at least at the state level. Nearly 40,000 people in the United States died from a firearm-related injury in 2016.[1] Well over half of those were suicides. This accounts for an outsized proportion of violent gun deaths globally. The United States had 4.3 percent of the world's population in 2016, but 35.3 percent of firearm suicides and 23.1 percent of firearm homicides.[2] In 2017 firearms were the leading cause of death for black children and teens.[3] The high level of gun violence in this country is not inevitable—it is unique among developed countries.

Gun policy is, however, constrained by law and politics. Some policies—like a complete gun ban—would violate the Second Amendment. And even clearly constitutional, commonsense proposals to reduce gun violence have faced stiff political headwinds. The federal government has not passed major gun legislation in many years.[4] Only after the February 2018 shooting at a high school in Parkland, Florida, has there been significant movement at the state level—especially with the passage that year of red flag statutes in eight states.[5]

This book builds on that momentum by proposing new kinds of interventions, which we call "choice-enhancing" gun control. This approach has two central attributes: it is decentralized, and it tends to expand individuals' freedom. Traditional gun control is top-down state control. The government decides which guns and people should be restricted, then attempts to enforce these restrictions. For example, a traditional command-and-control approach would mandate that everyone must purchase a safety lock or that no one may purchase a bump stock.

Our proposals instead empower people. The bottom-up approach first searches for individual members of society who have sufficient information and incentives to take action to reduce gun violence. It then tries to give these decentralized actors new choices. Our choice-enhancing proposals are thus deeply libertarian. Instead of imposing one-size-fits-all rules on society, they give individuals the liberty to reduce the risk of gun violence. This book shows how inviting participation and expanding and restructuring personal choices can reduce gun violence.

This approach is not a panacea. And it should not replace all traditional prohibitions and mandates. But our proposed interventions are a powerful complement to existing regulations. Libertarian gun control is not an oxymoron. This book provides a blueprint of how to make progress on gun violence without offending either the Supreme Court's current interpretation of the Second Amendment or the general public's sense of justice. One of our core proposals (voluntary self-restriction) has already passed on a bipartisan basis in one state and has been introduced in nine others, including red states like Alabama, Louisiana, and Tennessee. In other words, there are reasons to think our core ideas might actually be implemented. This book is not a fanciful wish list; it is a to-do list.

We apply the bottom-up ideas of libertarian decentralization to propose ten different policies that could be adopted at the state level. You may not like all of the proposals. But they do not rise and fall together. They are modular. Reasonable readers might embrace some, reject others, and amend or modify still others to their liking.

The first, and most important, gun control proposal is a kind of self-control. Part 1 (comprising Chapters 1 to 3) explains and justifies a voluntary self-restriction proposal, Donna's Law, whereby individuals would be empowered to temporarily suspend their ability either to purchase or to purchase and possess firearms. Donna's Law gives people a new choice that they have not had before—the option to cede their Second Amendment rights. Prior research demonstrates that even a short delay in gun acquisition can reduce suicide, and findings presented here for the first time demonstrate that a large percentage of the population would self-restrict in this manner.

Donna's Law is one of the few measures that is particularly focused on reining in the tragedy of gun suicides. The public's attention is consumed with the 300 or 400 lives lost annually to mass shootings, but gun suicides claim more than fifty times this number year after year.[6] Banning high-capacity magazines will have no impact on the 20,000 Americans who kill themselves with guns each year. Our surveys show that people who have been previously diagnosed with mental illness are particularly likely to durably waive their right to bear arms. Donna's Law allows these people, and anyone else, to take action to protect themselves.

Many lives could be saved without any new government mandate. Washington State enacted a version of Donna's Law on a bipartisan basis, and bills have been introduced in many other states. Our survey finds that well over 60 percent of the general population support the proposal, including a majority of gun owners. In Chapter 3, we offer an insider's look into the legislative process as a case study in lawmaking, and also as a road map for advocates in other states. Appendix B presents an authorizing statute that can also serve as model legislation.

Part 2 (comprising Chapters 4 to 6) then makes the case for four additional interventions that can enhance associational freedom. The law can also enhance people's freedom by giving them better ability to make more informed associational choices. While the title of this book, *Weapon of Choice*, might initially strike readers as referring solely to the choice that people make to disarm themselves, Part 2 shows how other people's choices can also lead to disarmament. It focuses on harnessing others' associational preferences, which gives non–gun owners an ability to make better-informed associational choices. People can defend themselves not just by arming themselves, but by choosing not to associate with others who are armed.

Part 2 explores how something as simple as an email option can help create an associational marketplace. At the time of registering to waive gun rights with the Donna's Law platform discussed in Part 1, individuals should also have the option of entering the email addresses of people whom they would like the registry to contact verifying that they have waived their Second Amendment rights (as well as notifying those contacts if they subsequently move to rescind that waiver). Chapter 4 describes how the email option could operate to level the evidentiary playing field, making it easier for a landlord or loved one to verify that you are unarmed.

Properly structured, an email option can make the Second Amendment right to bear arms contend with the First Amendment associational rights of others. As Justice John Paul Stevens recognized in *McDonald v. Chicago:*

> In evaluating an asserted right to be free from particular gun-control regulations, liberty is on both sides of the equation. Guns may be useful for self-defense, as well as for hunting and sport, but they also have a unique potential to facilitate death and destruction and thereby to destabilize ordered liberty. *Your* interest in keeping and bearing a certain firearm may diminish *my* interest in being and feeling safe from armed violence.[7]

The associational choices of landlords, insurers, friends, and neighbors can appropriately induce the disarmament of others. Chapter 5 explores the legal and moral limits to associational markets and describes how we would limit associational discrimination by economic actors to those with plausible self-defense interests. We include in Appendix B a model of this associational marketplace extension of Donna's Law.

Chapter 6 then applies the idea of associational choice to owners of real property. While state and federal law have out-lawed carrying guns to dozens of different kinds of places, such as schools, sports arenas, and parks, our laws have not sufficiently empowered private property owners to render their homes and businesses gun free. In most states, a houseguest or refrigerator repair person is free to carry a (possibly concealed) firearm onto your property unless you explicitly object. The bizarre inefficiency of the law can be seen in many rural areas where landowners need to have "posted" signs at regular intervals on the border of their property to stop armed strangers from legally entering their land and hunting. An easy fix would be to follow the lead of South Carolina and Alaska and flip the default to what most people want. Carrying a firearm onto someone else's property should be criminal trespass unless the property owner explicitly consents. This chapter also describes how property law can be used to allow property owners to create durable gun-free zones. Inspired by the creative "land buyback" of the Westport, Missouri, business district, we propose a mechanism where a supermajority of residents could privatize the streets and sidewalks in their neighborhood to render the neighborhood a gun-free zone.

Part 3 (comprising Chapters 7 to 9) continues our decentral-izing project, but with a focus on informational choice. These chapters detail how, instead of harnessing associational prefer-ences, we can better harness dispersed knowledge of ordinary citizens to promote gun safety. Chapter 7 begins by describing how red flag statutes represent an important evolution of gun reg-ulation related to mental health. In large part, this is an evolu-tion from diagnosis- and treatment-based restrictions toward symptom-based restriction. Instead of prohibiting people who have been diagnosed with a mental health disorder or who have been treated with involuntary commitment from purchasing or owning guns, red flag statutes are focused on symptoms that are associated with dangerousness. Department of Motor Vehicles procedures provide a motivating analogy. The eye exam prerequisite for a driver's license does not diagnose *why* you can't see (or suggest a treatment); it is sufficient to restrict your driving rights that your poor sight is a symptom that indicates driving dangerousness. Seeing the analogous symptom-based nature of red flag adjudication allows us to expand and decentralize the process. Like a failed eye exam, some violence-related symptoms should be sufficient in and of themselves to warrant gun removal. Specifically, we argue that paranoid delusions and threatening hallucinations have ample evidence-based indicia of risk to justify temporary gun removal orders. An appreciation of symptom-based restriction makes it easier to train a wider proportion of the populace to look for warning signs of these risks. Relying solely on treatment- and diagnosis-based restrictions can create bottlenecks where mental health workers are unable to reach large parts of the population. But just as eye exams can be conducted by a broader swath of minimally trained people, succinct validated questionnaires can be administered by police (or employers or schools) to better assess when to raise a red flag.

Chapter 8 proposes a new form of gun removal petition to confiscate guns from unlawful possessors. We estimate that more than 20 percent of Americans are disqualified from owning firearms, but millions of these Americans nonetheless possess them. We document how federal and state efforts to disarm unlawful possessors have been sorely lacking. Private individuals are often well placed to come forward to protect themselves and their community from such contraband ownership. A well-crafted "unlawful possession" petition process can usefully complement domestic violence and red flag petition processes. Unlawful possession adjudication is in some ways an extension of our symptom-based restriction idea, because the state would be removing guns from individuals who fall into categories that by statute have been deemed too dangerous to bear arms.

Our unlawful possession petitions are also freedom enhancing because they give community members a new choice—the option to trigger a process that can lead to a gun removal order. The confiscation of the gun does not burden the respondent's freedom, because the unlawful possessor—say, the underage teen or felon—had no legal right to possess the gun in the first place.

We also propose that these petition processes be integrated with the federal background check system (the National Instant Criminal Background Check System, or NICS). Anyone subject to a red flag or unlawful possession removal order should have their name entered automatically in the background check database so that they will be prevented from reacquiring guns from gun dealers. Bizarrely, several states with red flag statutes do not alert NICS when a person becomes subject to a gun removal order.

Finally, Part 3 proposes to modernize the prohibited possession categories and better incentivize red flag and unlawful possession petitions. Chapter 8 describes how states can tailor the unlawful possession petition to exclude categories of individuals (such as recreational cannabis users) who have not been shown to have elevated risk of gun misuse. More importantly, it identifies six additional categories of people (such as anyone convicted of a DUI, DWI, or other alcohol-related offense) that have been empirically shown to pose firearm risks. These categories should be adopted as "state prohibitors" that not only bar included individuals from purchase and possession, but also make them potential respondents in unlawful possession adjudications. And in addition to subjecting the unlawful possession categories to better evidence-based tailoring, we propose enhanced incentives to better encourage informed citizens to come forward with petition-relevant information. Specifically, Chapter 9 describes not only how gun bounties for providing unlawful possession evidence can incentivize gun removal, but also how bounties have, in a variety of trial programs, resulted in the forfeiture of other forms of contraband, including illicit drugs and money. We also argue that red flag regulations should incorporate mandatory disclosure of symptomatic risk by employers, colleges, and other organizations that are likely at times to have knowledge of the behavior of members of their community. Unleashing the siloed knowledge of individuals and organizations can further the straightforward and broadly supported public health goal of disarming high-risk individuals.

Our title, *Weapon of Choice,* thus captures the substance of many of our proposals. Giving people new choices can lead them to disarm themselves, or to unleash their preferences or information in ways that disarm others. But policies that expand choice can also be rhetorically disarming to both sides of this issue. Liberty-loving gun rights advocates are hard pressed to oppose the rights of property owners to do what they will with their land or to oppose the rights of individuals to choose not to carry a firearm. In some states, even the National Rifle Association has not risen to object to Donna's Law.

Likewise, gun control advocates can get behind the proposals in this book without demonizing their opposition. We are not trying to "weaponize" choice in order to eliminate responsible gun ownership. We respect the fact that millions of law-abiding Americans cherish the right to keep and bear arms. Their choices count as much as the choices of others to disarm or to be in gun-free environments. In a policy space riven by political division and deadlock, liberty-enhancing gun control that better brings to bear the choices of all Americans can forge new coalitions of support.

We emphasize decentralized choice not merely because it makes our proposals more politically palatable. Decentralization is valuable because centralized governmental authority is not always best placed to decide whose gun rights should be limited. Sometimes the best person to decide is you. That's why Donna's Law gives you the option of durably waiving your Second Amendment rights. Sometimes the best person to negotiate for your disarming is a loved one or neighbor or landlord, who can insist upon email verification as a condition of continued association. Sometimes it is one of the myriad people you come in contact with at home or school or work or place of worship who comes to know that you harbor paranoid delusions or unlawfully possess a firearm. Giving a broad swath of citizens practicable ways to contribute to gun safety can save thousands of lives a year—if government can muster the political will to act.

EMPOWERING SELF-RESTRICTION

DONNA'S LAW

On June 26, 2018, Donna Nathan killed herself with a gun she had purchased earlier that morning, ending a thirty-year battle with bipolar disorder and depression. Nathan fought right up until the end, admitting herself three times to inpatient psychiatric treatment in 2018. She had not been fighting alone. Her family paid for the best private mental health care in New Orleans and provided her with a beautiful house in a good neighborhood. Her partner of twelve years, Patrick Burke, took a leave of absence from his job to care for her: "She and I were so much in love. It wasn't enough."[1]

Nathan had sought psychiatric care precisely because she wanted treatment for her suicidal thoughts and prior impulsive suicide attempts. By voluntarily admitting herself, she willingly accepted the limitations on liberty that come with a psychiatric hospitalization in exchange for safety and the prospect of clinical improvement. What she could not limit, what the law did not allow her to limit, was her ability to quickly purchase a gun. That should change. People at risk for suicide, like Donna, should have the option to make it more difficult for themselves to buy a firearm during a suicidal crisis.

Allowing people to sign on to a do-not-sell list could have saved Donna Nathan. Her daughter, Katrina Brees, believes that her mother would have signed up and that doing so could have saved her. In this chapter, we show that Nathan is not unique.

What we propose is likely to save many other lives. Our research suggests that tens of thousands of people would sign up and hundreds of lives would be saved each year. By comparison, the costs of implementation, we will show in Chapter 3, are quite modest.

SIGNING UP WOULD SAVE LIVES

Restricting access to firearms during a suicidal crisis saves lives. This section highlights the key research findings. To summarize, most people who are contemplating gun suicide but are denied access to a gun do not switch to an alternative method. Some do switch, but other methods are less deadly than firearms, and the vast majority of individuals who survive a suicide attempt do not end up dying by suicide. Requiring an individual purchasing a firearm to wait for a period of time before receiving the gun has been shown to reduce firearm suicide with no significant substitution of other methods. And not having a firearm in the home is associated with a significantly lower overall suicide rate.

A mere delay in the ability to access a firearm can be enough to save a life. Suicide is often impulsive. For many people, the period of real risk for suicide is "relatively brief," lasting minutes, hours, or days, "but rarely longer."[2] One study of suicide attempt survivors (various means) found that for nearly all, the period between the decision to attempt suicide and the attempt was less than one week.[3] A study of thirty survivors of firearm suicide attempts found that more than half had suicidal thoughts for less than a day.[4]

The suicidal impulse is often not just fleeting, but also nonrecurring. More than 90 percent of suicide attempt survivors go on to die from something other than suicide.[5] In other words, most do not attempt suicide again and again until they are successful. Rather, the vast majority impulsively attempt suicide, then subsequently change their minds. The short deliberation period and post-attempt decision to live make sense given what we know about the motivations for suicide.

Certain categories of people are at an elevated baseline risk level. One review of seventy-six studies found that the median proportion of suicides involving a mental disorder was around 90 percent.[6] One meta-analysis concluded that "virtually all mental disorders have an increased risk of suicide."[7] However, the high suicide risk phases of most disorders are temporary.[8] Advances in medicine may even reduce the duration of those phases. One promising new pharmacological intervention is intranasal esketamine, which has the potential to quickly reduce suicidality.[9] Mental illness may not be curable, but the worst times pass, and most people have periods of relative stability.[10]

Firearm suicide, in particular, is often driven by life crises within the past week, relationship problems, and alcohol use.[11] "The choice of a firearm as a suicide method appears to be precipitated by stressful life events."[12] Because such triggers come and go, firearm suicide "appears far more unpredictable and impulsive" than suicide by other means.[13] But importantly, these causes usually abate with time. The acute effects of alcohol are temporary, and distress over life crises usually diminishes over time. The likelihood of attempting suicide decreases as the temporal distance from the triggering event increases.

Surviving the suicidal moment usually avoids suicide altogether, and the chance of survival goes up dramatically if there is no readily available firearm. It is known that having a firearm at home increases suicide risk.[14] This may be, in part, because firearm suicide attempts succeed in 85 percent of cases, as compared with an overall fatality rate for other methods of only 4 percent.[15] People who shift to a non-firearm method of attempting suicide are much more likely to survive.

But, contrary to popular belief, substitution of methods is actually infrequent.[16] Restricting access to firearms does not appear to cause an increase in non-firearm suicide.[17] Reducing Israel Defense Forces soldiers' access to firearms on weekends led to a 40 percent reduction in suicides.[18] Weekend firearm suicides declined, with no significant uptick in weekday or non-firearm suicides. In that case, what essentially amounted to a two-day delay period for firearm access substantially reduced suicide; it did not merely delay firearm suicide or shift individuals to other means.

The evidence overwhelmingly shows that keeping firearms altogether out of reach of individuals at high risk of suicide saves lives.[19] But would a restriction limited to immediate purchase have a significant effect? Very likely yes. The National Research Council (NRC), citing two studies, has stated that "a small but significant fraction of gun suicides are committed within days to weeks after the purchase of a handgun."[20]

The first of those studies concluded that "some persons may purposely buy a handgun to commit suicide."[21] The basis for this conclusion was the finding that suicide risk was highest during the first year after handgun purchase.[22] The second study found that the rate of firearm suicide in the first week after the purchase of a handgun was fifty-seven times as high as the rate in the general population.[23] A study of firearm suicides in Wisconsin found a sharp increase in risk of suicide within one week of gun purchase.[24] And an older, two-site Tennessee-Washington study found that 3 percent of suicide victims used a firearm obtained within two weeks.[25]

Against this backdrop, it is not surprising that laws mandating a delay between purchasing a firearm and receiving it (a "waiting period") appear to reduce suicide. One study found that waiting periods are associated with statistically significant lower (2–5 percent) rates of firearm suicide.[26] Equally significant, there was no evidence of substitution to non-firearm suicide methods: non-firearm suicide rates were not significantly impacted. Another recent study found an even larger, but not statistically significant, reduction in suicide associated with waiting periods (7 percent).[27] In other words, waiting periods have the potential to save hundreds of lives each year. Temporarily restricting one's own ability to purchase a firearm is essentially an opt-in waiting period. As long as significant numbers of people opt in (and we show below many people want to), saving many lives is very likely.

We will outline various implementation choices in Chapter 2, but one critical choice is whether to allow individuals to sign up for penalties on their own gun possession, not only to opt for a delay in purchasing a gun. There may be downsides, but a ban on possession has the potential to save more lives than a ban on purchase only. The impact of a purchase-only restriction, while significant, is basically limited to suicides involving recently purchased firearms. The vast majority of suicides involve weapons that were not recently purchased.[28] Allowing individuals to waive their right to possess a firearm may lead them to give up firearms already in their possession. Having a firearm in one's home greatly increases the risk of suicide, and a voluntary possession ban has the potential to eliminate that risk, thereby saving many more lives than a purchase-only restriction would. The evidence described above overwhelmingly shows that keeping firearms altogether out of reach of individuals at high risk of suicide saves lives. The critical factor again is how many people would actually sign up.

Before describing our efforts to gauge the popularity of Donna's Law, it is worth noting two additional, indirect mechanisms by which the proposal might save lives. Any implementation scheme will have to include health care provider and public education campaigns promoting self-restriction of access to firearms. These campaigns will publicize existing research showing that curbing access to firearms can prevent suicide. Thus, even those who do not register may be persuaded to voluntarily relinquish or lock up their firearms. A second indirect pathway is to counter hopelessness and thereby prevent suicide attempts with guns or other methods. Providing an avenue for people concerned about suicide to reduce their own risk of self-harm may alleviate the despair and anxiety that pushes them toward suicide. A "safety plan" is a list of coping strategies and sources of support that patients develop for use before or during a suicidal crises.[29] Like other aspects of safety planning focused on self-help, the proposal would "enhance patients' self-efficacy and can help to create a sense that suicidal urges can be mastered," which in turn "may help [patients] feel less vulnerable and less at the mercy of their suicidal thoughts."[30] In short, allowing people to protect themselves in this way may give them back a sense of control over their lives.

MANY PEOPLE WOULD SIGN UP

The positive impacts described above would materialize only if people participate. Our research suggests that many people would sign up. Large percentages of respondents in three separate surveys indicated that they would participate in the program if it were available.

Our first study asked 200 individuals receiving psychiatric care, in both inpatient and outpatient settings, whether they would sign up for either a seven-day delay version of the proposal or a version that would restore gun purchase ability only after a seven-day delay and a judicial hearing.[31] Forty-six percent of respondents said that they would sign up for one or both versions (see Table 1.1). Predictably, having present access to a firearm was strongly associated with declining to sign up. Other covariates— including demographic variables, score on a suicide risk instrument (SBQ-R), and specific mental health diagnoses—were generally not statistically significant. The bottom line of this study is that nearly half of a group of individuals at relatively high risk of suicide said that they would voluntarily restrict their ability to purchase guns. One important limitation of this study is that it employed a convenience sample in a single state (Alabama) and therefore may not be representative of all people being treated for mental illness.

Our next study confirmed the popularity of self-restriction in a broader sample.[32] This time we administered an online survey

Table 1.1. Surveys of Willingness to Participate in Donna's Law

Study	Alabama[1]	Amazon mTurk[2]	YouGov[3]
Respondents	200 inpatient and outpatient psychiatric patients	1,050 adult Internet users	1,000 adult U.S. nonveterans and 1,000 adult U.S. veterans
Sample type	Convenience	Convenience	Representative
Proposal	Purchase-only restriction with 7-day or judicial hearing option	Purchase-only or possession-too restriction with 7-day or judicial hearing option	Purchase-only or possession-too restriction with 21-day option
Percentage willing to volunteer	46% either option	~30% overall	~29% overall

1. Fredrick E. Vars et al., *Willingness of Mentally Ill Individuals to Sign Up for a Novel Proposal to Prevent Firearm Suicide*, 47 Suicide and Life-Threatening Behav. 483 (2017).
2. Ian Ayres and Fredrick E. Vars, *Libertarian Gun Control*, 167 U. Pa. L. Rev. 921 (2019).
3. Ian Ayres and Fredrick E. Vars, YouGov survey conducted for this book.

to 1,050 Internet users. Each respondent was presented with only one version of the proposal, either restoration upon request and a seven-day delay or restoration only after review by a judge. In this study, however, respondents were randomly assigned to subgroups, one presented with a purchase-only restriction and the other offered the opportunity to restrict both purchase and possession.

Combining all subgroups, 30.8 percent responded that they would be willing to add their names to their state's no-guns list. The seven-day delay option was more popular than the judicial review version, but there was essentially no difference in the popularity of the purchase-only and purchase-plus-possession bans. Two powerful predictors of willingness to participate were (1) having a mental health diagnosis (these respondents were more

likely to want to participate) and (2) having current access to firearms (these respondents were less likely to want to participate).
It appears that individuals who know they are at elevated risk of
suicide due to mental health problems are more likely to want to
restrict their own access to firearms. And those who already possess guns are less likely to give up their gun rights.

These two studies both suggest that many people would participate in a gun self-restriction program. Estimating the precise
percentage is difficult because neither study used a nationally representative sample. The online survey respondents differed sys-
tematically from the general population, as they were much more
likely to be male, single, and white, and to hold a college degree.
We therefore embarked on a third study, using a nationally representative sample of the general population.

We selected YouGov to administer the survey because its panel
has been shown to more accurately reflect the general U.S. population.[33] The respondents were matched to a sampling frame on
gender, age, race, and education. The frame was constructed
by stratified sampling from the full 2016 American Community
Survey one-year sample, a large government sample representative of the overall population. Responses were weighted using the
four demographic variables listed above as well as region (Midwest, Northeast, South, and West) and 2016 presidential vote
choice. The resulting weighted sample of 1,000 responses from
nonveteran adults closely matches the overall population (Appendix A, Table A.1). Through YouGov, we surveyed a second
sample of 1,000 respondents representative of the U.S. adult veteran population. We report the nonveteran results first.

Our key variable of interest was willingness to sign up for a
suspension of one's ability to purchase, or to purchase and possess, a firearm.[34] Nearly one-third (31.1 percent) said they would
sign up for a purchase-only restriction (4.0 percent margin of
error). A slightly lower percentage (29.1 percent) said they would
sign up for the purchase and possession restriction, but the difference was less than the margin of error (4.0 percent).

What is perhaps most striking is how few variables had a significant impact on willingness to sign up.[35] Donna's Law is attractive more or less across the board. This may reflect the reality that suicide affects every demographic. There were, however, some notable exceptions where respondent characteristics did significantly impact the likelihood that they would sign up. Respondents with a relatively high suicide risk (measured by a modified version of the Suicide Behaviors Questionnaire-Revised, or SBQ-R, score) expressed statistically increased willingness to sign up. This finding helps makes the case for Donna's Law. As we would hope and expect, people who are at greatest risk of self-harm are more willing to waive their gun rights.

Figure 1.1 summarizes the core associations derived from our regression analysis.[36] People with a mental health diagnosis were nearly 70 percent more likely to sign up (OR = 1.688; $p < 0.05$), confirming our previous findings. On the other hand, this study confirmed that individuals with gun access, not surprisingly, are significantly less likely to sign up (OR = 0.590; $p < 0.05$). It is worth emphasizing that even among people who currently have guns in their home, the sign-up rate was more than 20 percent, suggesting that even some people who currently have access to firearms may be persuaded to give them up.[37] The strongest negative correlates of sign-up were being a political independent (OR = 0.493; $p < 0.01$) and having voted for Donald Trump in the 2016 presidential election. Trump voters were less than half as likely to self-restrict as Hillary Clinton voters (OR = 0.407; $p < 0.01$). Given Trump's forceful embrace of gun rights, this finding was perhaps predictable.

This Trump-Clinton disparity suggests a second potential motivation for participation: political expression. Gun policies that are popular among the general public often fail in state and federal legislatures. Waiting periods and background check bills are prime examples.[38] People who support such policies could bypass nonresponsive lawmakers by opting for a waiting period, or possession restriction, on their own. While names of those who have

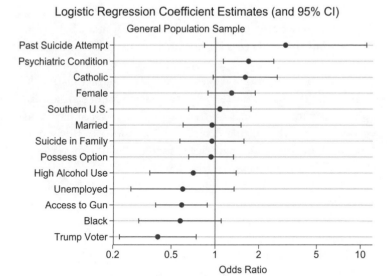

Figure 1.1. YouGov Survey—Willingness to Participate

signed up will be kept confidential, anyone is free to announce their participation, and our proposal amplifies those individual voices by publicly reporting overall participation figures.[39] Mass shootings predictably lead some segments of the population to purchase weapons. But after mass shootings like those at Newtown or Las Vegas or Parkland, other segments of the population want to be able to express their support for gun control laws. The ability to move the aggregate statistic of gun waivers could thus be a way for like-minded Americans to make common cause and express solidarity with one another.

Veterans

In April 2019, at a Veterans Affairs clinic in Austin, Texas, hundreds of people witnessed a veteran shoot himself to death.[40] He was one of three veterans who killed themselves on VA properties in a single week.[41] An estimated twenty veterans die each day from suicide.[42] The suicide rate among veterans is 50 percent higher than for nonveterans.[43] For these reasons we were interested in the potential impact of the proposal among veterans. One might speculate that veterans, who have been trained to use firearms and who may have lived with a firearm as a companion and tool, would be unwilling to restrict their own gun access.

We administered the nonveteran survey questions to an independent sample of 1,000 veterans. Veteran respondents also answered service-related questions. Overall, 21.7 percent (margin of error 3.6 percent) of veterans said they would sign up for the purchase-only restriction. The purchase and possession option was less attractive, with a 14.3 percent sign-up rate (margin of error 3.1 percent). Unlike the general population, veterans were significantly less likely to give up their right to possess a firearm than to give up the right to purchase one. And while veterans were significantly less likely than nonveterans to express willingness to sign up for either version of the proposal, many in this high-risk group were willing to put distance between themselves and firearms.

As with the nonveteran population, current gun access $(OR = 0.339, p < 0.01)$ and voting for Trump $(OR = 0.329, p < 0.01)$ were strongly associated with lower likelihood of signing up. Having a psychiatric diagnosis was not a significant predictor of signing up. Veterans who had been on active duty were more likely to sign up $(OR = 4.741, p < 0.05)$, but veterans who had been deployed were significantly less likely to sign up $(0.587, p < 0.05)$.

Estimated Lives Saved

When the veterans and nonveterans are combined using appropriate weights, the overall sign-up rate for the purchase-only restriction was about 30 percent. This high sign-up rate suggests that this version of Donna's Law could save hundreds of lives each year. Again, one way to conceptualize the revocable purchase-only restriction is as an optional waiting period. As noted above, two recent studies estimate that a mandatory, across-the-board waiting period is associated with a 2–7 percent reduction in

suicide.[44] In 2014, there were 23,017 suicides in states that did
not have a waiting period. (Waiting period states are excluded
from this calculation because they are already experiencing the
suicide reduction effect associated with a delay period for firearm
purchases.) If Donna's Law were adopted in states without waiting
periods, and 30 percent of people signed up, the purchase-only
restriction could be expected to save somewhere on the order of
140 to 490 lives each year (23,017 suicides × 30 percent of people
opting for waiting period × 2–7 percent reduction in suicide associated with waiting period).

The effect of waiting periods, however, is limited because most
gun suicides do not involve recently purchased guns. Convincing
people to give up guns they already own has the potential to make
an even bigger dent in the suicide rate. Our results suggest that
this is entirely possible. Thirteen percent of respondents in our
study who said they would sign up for a purchase and possession
restriction were gun owners. To comply with the restriction, these
individuals, 3.8 percent of the sample, would have to give up their
guns. Eliminating gun access in the home is associated with a significantly lower risk of suicide—about a 70 percent reduction[45]—
so getting rid of existing guns even from a small percentage of
homes could dramatically reduce suicide. Using 2017 suicide statistics, we estimate roughly 1,245 lives saved (47,178 suicides
in 2017 × 3.8 percent of respondents who would give up their
gun × 70 percent reduced suicide risk from not having gun access).[46] This estimate is for a purchase and possession ban that
requires the relinquishment of current firearms, but, of course,
some who sign up for a purchase-only restriction might also
choose voluntarily to relinquish existing guns.

These estimates should be interpreted with caution. They rely
on several assumptions. Probably the most unrealistic assumption
is that survey respondents who say they would sign up would actually do so if given the opportunity. Saying yes on a survey is
easier than completing an actual sign-up process, even with the
most user-friendly registration website (described in Chapter 2).

Then again, public service announcement campaigns might be effective in stimulating even more demand than we uncovered in asking respondents to consider waivers for the first time. A second critical assumption is that the impact of a waiting period or relinquishing a current firearm is the same for people who sign up as it is in the overall population. The effect of this assumption is unclear. The actual life-saving impact may be greater, since relatively high-risk people with mental illness are more likely to choose to register. On the other hand, those willing to give up gun access may be safer with guns already—for example, by using gun locks or by giving guns to friends for safekeeping in times of crisis. Precision in this context is unattainable, but we believe our estimates give a general sense of the potential impact of Donna's Law.

It is too late for Donna Nathan, but Donna's Law would likely save many other lives, hundreds each year in our estimation. Without knowing this estimate and likely without any familiarity with Donna's Law, majorities of gun owners already support it. As part of the YouGov survey, we asked each respondent whether "states should pass laws allowing people to voluntarily put their names on a list." A majority of gun owners said yes. Donna's Law appeals across traditional fault lines and, if adopted, could save many lives. Providing people with this new way to protect themselves from suicide is our purest example of how government can facilitate individuals to disarm by choice. Indeed, even calling Donna's Law "gun control" is in some ways inapt—it is more accurately described as self-control.

2

ANALOGIES, CHOICES, AND CONSTRAINTS

Self-restriction of gun rights would represent a paradigm shift in the gun policy debate, but there are successful analogies to other contexts. These analogies can help inform the host of implementation questions that must be addressed. No matter how these implementation questions are answered, Donna's Law does not violate the Second Amendment.

The classic example of binding oneself against future bad decisions is Ulysses, who ordered his men to tie his hands to the mast so that he would not succumb to the Sirens' song.[1] Self-binding can be a good strategy, and not just for classical heroes.[2] People who worry about loss of future control seek out a variety of disabling devices—including bariatric surgery (which makes it uncomfortable to overeat) and Antabuse (which makes it unpleasant to drink alcohol). Users of the commitment website stickK.com (cofounded by one of us) have voluntarily put more than $40 million at risk, collectively, to increase the chance that they will follow through with their goals.[3]

States can and have played important roles in providing citizens with ways to voluntarily restrict future behavior. For example, state recognition of marriage can be seen as enhancing individual liberty by facilitating the ability of people to make more durable relationship commitments. Two state policies in particular are analogous to firearm self-restriction: self-exclusion from gambling and advance directives.

SELF-EXCLUSION FROM GAMBLING

Under gambling "self-exclusion" programs, individuals commit not to gamble, usually for a set period of time. The vast majority of jurisdictions with legal casino gambling have state-prescribed regulations allowing self-exclusion.[4] Tens of thousands of people have signed up, multiples more than seek professional assistance.[5]

Gambling self-exclusion programs work as follows. To get on the gambling self-exclusion list in New Jersey, for example, individuals must complete a form and appear in person at the New Jersey Division of Gaming Enforcement with photo identification. They may opt for a one-year, five-year, or lifetime ban.[6] Even after the temporary period expires, removal from the list is not automatic. "A person who has chosen the one or five year exclusion must also make a request for removal, however it also must be accompanied by a letter from a mental health professional certifying that the individual is not suffering from a gambling problem."[7] There is no provision to revoke a lifetime self-exclusion. Casinos may refuse to accept wagers from listed persons and may ask the person to leave the gaming area. If someone slips through the cracks and does gamble, that person is prohibited from collecting winnings.[8] Details vary from state to state, but the New Jersey program is fairly typical.

The primary goal of self-exclusion is obvious: to stop problem gambling. Research suggests that such programs have made significant strides toward that goal. Most participants in Missouri's lifetime self-exclusion program did not abstain permanently from gambling after enrolling, but did experience positive effects.[9] Nearly 80 percent exhibited "probable pathological gambling" in the six months before enrollment, as compared with just 15 percent in the six months after.[10] A 2014 review of studies from over a dozen jurisdictions reported a reduction in "psychological difficulties including depression and anxiety" related to problem gambling and that enrollees "feel they have more control of their circumstances."[11]

The analogy between gambling and suicide, while imperfect, is still instructive. Both the compulsion to gamble and suicidal ideation typically ebb and flow.[12] Many thousands of problem gamblers have voluntarily chosen to protect themselves against future self-destructive behavior. It should not be surprising that so many of our survey respondents, especially those with mental health problems, similarly wanted to protect themselves against suicide by restricting their own gun access. While the effectiveness of self-exclusion in both contexts depends on enforcement, restricting gun purchase is arguably easier than gambling exclusion. As discussed below, the firearm purchase background check system could easily implement gun self-exclusion in all fifty states, at least for purchases from licensed dealers.

It is not easy to get off the no-gambling list in many states. New Jersey's irrevocable exclusion periods of one-year, five-year, or even lifetime durations are typical. These options could certainly be added to Donna's Law, although the findings above suggest that much of the suicide prevention benefit can be achieved with shorter periods, even just days or weeks. New Jersey's requirement for assessment by a mental health professional in order to be *removed* from the self-exclusion list could also be appropriate for a no-gun registry. Given the life-and-death stakes associated with reinstatement of gun purchase rights, reinstatement could even require judicial approval. Either mental health assessment or judicial approval could be mandatory or merely options that could be selected by an individual at the time of registration.

The gambling analogy suggests that gun self-exclusion could be privatized, but only as a second-best option to legislation. In states without a no-gambling list, some casinos have instituted self-exclusion programs on their own.[13] This is obviously more effective in areas where casinos are far apart or where every casino in the area has a self-exclusion program. Gun dealers are much more numerous than casinos—as of December 2017, there were 81,187 federally licensed gun dealers[14]—so one might question whether a gun self-exclusion program by one retailer could make a difference. In some markets, retailers would probably have to combine forces into a joint program in order to have a significant effect. But in other markets, a big retailer is the only game in town. One need not look far down the alphabet to see this: in 2017, a Walmart was the only federally licensed gun dealer in Aberdeen, Maryland; Algood, Tennessee; Alma, Michigan; and Argos, Indiana.[15] And the notion that a gun retailer would impose restrictions on sales beyond those required by law is not far-fetched: after the Parkland shooting, Dick's Sporting Goods raised the minimum age for firearm sales and stopped selling assault weapons. Still, a public program binding on every retailer in every state would be superior to whatever patchwork quilt the market might produce on its own.

ADVANCE DIRECTIVES

Advance directives present another parallel to Donna's Law. Advance directives allow individuals to make medical decisions in advance that will be respected in the event that the individual loses the capacity to make decisions in real time. All states recognize some form of health care advance directive.[16] Advance directives promote patient autonomy, reduce health care expenditures, and decrease stress for family members. Over one-third of Americans have an advance directive.[17] The problem of patient incapacity to make medical decisions is closely analogous to the problem of a prospective gun purchaser driven by suicidal impulses. In both situations, earlier well-considered preferences should control, not fleeting irrational thoughts. The stakes in both circumstances can be life or death. The fact that every state recognizes advance directives indicates that every state agrees people ought to be able to direct future decisions. And the fact that so many Americans have executed advance directives further suggests that there would be demand for firearm self-restriction, at least among those prone to suicidal thinking.

Some state statutes authorize advance directives only for end-of-life decision making. Other states authorize special advance directives for psychiatric care. The psychiatric advance directive, or PAD, has been defined as "a legally enforceable document that sets forth a person's wishes concerning psychiatric treatment in anticipation of the event that he or she may later become incompetent to make informed health care decisions."[18]

A primary goal of PADs is to avoid the need for coercive treatment. One early advocate of PADs asserted that "acting and being treated as self-determining individuals with a significant measure of authority over their own fate, instead of as powerless and incompetent victims of forces beyond their understanding and control, can be therapeutically advantageous to mentally ill patients."[19] That prediction has been validated through research. One recent study found that people with PADs were significantly less likely to experience coercive crisis interventions, such as forced medication and hospitalization.[20] Giving individuals control over their own access to firearms is similarly empowering and may itself counter the feelings of helplessness at the root of many suicides. Self-restriction may also avoid the need for forcible gun confiscation in dangerous emergencies.

Some jurisdictions require that PADs be both witnessed and notarized.[21] Yet "research indicates that although approximately 70% of patients with mental illness would want a PAD if offered assistance in completing one, less than 10% have actually completed a PAD."[22] One reason patients give for not completing a PAD is "trouble notarizing the document while obtaining appropriate witnesses."[23] Adding a web-based (or even text) sign-up platform for Donna's Law could allow a greater number of interested individuals to take advantage of the opportunity—and save more lives.

Advance directives are sometimes not available to health care providers when decisions need to be made.[24] To alleviate this problem, one of us has advocated an accessible national registry of advance directives.[25] As will be discussed below, a national registry of individuals barred from purchasing a gun already exists, so one can more easily self-restrict gun purchase nationally. There is no need to create a new database.

IMPLEMENTATION

Systems to allow people to set restrictions on their own future behavior already exist in multiple contexts. The basic architecture for firearm self-restriction could be easily built. Federally licensed firearms dealers (and other sellers in some states) are already required to perform a background check before selling a firearm. All that is needed, therefore, is a new mechanism for individuals to add and subtract their own names from the existing background check system. Some states supplement the federal check with their own databases. Whether or not a state has opted to be the "point of contact" for background checks, the names of Donna's Law registrants should be provided to the federal database so that registrants would then be barred from purchasing a firearm in all fifty states, not only in their state of residence. Beyond this basic framework, a host of implementation decisions remain. Key considerations are voluntariness and confidentiality, as well as scope and duration of restriction.

Voluntariness

Participation should be voluntary and confidential. To ensure that participation is truly voluntary, people must be clearly informed about the consequences of signing up. These consequences—what exactly is prohibited and for how long, what the process is to end participation, and so forth—should be communicated as part of any public education campaign and by health care providers and others who suggest participation. But such material and oral explanations are not enough; sign-up forms and websites must contain clear and complete explanations.

Another aspect of voluntariness is assuring that no one can successfully register someone else. Simply mailing in a signed form without identification would not provide adequate assurance of participant identity. One possibility is to require notarized forms. Notarization is commonly accepted as sufficient identity verification in many high-stakes transactions. There are 4.4 million notaries nationwide,[26] and some companies provide online notarization recognized in all fifty states.[27] Still, locating and paying for notarization would almost certainly deter participation by many interested individuals.

A second alternative is to require in-person registration at a government office. A photo identification or other sufficient evidence of identity would be checked at the time of registration. As will be discussed in Chapter 3, Washington State requires participants to register in person at the county clerk's office. The courthouse may be easier to find than a notary, but many potential participants will again likely be deterred due to barriers such as time, distance, and lack of anonymity. Both the notarization and in-person government options require a face-to-face encounter in which individuals must disclose to another person their intent to register. Suicide, mental illness, and firearms are sensitive issues, and many people may be willing to participate only if they can do so in private.

The privacy of a doctor's office or other health care provider location is a much better alternative for in-person registration than a county courthouse. Patients who have already decided to disclose their conditions to a health care provider would be more likely willing to also disclose their preference for a firearm self-restriction. Providing the self-restriction option at the doctor's office has the potential to reach many people at risk of suicide. One review found that 45 percent of suicide victims had seen a primary care physician within one month of dying and that 77 percent had done so within the last year of their life.[28]

Allowing sign-up through a secure Internet portal in addition to other sign-up options would better protect privacy and lead to greater participation.[29] Online identity verification is now standard and reliable, as demonstrated by hundreds of online finance and commerce websites as well as online government portals administered by the IRS and the Social Security Administration.[30] Even Facebook developed and launched an online mechanism to verify the identity of individuals attempting to place policy-related advertisements, under pressure following Russian interference with the 2016 presidential election.[31] Both of our model bills would require states to create an Internet platform that takes sufficient measures to ensure the identity of registering individuals.

Confidentiality

A participant should be able to rely on confidentiality. As noted above, Donna's Law can implicate highly sensitive issues. Stigma around suicide and mental illness is rampant, and discrimination is a genuine possibility. A fear of disclosure could suppress participation. Though no system can eliminate entirely the risk of a data breach, the federal background check system is very secure. Indeed, we can find no reported instance of breach. Donna's Law would require a similarly secure new interface for registration, but regardless of which registration system is selected, the repository of data would remain the existing, and historically robust, federal background check system.

Confidentiality would be waivable: participants could, of course, choose to disclose their participation. Indeed, the system should facilitate such disclosure in at least one way. At the time of sign-up, the participant would have the option of listing individuals to be contacted should the participant later request removal from the system. These trusted individuals would be able to check in on the well-being of the participant before the suspension of gun purchase ability would be revoked. A participant might list friends, family, or even health care providers. We refer to this option as "back-end notification."

Another, more controversial possibility would be "front-end notification." As the name suggests, pursuant to this option, participants could credibly communicate at the outset that they have signed up for a gun restriction. For example, a participant could list an email address, and the system would immediately upon registration send an email to that address. If this option were available, third parties might refuse to deal with an individual unless an email verified her registration. Discrimination based on participation status could (and should) be limited, but front-end notification is a key building block for the associational marketplace extension of Donna's Law outlined in Chapter 4. Both of our model bills include back-end notification, but only the second model bill includes the more controversial front-end email notification.

Scope of Restriction: Purchase or Possession

A related but independent question is whether to restrict solely gun purchase ability or to include also a prohibition on gun possession.[32] This is a highly consequential decision. On the one hand, the vast majority of gun suicides do not involve recently acquired firearms. A possession ban might persuade some people who have guns to relinquish them, which could prevent some of these suicides. On the other hand, what is the point of restricting gun purchase by signing up for the program if you already have a gun? A person who is willing to give up their right to buy a gun probably does not own a gun, or if they do, would be willing to voluntarily give it up. Adding the threat of criminal sanction likely would not be needed.[33]

There may be other negative consequences of allowing individuals to criminalize their own gun possession. Under other statutes, possession has been interpreted broadly and in ways that individuals may not anticipate. Having someone else's gun in the glove compartment of a participant's car may constitute a crime.[34] Such unexpected outcomes could support a claim that the waiver of gun rights was not voluntary or knowing. But even in the center of the proscribed conduct—a participant intentionally holding a gun—the wisdom of criminalization is arguable. If a mentally ill individual illegally acquires a firearm in an unsuccessful suicide attempt, is jail or prison the right place to send them?

There are several responses to these arguments. Perhaps the most fundamental is that they are paternalistic. If adequately informed individuals want to prohibit their own gun possession (and many do, as we showed above), then they should be allowed that choice. And giving them that choice increases the choices available to people around them. A possession ban is a second building block for the associational marketplace. A landlord might conclude that the apartment building is safer if no one possesses a gun. Tenants being prohibited from purchasing firearms is helpful, but does not ensure a gun-free building. A possession ban could. Our second model bill calls for registration to prohibit both purchase and possession, but again reasonable legislators might just choose to limit purchase via the NICS background check system, as provided in our first model bill.

Duration and Durability

A final design question concerns the duration and durability of the restriction. To prevent impulsive suicide, a brief delay period is sufficient. Our model Donna's Law bill includes a twenty-one-day delay between a request for removal and reinstatement of gun purchase ability. Some suicides are less impulsive, and suicide risk is highest during the period after a crisis. For those reasons (and building on the no-gambling analogy), a bill introduced in Wisconsin allows participants to choose a one-, five-, or twenty-year term.[35] Of course, an irrevocable lifetime ban could also be made available.

An alternative approach is to assess suicide risk rather than to rely on time-limited restriction alone. One possibility, similar to some no-gambling programs, is to require a declaration from a health care provider that the participant is not at elevated risk of suicide. Two bills (California and Massachusetts) borrow the more familiar civil commitment standard "danger to self or others." Health care providers may understandably be reluctant to vouch for patients in this way. A judicial hearing could supplement or supplant the written health care provider declaration requirement.

DONNA'S LAW WOULD NOT VIOLATE THE
SECOND AMENDMENT

The proposal is clearly constitutional.[36] The Supreme Court in 2008 announced that the Second Amendment protects an individual's right to keep and bear arms.[37] But the Court made clear that right is not unlimited.[38] The Second Amendment case *Silvester v. Harris* is closest on the facts to the twenty-one-day purchase delay. Plaintiffs in *Silvester* argued that California's ten-day waiting period to purchase a firearm violated the Second Amendment. The Ninth Circuit rejected that argument. The court held first that the waiting period imposed a burden on Second Amendment rights, but not so great a burden as to justify more than intermediate scrutiny. The court held that the waiting period passed intermediate scrutiny because it provided a cooling-off period to deter violence and suicide.[39]

Silvester points to the first of four sufficient reasons why Donna's Law does not violate the Second Amendment. Restricting one's own ability to purchase a firearm with an automatic but delayed revocation option is functionally equivalent to a self-imposed waiting period. If a mandatory waiting period does not violate the Second Amendment, which *Silvester* squarely holds, then neither does a less restrictive, optional waiting period. If the government can constitutionally deny immediate access to a new firearm, surely it is constitutional for the government to expand individual choice by allowing people to opt for a firearm purchase delay. People who want to keep their gun rights or for any reason do not trust the government can simply refrain from registering.

The next closest line of cases involves firearm restrictions based on the perceived dangerousness of certain categories of individuals, such as convicted felons. Restrictions of this kind have been upheld time and time again.[40] An optional and temporary measure is less restrictive than a mandatory restriction premised on someone else's judgment that the restricted category is "dangerous." In other words, Donna's Law's constitutionality follows a fortiori from the constitutionality of dangerousness restrictions. The dangerousness cases all involve prohibitions on both purchase and possession, so they strongly support the constitutionality of the purchase-and-possession version of the registry.

A third argument in favor of constitutionality rests on the proposition that "the Second Amendment's guarantee of an individual right to keep or bear arms in self-defense should include the freedom not to keep or bear them at all."[41] Firearm self-restriction would provide a tool to strengthen this right not to bear arms—by binding oneself against impulsively buying arms in the future. The animating principle of the Second Amendment is self-defense.[42] One ought to be able to defend oneself against suicide.[43] This self-defense imperative applies both to recently purchased and already possessed guns, so the right not to bear arms should protect both the purchase-only and purchase-and-possession alternatives.

Finally, individuals who restrict their own ability to purchase firearms generally waive their Second Amendment rights. Waivers of constitutional rights "not only must be voluntary but must be knowing, intelligent acts done with sufficient awareness of the relevant circumstances and likely consequences."[44] Sign-up systems for a Donna's Law should include clear and prominent explanations. The consequences of a purchase-only restriction are plain and easily understood. As suggested above, the scope of a possession ban is less straightforward, and explanations may need to be more detailed.

The constitutional analysis varies depending on the duration of the restriction, but the outcome does not. Even a lifetime, irrevocable ban is likely constitutional.[45] Clifford Charles Tyler was involuntarily hospitalized in 1986 for a depressive episode following an emotional divorce.[46] As a result of his civil commitment, he was barred by federal law from possessing a firearm. Nearly thirty years later, Tyler was not mentally ill and challenged the restriction on gun possession under the Second Amendment.

The Sixth Circuit, sitting en banc, upheld the challenge, concluding that the government had not shown that a lifetime ban was substantially related to the government purpose in preventing suicide. Research showing an elevated short-term risk of suicide was not sufficient, the court held.

At first blush, this result would seem to cut against the constitutionality of a permanent waiver version of our proposal. But there is a critical distinction: Tyler lost his gun rights against his will; participants in our program give away their gun rights voluntarily. In this way, our proposal is closer to the ban on gun possession by convicted felons, which has been upheld against durational objections. A district court reaching the same result as the Sixth Circuit in *Tyler* explained: "An involuntary commitment is premised on mental illness rather than a deliberate choice to break the law and forfeit civil rights."[47] Holding someone accountable permanently for their intentional actions is different from imposing lifelong consequences for a purely involuntary condition. Full autonomy includes the power to make an irrevocable as well as a revocable waiver.

In this chapter, we showed that there are successful examples of self-restriction in two contexts, gambling and psychiatric advance directives, we delineated design choices and defended our basic and extended models, and we established that firearm self-restriction, under the various implementations we discuss, is constitutional. In Chapter 3 we chart the course of Donna's Law in state legislatures, distilling key lessons.

3

LABORATORIES OF DEMOCRACY

Justice Louis Brandeis's "laboratories" of democracy are places of remarkable invention.[1] In this chapter we report on our personal experiences lobbying state legislators to introduce and move forward with versions of Donna's Law in nine early states.[2] No two versions of the bill or pathways to introduction are identical. We outline the diversity of implementation decisions reflected in these states and also distill several common political factors impacting state introduction efforts. Our hope is that these stories can guide future efforts, or at least illuminate a few avoidable pitfalls.

EXPERIENCES IN THE STATES

Tennessee

We found our first sponsor in Tennessee. While a student in law school, Lee Harris worked with us on a project examining taxicab tipping.[3] As a law professor, Harris gave a talk at the University of Alabama law school, where Fred teaches. In late 2016, Harris was the Tennessee Senate Minority Leader, so Fred reached out with an email. Harris responded the same day, "This is a great idea. . . . I would love to draft something on it and see where it goes."[4]

The bill we crafted together provided for a purchase-only ban, web-based registration, integration with National Instant

Criminal Background Check System (NICS), a twenty-one-day reinstatement period, and privacy and antidiscrimination protections. These have been the key components of essentially all of the draft bills we have offered legislators in each state.[5] Bills in other states were drafted without our input and vary substantially.

Harris managed to get a committee hearing for the bill in early 2017. For a while it seemed that the bill would move forward without significant pushback. However, literally the day before the hearing was scheduled to take place, the Tennessee Bureau of Investigation (TBI) raised an objection. While the nature of the objection was never entirely clear, we did identify a potential problem: the bill allowed for residents of states other than Tennessee to register. Apparently, the TBI believed that it was not allowed to use NICS to limit the ability of nonresidents to purchase firearms. We have avoided this issue in all bills introduced since, but the effort in Tennessee stalled, and the bill has not been reintroduced. Harris is no longer in the legislature; he is mayor of Shelby County, which includes Memphis.

Alabama

Our earliest and most sustained advocacy efforts have been in Alabama, where Fred is a law professor. After numerous unsuccessful direct contacts with legislators beginning in 2015, Othni Latham, director of the Alabama Law Institute (ALI), suggested reaching out to Representative Allen Farley in 2017. Farley was then serving as chair of an Alabama firearms law commission and was immediately interested in the proposal. He arranged for Fred to present to the commission and to the Republican House caucus.

Interestingly, Farley was not the first to introduce the bill in Alabama. Shortly after the February 2018 Parkland shooting, Senator Trip Pittman, a lifelong member of the NRA, asked ALI if they knew of any gun legislation that might be palatable in a pro–gun rights state. ALI offered our bill, which Pittman introduced. We then reached out to Pittman, and he invited Fred to present the bill to the Senate Judiciary Committee, which Fred did. The bill passed out of committee, but time ran out in the session. Pittman is no longer in the legislature, but Representative Farley remains committed to the bill.

We have been closely involved in drafting and redrafting the Alabama bill. The original version was essentially identical to our original model. Features were added after they were proposed in other states. Modeling the Washington bill (explored in more depth below), Alabama lawmakers added a provision that gives a participant the option of listing individuals who should be contacted if the participant requests that their ability to purchase guns be reinstated ("back-end notification"). This safety net ensures that people close to the participant can intervene if they suspect that the participant is reversing their status with the intention of doing harm to themselves or others. Lawmakers have also strengthened privacy and nondiscrimination provisions as they develop in other states.

Because the expense associated with a web-based sign-up platform has proven fatal in other states, Alabama's current version provides for two less expensive sign-up alternatives in case the legislature balks at the price tag of the web-based platform: (1) in-person registration with the court clerk; and (2) mail-in registration by notarized form. These options also provide access to the program for individuals who lack Internet access and should be retained even in states that create a web-based registration platform.[6]

California

Fred played intramural soccer in law school with our California sponsor, Assemblyman Rob Bonta. A brief exchange of voice-mails and emails was enough to prompt Bonta and his team into action. We offered Bonta a different draft bill than our standard model. California already has a mandatory ten-day waiting period before an individual can purchase a firearm. As such, the standard proposal of a twenty-one-day optional waiting period seemed almost redundant. We took the opportunity to experiment with other kinds of "cooling-off" periods, and proposed that once registered, a participant could reinstate their ability to purchase a gun only by showing at a court hearing that "he or she is not at elevated risk of suicide."

Bonta engaged allies in the gun regulation community, including representatives of Giffords Law Center and the Brady Campaign. After extended substantive discussions, a new reinstatement regime was conceived. At any time one year or more after registration, a participant could request removal. That request would automatically take effect twenty-one days later. During the first year, removal required a declaration from a health care professional confirming that "the person does not present a substantial risk of harm to self or others with a firearm." Because this standard closely tracks the civil commitment standard, we hoped that it could be more easily and predictably applied than an "elevated risk" standard. In addition, avoiding a judicial hearing would protect privacy and lower costs. Finally, we thought that automatic removal after a year might be more attractive to participants and less offensive to gun rights advocates.

A key sticking point in California was cost. The California Department of Justice (DOJ) reported that start-up costs would likely peak at nearly a million dollars in year two of the program. In addition, DOJ estimated maintenance costs "in the low hundreds of thousands of dollars." The Department of Public Health's annual advertising fees alone would add up to $120,000. Strenuous efforts to fully understand and bring down those estimated costs were unsuccessful. The bill was replaced with a bill commissioning a study of the idea. That bill passed the legislature, but was vetoed. The governor, Jerry Brown, called the idea "interesting," but concluded that it could be studied through alternative, existing avenues.

Illinois

Our connection in Illinois was Mark Heyrman, then a professor at the University of Chicago law school. Heyrman is deeply involved in mental health policy in Illinois, and his connections generated a sponsor, Representative Will Guzzardi. The concise Illinois bill allowed individuals to register for a newly created database by a notarized form and required a seven-day delay for reinstatement.

The bill encountered remarkable opposition. A total of 1,364 opponents filed "witness slips." A witness slip is a position statement on a bill and may or may not be accompanied by a request to testify at the hearing. A proponent of the bill speculated that the committee simply did not know how to handle this volume. That was exactly the intent of the group Gun Rights 4 Illinois, which hosts a webpage encouraging and facilitating the submission of witness slips. The goal was expressly stated: "If 2.5 million gun owners in Illinois each filed a slip, we could block every anti-gun bill."[7] Some highly motivated individuals appear to have submitted witness slips against every bill opposed by the organization Gun Rights 4 Illinois. The bills listed on the webpage right above and right below the voluntary bill had 1,414 and 1,378 opponent slips, respectively. Again, 1,364 slips were filed against the voluntary bill. These numbers strongly suggest that there was not individualized evaluation of the proposed bills. Going forward, the legislature will have to recognize that the witness slip process may not be an accurate gauge of considered judgment.

Oregon

The Oregon bill resulted from a face-to-face meeting between constituents and their representative. Fred's parents are campaign contributors to State Representative Dan Rayfield. They asked for and successfully scheduled a meeting, at which they hand-delivered a binder of supporting materials and put Fred on speakerphone to make the pitch. Rayfield was enthusiastic.

The Oregon bill resembled other versions, but incorporated remedies and procedures from state antidiscrimination law. Rayfield introduced the bill in two consecutive sessions. The bill did not make it into the omnibus gun package either session, due to other priorities and perhaps also because the web-based interface would require appropriations. In the second session, Rayfield simultaneously pursued an alternative pathway of pushing the bill as a stand-alone with bipartisan support. Those efforts were also unsuccessful, perhaps coming too late in the session.

Louisiana

In her home city of New Orleans, Donna Nathan purchased a gun and used it to kill herself the same day. Two days later, Donna's daughter, Katrina Brees, posted on Facebook: "People suffering from bipolar and depression have no way to protect themselves from a suicidal gun purchase in Louisiana."[8] A reporter at the New Orleans *Times-Picayune* put Katrina in touch with us. We shared our draft bill and recommended that she find a sponsor in the Louisiana legislature. We advised her that Republican sponsorship, or cosponsorship, is ideal in every state, but particularly in red states like Louisiana.

Katrina found a sponsor through an unlikely path. Before her mother died, Katrina had been commissioned by the Republican Party to create sculptural work for their convention. Through this process she got to know the former head of the Republican Party and his partner, a former mayor of a city near New Orleans. Katrina did not raise the issue with them; they raised it with her after reading about her efforts in the paper. They connected her to State Senator Danny Martini, who in turn recruited Representative Jimmy Harris.

Representative Harris's bill was the first to propose a ban on purchase and possession, not just firearm purchase. Katrina does not know who made this change or why. It may have been inadvertent, or it may reflect a policy judgment that a possession ban could lead some individuals to disarm and thus save more lives. Just days before a scheduled hearing, the bill was pushed over to the next session. The stated concern was the cost of setting up a web-based interface.

Figure 3.1. Donna Nathan (right) and her daughter Katrina Brees
(Courtesy of Patrick M. Burke)

Massachusetts

The Massachusetts bill actually got its start in Norman, Oklahoma. Joseph Ostas had grown up an outgoing and happy child. As he got older, however, Joseph struggled with anxiety, depression, and mild Asperger's syndrome. He spent years trying different psychiatric and prescription therapies, and admitted himself to mental health facilities six times to seek help and treatment. While sometimes Joseph seemed to be doing better, he ultimately lost the fight at the age of twenty-four.

What is perhaps most tragic is that everyone could see how the defeat would come. Joseph had suicidal thoughts, which led him twice to purchase a firearm. Joseph's parents pleaded with the local gun shop in Norman not to sell him another gun. Their pleas were in vain. On August 15, 2016, Joseph bought a gun from that shop and used it to kill himself the same day.

A short time later, one of Joseph's friends, Reed Shafer-Ray, talked to Joseph's mother, Andrea Scopelitis, about how to prevent similar tragedies in the future. Reed described the Extreme Risk Protection Order (ERPO, aka red flag law), whereby family members could petition a court for a removal of gun rights from a family member in crisis. To Reed's surprise, Andrea expressed unease about what she saw as an intrusion on personal autonomy. The two of them conceived the idea of voluntary self-restriction, unaware of its prior development elsewhere.

Reed was well positioned to find a sponsor for legislation in Massachusetts. Then an undergraduate at Harvard University, he was legislative director for the Harvard Democrats and knew Massachusetts state representative Marjorie Decker well. He pitched her on both the ERPO and voluntary self-restriction ideas, and she ended up drafting two separate bills. When asked whether his preexisting relationship with Decker helped him get his proposals off the ground, Reed did not hesitate: "Oh, yes, a hundred percent." In stark contrast, Reed and Andrea's efforts in Oklahoma, where they had no prior relationships with legislators, fell flat.

Unfortunately, Representative Decker's bill included some poor drafting decisions. Most significantly, the bill mandated that in order to participate, a person must acknowledge that they "[have] a psychiatric disability and [are] a danger to themselves." Bills in other states allow participation by anyone and require no such personal disclosures. The closest analog to this eligibility standard in Massachusetts law is involuntary hospitalization, which requires mental illness and a likelihood of serious harm.[9] Forcing a registrant to acknowledge that they have a psychiatric disability is worse than unnecessary because it would almost certainly dissuade participation.

Other aspects of Decker's bill were more reasonable. The reinstatement provisions similarly echoed the same standard that is applied to those involuntarily hospitalized in Massachusetts. After five years, a court may restore firearm rights if the person is found not to be dangerous.[10] The Massachusetts bill also broke new ground by promoting enrollment in three affirmative ways: (1) requiring distribution of the sign-up form to acute-care hospitals and satellite emergency facilities; (2) requiring such facilities to present the form to voluntary patients believed to be suffering from depression; and (3) requiring suicide hotlines to refer callers to the form. The bill also exempts the list from public records laws, which may promote enrollment by protecting enrollees' confidentiality.

Wisconsin

Our involvement in Wisconsin has been limited. Representative Melissa Sargent built her voluntary handgun purchase prohibition bill on the model of gambling self-exclusion.[11] Under her bill, one can elect for a one-year, five-year, or twenty-year exclusion period. After the full period selected, revocation is automatic upon request. The first year, exclusion is irrevocable under all three options. After the first year but before the five- or twenty-year periods have run, handgun purchase ability can be restored only with an affidavit from a psychiatrist or psychologist stating that the person can possess a firearm without posing a danger to self or others. Sargent first introduced her bill in October 2017.

Washington

Our effort in Washington State was multipronged. In the fall of 2015, Fred blogged about the idea on PrawfsBlawg, a site for law professors.[12] Those posts led Fred to speak with Professor Charlotte Garden, who was visiting Alabama from her home institution, the Seattle University law school. When asked if she had any connections in policymaking circles, Professor Garden connected Fred with a Washington State Senator, Cyrus Habib, who was also on the faculty at Seattle. After exchanging emails with Fred in late 2015, Senator Habib called to express interest in the idea and to discuss it. For whatever reason, that conversation did not generate a bill.

The project seemed indefinitely stalled until April 2016. Jennifer Stuber, a professor at the University of Washington, published an op-ed in the *Washington Post,* where she described forging common ground on the topic of suicide prevention on a telephone call with a representative of the NRA.[13] After reading the op-ed, Fred emailed Professor Stuber, describing the proposal. She called it a "fantastic idea" and was later crucial in building the bipartisan coalition that ultimately succeeded in Washington State.

But the most essential driver for the bill in Washington State was State Senator Jamie Pedersen, who would become the bill's architect and sponsor. Senator Pedersen knows Ian because they were both members of the Yale Russian Chorus, and he learned of the idea from Ian. Senator Pedersen has emphasized that seeing Ian's name attached to the idea was a big factor in his decision to pursue it. Ideas offered by strangers are understandably discounted; an idea backed by a friend who is also a law professor might be taken more seriously. As Senator Pedersen explains, a connection to the sponsor is an important validator: it says that "this person isn't crazy."

Fred and Jamie started an extensive email correspondence about the bill after it had been drafted and introduced, around the time it was scheduled for its first committee hearing. The Washington bill allows people to voluntarily waive their gun purchase rights by registering in person at the county clerk's office. Individuals can revoke the waiver (i.e., restore their gun purchase rights) after seven days in the same manner. Neither Fred nor Ian influenced these implementation choices.

Senator Pedersen called Professor Stuber early in the drafting process. After the gun suicide death of her husband, Stuber had become a leader in suicide prevention, particularly in promoting measures that appeal to both gun owners and proponents of stricter gun regulation. She had been instrumental in removing legal hurdles for a person in crisis to temporarily give their gun to a trusted friend or family member. Stuber's prior work may have been the inspiration for the Washington bill's most significant innovation, what we call back-end notification: allowing a person at sign-up to designate a trusted individual, who would be notified in the event that the enrollee requested to reestablish their gun purchase rights. While the designated individual would not have the power under the bill to prevent a gun purchase, they would be able to assess the mind-set of the participant and intervene as appropriate.

The transfer-in-crisis paradigm also appears to have influenced the delay provisions of the bill. In Washington, a person who signs up for self-exclusion may not request to have their purchase ability restored for seven days. After that, restoration requests are accepted, and restoration must happen within seven days. In theory, the state could move very quickly, restoring gun purchase ability on the same day as the request is made. Washington's bill could be described as primarily designed to get an individual through one crisis, not to delay purchases down the road, though requiring a trip back to the courthouse to restore gun rights could deter impulsive suicide indefinitely.

Senator Pedersen also chose to require in-person registration at the county clerk's office. This provision will likely deter some people from registering who otherwise would have if given the option of registering at home through a web-based portal. When asked about this tradeoff, Senator Pedersen explained that in-person registration seemed appropriate given the serious nature of the decision to waive. He added that whereas a website would almost certainly have required appropriations review, using the county clerk was inexpensive enough to avoid this step. Avoiding the appropriations committee increases the likelihood of passage fivefold, Pedersen estimates.

The bill (SB 5553) was first heard in Washington State's Senate Committee on Law and Justice in January 2017. Gun rights organizations opposed the bill on two grounds: (1) the seven-day delay period for reinstatement was too long in case of an emergency need for a firearm; and (2) health care providers and others might coerce participation. The committee chairman did not call a vote. The brief delay period is precisely what prevents suicide, so there was no compromise on that point. But before the next legislative session, Senator Pedersen addressed the coercion issue by adding language bolstering privacy and expressly prohibiting discrimination based on registration status. These modifications muted opposition.

Serendipity played a major role as well. Democrats took control of the state senate in a special election in November 2017.[14] Senator Pedersen became chair of the relevant senate committee, ensuring that SB 5553 would get a committee vote in the next session. Not only did SB 5553 pass committee; it received bipartisan support at every stage of the process. The only significant amendment was to use the federal NICS database rather than just state lists. This means that a participant who resides in Vancouver cannot simply drive over the bridge to Portland, Oregon, to purchase a gun. Governor Jay Inslee signed the bill into law on March 21, 2018.[15] To close a last circle, then–Lieutenant Governor Habib also signed the bill in his capacity as president of the senate two and a half years after our first contact.

Through the skillful and tireless efforts of State Senator Jamie Pedersen, the proposal took effect in Washington State on January 1, 2019. This success story was made possible by personal connections, shifting state politics, prior advocacy on suicide prevention bringing together both sides of the gun debate, and a willingness to modify the bill in response to criticism. The story is not over: efforts continue to achieve statewide implementation and to encourage participation.[16]

LESSONS

In our experiences drafting and lobbying for different iterations of the bill, we encountered commonalities in both the actual policies contained in the bill and the strategies used to lobby for the bill's passage. While each state's political process is unique, we believe that many of these general lessons will be useful to concerned citizens, academics, and advocates alike.

Policies

States really are laboratories of democracy. The initial proposal has been improved with each iteration as thoughtful people engage with it and modify it to better fit the circumstances in their state. For example, Massachusetts has led the nation by requiring acute-care hospitals and satellite emergency facilities to provide individuals reasonably believed to be suffering with depression with the opportunity to register.[17] The commonwealth bill would also require state-funded suicide hotlines to inform callers about the registration option.[18]

The best example of state innovation is the option in the State of Washington's law for registrants to designate a third-party contact to be notified "if a voluntary waiver of firearm rights is revoked." A person so notified would have an opportunity to check in with their friend or family member to ensure that they were not motivated by suicidal intent when deciding to rescind. By restricting registry notifications to this back-end moment of potential rescission and not providing notifications of sign-up (or "front-end" notification), the Washington law precludes economic and noneconomic actors from conditioning their association on the registry verifying that a waiver is in effect. A Washington landlord might only want to rent to tenants who have registered to waive their firearm rights, but in Washington the landlord will only learn if a registrant attempts to rescind her registration. Back-end notifications are still valuable because they can provide friends, family, and health care professionals with notice that this person was once registered and will soon be capable of again purchasing firearms. Recipients of these back-end notifications have the opportunity to inquire and potentially intervene to save the registrant's life.

In Chapter 4, we argue that some states may actually want to allow limited types of discrimination as the foundation of an associational marketplace. But Washington has chosen to prohibit discrimination while still allowing for a safety net in the form of optional back-end notification. We feel a mixture of both humility (as academics) and pride (as citizens) that this innovation of back-end notification sprang not from our minds but from the mind of an elected state official and his collaborators.

Other variations respond to differences in states' existing gun laws. Massachusetts already requires a license to purchase a firearm, and getting a license already slows down gun purchase, so reinstatement after a mere delay period may have little marginal effect.[19] Representative Decker's decision to require a court hearing to reinstate gun purchase ability therefore is a reasonable response (although the requirement for court review may dampen people's initial willingness to register). California's bill included a similar requirement for a similar reason. A state's existing gun regulations should be, and have been, factored in when crafting a bill in that state. Other state bills have varied durability of registration along other dimensions. The Wisconsin registry, for example, makes mental health professionals the gatekeepers with regard to registrant rescission. After Wisconsin's yearlong irrevocable period, registrants may remove themselves from the database by submitting to the state's Department of Justice a request for removal and an affidavit from a licensed psychiatrist or psychologist saying that the individual would not pose a threat to themselves or others should they possess a firearm.[20]

Not every innovation has been a success. Some states have included participation restrictions that we believe will decrease the number of people who enroll in the program. Massachusetts's bill requires individuals registering to acknowledge that they have a psychiatric disability and are dangerous. This requirement is deeply misguided. Limiting registration to this class of people unreasonably discriminates against individuals who do not fit within these qualifying categories. Moreover, it needlessly stigmatizes registrants without any credible offsetting benefit. People without a documented disability could also benefit from participation, and people with a mental illness may be justifiably concerned about disclosing their diagnosis to the government. Such a provision will likely discourage many from participating in the registry. We don't mean to suggest that this was the intent of the drafters of the Massachusetts bill. To the contrary, the misemphasis of the Massachusetts bill may be due to the fact that it was drafted in response to a specific suicide involving both mental illness and extreme suicide risk.

Illinois would require notarization as the only registration option. The difficulty of finding a notary and the added pressure of having to "out" oneself to others would likely suppress participation. For this reason, we have strenuously urged the creation of an online or text registration option, which removes both logistical and privacy obstacles.

Other states have included design details that tend to limit the scope of self-exclusion, dampening the program's efficacy. For example, some bills use state databases rather than NICS to record a person's registration status. A state registry would generally prevent people from purchasing weapons only in the state in which they are enrolled. However, it would still allow them to drive to the next state over and purchase a firearm without having to revoke their registration status. In contrast, NICS has a national effect and applies to gun purchases in all states and is thus a more effective self-restraint mechanism. During the legislative process, the Washington bill switched from using state databases to using NICS.

The bills in Washington and Wisconsin also do not allow for enough of a cooling-off period for individuals who request to be removed from the self-exclusion list. After the first seven-day prohibition on gun purchase in Washington and a longer prohibition period in Wisconsin, a participant could be removed from the list on the same day that they make the request. This does not provide enough time for individuals to reconsider what might have been a rash and dangerous decision made in haste.

In addition, Wisconsin's bill applies only to handguns, ignoring the large number of people who use shotguns and even rifles in

suicide attempts.[21] While certainly a handgun registry is better than
nothing, future efforts should look seriously to expanding the
scope of the bill in order to increase its effectiveness.

Perhaps the most consequential decision a state can make is
whether to allow individuals merely to prevent their own gun
purchases or also to prohibit their own gun possession. The first
Louisiana bill opted for a ban on possession as well as purchase.
The argument to do so is to get guns out of the homes of people
at risk for suicide and to prevent many more gun suicides. One
argument against this is that people might be deterred from
signing up. Also, a person who illegally obtains a gun to attempt
suicide probably doesn't belong in prison. Other states appear
poised to follow Louisiana's lead, potentially creating a natural
experiment in our laboratories of democracy.

Lobbying Strategy

Our experience suggests that a personal connection to a legislator
is a powerful factor in securing a motivated sponsor. One might
hope that the merits of an idea, standing alone, would be sufficient for success. But put yourself in the position of a legislator.
In addition to attending to the multitude of responsibilities of office, legislators often receive idea pitches in a broad range of areas
from countless constituents or other interested parties. It is unlikely that most legislators have the time or expertise to evaluate
each suggestion on the merits. They rely on proxies in determining
which ideas to pursue. We mistakenly thought that cold-calling
and emailing with our idea would be sufficient. A personal connection with a legislator was an important factor in most of the
states where a bill was introduced. Often the connection was to
a former classmate or student who had gone on to become a state
legislator.

At least one of two other ingredients has been present for the
bills that have advanced quickest and farthest. The first is having
an advocate who lost a loved one to suicide, because, as Reed puts

it, "it's their story that's actually going to compel people to become champions of the legislation in your given state." Katrina Brees in Louisiana is a prime example of a driven survivor-advocate. A key suicide prevention leader in Washington, Jennifer Stuber, is herself a survivor of her husband's gun suicide. People who have lost loved ones are both passionate advocates and can speak with particular authority. The history of Massachusetts's bill suggests, however, that the power of a particular tragedy can be a double-edged sword. The vividness of Joseph Ostas's tragic death helped motivate advocates for the commonwealth bill, but this same salience may have led the bill's drafters to focus too intently on the details of that one particular event (and to resist our repeated suggestions to expand coverage beyond people who acknowledge having "a psychiatric disability and [being] a danger to themselves").[22]

The second key factor is a sustained ground game. Securing a sponsor in a far-flung state has never been enough to get a bill enacted. What is needed is activism within the state. Our California and Washington sponsors successfully engaged suicide prevention and gun safety groups like Giffords Law Center and the Brady Campaign in California and the Alliance for Gun Responsibility and Forefront Suicide Prevention in Washington. These groups have the benefit of being more familiar with the state's policy and political landscape, and having important local connections with influential figures.

The pathway and destination for the proposal will vary from state to state. While this can generate innovation and improvement, it also can result in missteps and missed opportunities. Procedurally, the importance of personal connections in getting bills introduced is discouraging. And the wall of limited state resources has stopped several bills in their tracks. Persuading lawmakers of the potential of the idea is one thing; persuading them to devote funds to it is another.

Cost

Finally, funding has proved to be a powerful impediment. Bills in several states have failed because of the estimated cost of setting up a web-based sign-up platform. It is surely no coincidence that our only success to date came in Washington, which did not include a web-based option but instead required relatively inexpensive in-person registration. We remain committed to the goal of making secure registration as easy as possible while keeping costs reasonable.

The costs of online registration are modest in comparison with the number of lives potentially saved. Legislative efforts in at least four states have made it possible to estimate how much it would cost to save one life under our proposal. Table 3.1 summarizes these estimates. The variation in the estimates is striking, but the policy is cost-benefit justified even when taking into account the highest cost estimate in each state. The highest amount per life saved would be in the first year in Louisiana, around $16,000. This assumes that 3 percent of residents give up their existing guns. Even assuming instead that no one gives up their gun, the waiting period effect alone generates a cost-per-life-saved estimate of $90,000.

Reducing human lives to dollars is controversial, but looking solely at medical costs and lost productivity further supports the cost-benefit argument in favor of the proposal. It has been estimated that one suicide carries medical and economic costs of $1.3 million.[23] That means well over $1 million in purely economic savings per suicide averted. Add to that the inestimable emotional harm of a suicide, and the proposal pays for itself many times over. Moreover, after the first state sets up a web interface, subsequent states may be able to reduce costs by borrowing technology, thus further reducing implementation costs. There is no need to reinvent the wheel.

We recognize that some states may be unable or unwilling to allocate even the modest amount of money needed for imple-

Table 3.1. Estimated Cost to Implement Donna's Law (in thousands of dollars)

	Washington[1]	Tennessee[2]	Louisiana[3]	California[4]
Year 1	<50	235	≤358	777
Year 2	<50	91	≤200	1055
Year 3	<50	91	≤200	460
Year 4+	<50	91	≤200	271

1. Wash. Judicial Impact Fiscal Note, SB 5553. Washington State's bill did not include a web-based platform, and therefore the cost of implementation does not include the cost of programming and maintenance.
2. Tenn. Fiscal Note, SB 671–HB 962.
3. La. Fiscal Note, HB 101.
4. Cal. Assembly Committee on Appropriations Report, AB 1927.

menting web-based registration. Compromise may be necessary. Neither substance nor process must hew to some Aristotelean ideal. Our experience shows that there is enormous potential for creative adaptation by different states and demonstrates the power of sustained, collaborative advocacy.

In this chapter we discussed our experiences trying to enact Donna's Law in various state legislatures. Our efforts have yielded both substantive and procedural lessons. Procedurally, this chapter has shown the importance of a sustained ground-game, personal stories, and personal connections. Substantively, we've shown how legislators have generated new ideas for tailoring the bill in different states. The ingredients for political success appear more or less constant across states, but the implementation choices have been diverse. Our hope is that others will build on the existing groundwork to continue pushing for reform.

Postscript: As this book went to press in April 2020, Virginia became the second state to adopt Donna's Law. The Virginia law includes a mail-in registration option, provides that possession is

a fine-only misdemeanor, and requires notice of the law to all licensed counselors, doctors, nurses, and psychologists. Senator
Scott Surovell was the architect and champion. And earlier this
year, Utah became the eleventh state to introduce a version of
Donna's Law.

PART II

HARNESSING OTHERS' ASSOCIATION PREFERENCES

4

EMAILS AND THE
ASSOCIATIONAL MARKETPLACE

In Part 1 we laid out our case for how Donna's Law could enhance liberty and save hundreds of lives every year. In this chapter we suggest a simple, principled way to enhance the life-saving impact of the registry severalfold. We propose that individuals who register to waive their gun rights also be given the option to credibly communicate their waiver to others. Accordingly, our second model statute calls for the registration platform to give waiving individuals the option of providing email addresses for the platform to automatically notify of the individual's waiver.

Our email option facilitates an associational marketplace. Individuals who on their own would not be willing to self-exclude from gun ownership may voluntarily opt to waive their firearm rights in order to secure particular associational opportunities. Citizens routinely waive their First Amendment free-speech rights in order to associate with others. That's what happens, for example, when an engineer signs a nondisclosure agreement (NDA) as a prerequisite of being able to collaborate with a corporation, or when a citizen gives up the right to endorse candidates in order to take certain federal jobs under the Hatch Act.[1] Likewise, people might waive their Second Amendment rights in order to associate socially and economically with others. A government-sponsored no-guns registry with optional email notices to third parties can promote social welfare by forcing Second Amendment rights to

contend with the First Amendment's protection of private associational freedom. An individual would certainly be free to register anonymously by opting not to provide the registry with any
email addresses. But your insurance company may only be willing
to give you a discount on your homeowner's or renter's insurance if
you provide the registry with the insurer's email to verify that you
have waived your right to bear arms. Or you may only be able to
buy into a particular condo if the condominium association receives
an email from the registry verifying that you have registered.

The goal here is not to punish gun owners, but rather to better
inform market participants who have a reasonable interest in
defending their insurance reserves or real property. Our email proposal, for example, does not require that insurance companies offer
no-gun discounts. The forces of an associational market might
lead to either more or less gun possession. Insurance companies
would have an economic incentive to offer no-gun discounts only if
they expect that offering such discounts will increase their profits
by reducing expected necessary payouts.

This book's notion of gun control is "libertarian" not only in
that it gives an individual enhanced rights to durably commit to
not bear arms but also in that it allows a limited class of others
to condition their association on such a waiver. Our proposed
registry enhances both self-commitment liberty (by letting individuals bind their future selves) and market liberty (by letting
individuals make better commitments to others). Laurel has a
constitutional right to bear arms. But Hardy has a constitutional
right to choose whether or not to associate with Laurel, including
the right to only associate if Laurel is not armed. The goal of the
email option is to create an associational marketplace to resolve
these conflicting preferences. We imagine that some Hardys will
choose to associate with the Laurels of the world even though the
latter remain armed. But sometimes the Laurels will register to
credibly cede their Second Amendment rights in order to maintain their relationship with gun-eschewing Hardys. As in other

marketplaces, we imagine that the conceding party will sometimes receive some other consideration, a discount or concession on some other issue, to cut a deal. At other times, the parties will fail to reach an agreement to resolve the conflict the Laurels and will choose not to accept the other party's associational conditions. But in any case, informed association advances libertarian freedom.

Our discussion of Donna's Law in Part 1 was a freedom-enhancing approach that gave individuals a way to fulfill their preferences to waive their gun rights. This chapter pursues our "freedom-enhancing" agenda by giving individuals a new choice that can let them better fulfill their preferences about whether to economically and noneconomically interact with others. If a landlord prefers to rent only to people who have waived their gun rights, she can insist before renting on receiving a registry email verifying that the potential tenants have waived their rights. The email option thus gives other people some leverage, the right to withhold their association, as to whether a particular person retains the right to bear arms.

An associational market does not guarantee that fewer people will be armed. As an analytic matter, facilitating an associational market could lead to an equilibrium with greater gun ownership than we have in the present status quo. A landlord might be willing to rent only to armed tenants. But the option to condition association on owning a gun already exists and is easily verified: just show me your gun.[2] The email verification option levels the evidentiary playing field by allowing individuals to more feasibly condition their association on another person's waiver. Thus, while particular actors may or may not bring such pressure to bear, by making "no gun" contracting more verifiable, the email innovation should, as an empirical matter, lead to less gun ownership.[3] And more pragmatically, allowing insurance companies to give discounts on homeowner's and renter's insurance by itself might easily increase the demand for registration severalfold.

We recognize that allowing some third parties to condition their willingness to associate, including to economically associate via contracting, on a party not bearing arms raises constitutional and ethical concerns. Specifically, unfettered associational discrimination facilitated by state action might unduly burden an individual's Second Amendment rights.

We therefore propose banning *economic* associational discrimination based on whether a person has waived except by predefined individuals who can claim plausible self-defense interests in refusing to associate with someone who hasn't waived. Specifically, neighbors, cotenants, landlords, and homeowners' associations, as well as life and property insurers, have legitimate self-defense interests in conditioning their association on other people's waiver of the right to purchase and possess firearms. Accordingly, our proposal would only allow economic entities with residential or insurance self-defense interests to condition willingness to contract on waiver.

This exempted class is in fact narrower than the entire population of those who have credible self-defense reasons to screen for individuals who have not waived their right to bear arms. Employers, for example, have a substantial interest in preventing their employees from bringing guns to the job site and killing themselves or others. There have been numerous instances of employee-instigated workplace violence, including the 2019 Virginia Beach shootings, where an engineer who had resigned hours before the incident killed twelve employees at the municipal center building.[4] While mass shootings in the workplace are unusual,[5] attacks with fewer than four victims are quite common, resulting in 14,770 total workplace homicide victims between 1992 and 2012.[6] But in an abundance of caution, we do not propose authorizing employers to discriminate on the basis of a gun rights waiver.[7]

Outside the economic realm, citizens would retain the right to condition their social interactions on waiver. Reasonable citizens might, for example, prefer playdates for their children at homes with no-guns registrants. Individuals can also choose who they want to invite to dinner. If we can refuse to invite people because of the religion they practice, we certainly should be allowed to refuse to invite them because of their choice to bear or not to bear arms. The fact that both religion and bearing firearms are constitutionally protected from government interference does not mean that purely private individuals acting outside the market are similarly restrained.

Our model statute mandates that the registry "provide registrants with an email notification option that shall allow registered individuals to identify at the time of registration or thereafter one or more email addresses" and "separately ask whether a registrant wishes to provide the email addresses of his or her physician or healthcare provider."[8] The provision goes on to require that "[t]he [AGENCY] shall notify any such email addressees that the individual has registered his or her name with the [STATE] No Guns Registry and has thereby waived his or her right to bear arms, and the [AGENCY] shall also notify any such addressees if the individual subsequently seeks to rescind his or her waiver."

Even without this email option, waiving individuals could always exercise their free-speech rights by directly telling a third party that they had waived their right to purchase and possess guns. But the third party would have trouble verifying whether such waiver had actually taken place. Likewise, with or without the registry option, individuals are free to contractually promise not to purchase or possess firearms. But the possibility of contract damages would be an imperfect substitute for an email from the registry confirming that gun dealers are prohibited from selling to the registrant and that the registrant has subjected herself to potential criminal penalties for purchase or possession.[9] While any individual may claim (and even promise) to have waived their rights, email notifications from the government platform will more credibly indicate that they are committed to not bear arms.

The communication option that we have proposed is updatable across time in two ways. First, if a waiving individual later rescinds her waiver, the platform should automatically and immediately send emails to all previously designated addresses indicating that such waiver is being rescinded in twenty-one days. Notice of rescission will let recipients know that the individual will soon regain the right to bear arms. This allows recipients who were relying on the previous waiver to make different associational choices regarding the rescinding individual. Notice of rescission would also give recipients a chance to contact the individual and perhaps prevent a suicide attempt or other tragic outcome. This notice of rescission might be particularly valuable for health care professionals who, especially with regard to patients who had previously experienced suicidal ideation, might inquire into the patient's current mental health status.[10]

Second, the platform should allow waiving individuals to log on subsequent to their initial waiver and provide additional email addresses to the platform. The platform would immediately notify these additional addressees that the individual had waived her right to bear arms (and also notify these addressees if that individual subsequently initiated the process of rescinding her waiver). The platform would not, however, allow an individual to log on and remove the name of an addressee. Allowing for this option would undermine the impact of giving addressees notice of possible subsequent rescission.

FRONT-END, INTERIM, AND BACK-END EMAILS

This provision thus sets out three potential times when the registry would send out emails:

> (1) Front-end emails are sent at the time of registration (or if the registrant subsequently provides additional email addresses), notifying the addressees that the individual has registered;

(2) interim emails are sent if a registered individual attempts to unlawfully purchase a firearm, for example from Federal Firearms Licensees (FFLs), notifying the addressees of the attempted illegal purchase; and

(3) back-end emails are sent if the registrant subsequently seeks to rescind the registration, notifying the addressees of the date the rescission will take effect.

As a political matter, the full-blown email option with the possibility of front-end, interim, and back-end emails has been controversial. One person's informed association can be another person's coercive discrimination. Several of the registry bills to date forgo the email option altogether, and outlaw any attempts to discriminate on registry status in contracting.[11] However, Washington State senator Jamie Pedersen creatively forged an alternative email option that prohibits waiver discrimination while simultaneously retaining some of the core public health benefits of email notification. Pedersen's registry bill allows registrants to designate a third-party contact to be notified "if a voluntary waiver of firearm rights is revoked."[12] A more recently introduced California bill analogously allows registrants to "list up to five electronic mail addresses with the registry to be contacted promptly if the person subsequently requests that his or her name be removed from the registry."[13] By restricting registry notifications to the back-end moment of potential rescission, the Washington and California bills preclude economic and noneconomic actors from conditioning their association on the registry verifying that a waiver is in effect. A Washington landlord might only want to rent to tenants who have registered to waive their firearm rights, but in Washington the landlord will learn only if a registrant attempts to rescind her registration.[14] Back-end notifications are still valuable because they can provide friends, family, and health care professionals with notice that this person was once registered and will soon be capable of again purchasing firearms.

Recipients of these back-end notifications have the opportunity to inquire and potentially intervene to save the registrant's life.

Back-end and interim notifications, however, do not achieve all the associational benefits of our more fulsome email notification proposal. Front-end notifications sent at the time of initial registration are liberty-enhancing options that foster informed association in ways that allow others to better protect themselves. Front-end emails facilitate the associational marketplace by credibly signaling waiver of rights. A registry with just back-end notification would only send emails as the registrant rescinds her obligation not to bear arms. Accordingly, the landlord (whose email had been given to a registry by a tenant) would only learn after the fact that a registrant had previously given up the right to bear arms.

Nonetheless, we take the Washington State bill's use of back-end notice to be a humbling example of legislative creativity. After thinking and writing for years about alternative implementations of our self-exclusion idea, we had never considered the possibility of using an email option exclusively for back-end revocations. The ability of Senator Pedersen to devise a plausible improvement that had never occurred to us (or been mentioned at seminars on this idea given at over a dozen universities) is a success story for federalism. Creative state legislators confronting the necessity of forging a politically feasible coalition have conjured not just different forms of email notification, but different forms of durability and revocation. The state laboratory has succeeded in drafting different experiments far beyond our expectations.

NEGOTIATED WAIVER

The simple addition of an email option creates a substantial separate impetus for registering, what we term "negotiated exclusion." Part 1 of this book detailed theoretically and empirically why people might use the registry as a commitment device to keep themselves and others safe. Here we explore why individuals may also rationally commit to waive their Second Amendment firearm rights in order to induce others to associate with them. Some friends, neighbors, and even loved ones may be more willing to associate with individuals who credibly signal that they have foregone the right to bear arms. The potential demand for negotiated exclusion is suggested by analyzing Connecticut's Gun Violence Restraining Orders (GVROs), where roughly half of the petitions for gun removal come from family and friends.[15] Individuals who by themselves would not be willing to self-exclude from gun ownership may voluntarily opt to waive their firearm rights in order to secure or to continue particular associational opportunities.

The no-guns registry thus creates opportunities for a modern-day version of the central plot device in Aristophanes's *Lysistrata*—where some individuals voluntarily yield their right to weapons because of the threat of withholding various forms of interactions by friends and family.[16] In September 2006, dozens of women organized a sex strike in Pereira, Colombia, called *la huelga de las piernas cruzadas* (the strike of crossed legs) in an effort to encourage gang members to turn in their weapons.[17] We are skeptical that mass refusals of this kind could be effectively organized.[18] But friends' and families' demands to register as a prerequisite for playdates and family visits are not far-fetched.

The demand for negotiated self-exclusion might also be prompted by the threat by economic entities to withhold various forms of residential association. Homeowners' associations, co-op boards, and cotenants might condition occupancy upon individuals' waiver of their gun rights. It is hardly surprising that landlords, trying to collect late rent, have been shot by disgruntled tenants.[19] Some landlords, foreseeing this possibility, may prefer unarmed tenants.

Our proposed associational marketplace might even exhibit some aspects of a commodified marketplace. Some individuals might offer compensation if others will sign the registry. Or a tenants' association might mandate a financial forfeiture or eviction if a resident rescinds a required waiver.[20] Life insurers or home-owners' (or renters') insurers might give discounts to individuals who have credibly signaled that they had ceded the right to bear arms. While many suicides are impulsive, there is also evidence that those with life insurance are more likely to attempt suicide once the initial period of payout exclusion ends. Most states mandate that life insurance companies pay out when the cause of death is suicide if the death occurs after the first year or two of the policy.[21] Samuel Hsin-yu Tseng found that the "suicide rate quadruples after [this] exclusion period."[22] Life insurance companies, given the opportunity, might offer discounts to insureds who had provided registry verification that they had waived their right to own arms.[23] Similarly, competition might induce renter's and homeowner's insurance to offer discounts to waiving individuals, as there is some evidence that gun ownership increases the probability of burglary.[24] As explained by Philip Cook and Jens Ludwig:

> Guns in the home may pose a threat to burglars, but also serve as an inducement, since guns are particularly valuable loot. Other things equal, a gun-rich community provides more lucrative burglary opportunities than one where guns are more sparse. The new empirical results reported here provide no support for a net deterrent effect from widespread gun ownership. Rather, our analysis concludes that residential burglary rates tend to increase with community gun prevalence.[25]

While the incentive of individual insurance companies to provide waiver discounts may be muted because reducing community gun prevalence lowers the payouts of its rivals, a similar "lowering rivals' cost" effect has not stopped individual insurers from offering LoJack discounts.[26]

A no-guns registry with front- and back-end email notifications allows individuals to effectively communicate to others that they have committed not to purchase firearms. By serving as a central coordinator of these emails, the government can help provide the information necessary for individuals and businesses to make the associational decisions that best reflect their true preferences regarding gun ownership.

5

LIBERTARIAN CONTRACTING
AND ITS LIMITS

While giving individuals the unfettered, unilateral discretion to waive their right to bear arms is consonant with the libertarian embrace of self-authorship,[1] negotiated exclusion raises separate concerns about whether the government is burdening individuals' Second Amendment rights. From one perspective, where third parties induce waiver by threatening to withhold commercial or noncommercial association, no constitutional concerns are raised because state action is not involved. But the government does act as a facilitator with respect to the email option. The government facilitates the associational marketplace by credibly communicating waiver information (if so directed by the registrant) to third parties. This facilitation might constitute sufficient state action to ground a constitutional challenge.[2]

If a state created a similar option whereby women could have the state credibly communicate to third parties whether or not they have had an abortion, there would be valid concerns about whether this option would constitute an "undue burden" on the exercise of this fundamental right.[3] On the other hand, a government registry that allowed people to credibly communicate whether or not they exercised their right to vote in the last election would almost certainly pass constitutional muster. Indeed, many state governments, without constitutional challenge, compel such disclosure by actively publicizing whether individual citizens voted or did not vote in specific elections.[4] The constitutional jurisprudence of whether and when the government can compel disclosure of an individual's exercise of constitutional rights is not well specified. While mandated disclosure of voting is allowed, mandated disclosure of associational membership, in cases like *NAACP v. Alabama,* is prohibited.[5] It is not immediately obvious what differentiates these two rights such that the outcome should be different.

But our email option does not concern government-compelled disclosure. Instead it merely involves the government helping private individuals verify their registration to third parties of their choosing. Whether it is constitutional for a government to merely provide an individual the option of having the government disclose the exercise of a constitutional right has, to our knowledge, never been addressed by a court. The government sending an email does constitute a kind of state action. The government verifies that an individual has registered (or is revoking their registration), and the fact that the message comes from the state may give particular salience to this piece of information. Even though the government's action is triggered by and contingent on a private choice, it may not be immunized from constitutional scrutiny.

Imagine, for example, that the State of Louisiana gave candidates the option of having their race listed on election ballots and that the state did this for the purpose of facilitating private discrimination against African American candidates. In 1964, the Supreme Court in *Anderson v. Martin* struck down an analogous Louisiana statute that compelled the designation of a candidate's race on ballots.[6] The Court reasoned that "by directing the citizen's attention to the single consideration of race or color, the State indicates that a candidate's race or color is an important— perhaps paramount—consideration in the citizen's choice, which may decisively influence the citizen to cast his ballot along racial lines."[7] Though our hypothetical merely gives candidates the option of having the state report their race on ballots, it would similarly be constitutionally infirm. The illegitimate purpose of facilitating private discrimination "by directing the citizen's attention

to the single consideration of race" would still likely be impermissible notwithstanding that any discrimination would be the
by-product of state and private action. The Supreme Court in
NAACP v. Alabama, in striking down a compulsory disclosure
statute, emphasized:

> It is not sufficient to answer, as the State does here, that
> whatever repressive effect compulsory disclosure of names
> of petitioner's members may have upon participation by Al-
> abama citizens in petitioner's activities follows not from
> state action, but from private community pressures. The
> crucial factor is the interplay of governmental and private
> action, for it is only after the initial exertion of state power
> represented by the production order that private action
> takes hold.[8]

Similarly, it is the interplay of governmental and private action
with regard to the email option that raises the question of whether
"private community pressures" might unconstitutionally burden
individuals' exercise of their Second Amendment rights.

As in other areas, the constitutionality of government action
may turn on the government's underlying purpose.[9] The hypothetical Louisiana ballot option is unconstitutional because the
assumed purpose is to illegitimately facilitate private race discrimination. In contrast, a state facilitating credible disclosure
of whether a citizen voted would likely be constitutional if the
government purpose is to encourage voting, plainly a legitimate government objective.

The government need not passively accept how citizens choose
to exercise their constitutional rights, a fact further demonstrated
by the Supreme Court's abortion jurisprudence. For example, in
Planned Parenthood v. Casey, the Court held: "[W]e permit a
State to further its legitimate goal of protecting the life of the
unborn by enacting legislation aimed at ensuring a decision that
is mature and informed, even when, in so doing, the State expresses

a preference for childbirth over abortion."[10] Thus, even though abortion is a constitutionally protected right, the state may still try to influence individuals not to exercise it without unduly burdening the individual's exercise of that right.[11]

Given this jurisprudence, we think it would also be constitutionally permissible for a state to pass laws that have a purpose of expressing a preference for individuals not to bear arms. Gun deaths in the United States each year number in the tens of thousands—providing ample public health reasons to support the legitimacy of a government preference for reducing the prevalence of gun possession. Indeed, it is hard to imagine a court concluding that "protecting the life of the born" would not be as legitimate a state purpose as "protecting the life of the *un*born."

Opponents of the email option might nonetheless argue that pursuing this government purpose by using "private community pressures" unconstitutionally burdens the individual's right to bear arms. In *Buckley v. Valeo,* the Supreme Court rejected a facial constitutional challenge to certain mandated disclosures of campaign contributions, but nonetheless carved out a potential exception "where the threat to the exercise of First Amendment rights is so serious and the state interest furthered by disclosure so insubstantial that the Act's requirements cannot be constitutionally applied."[12] The Court worried that "compelled disclosure of party contributors' names will subject them to threats, harassment, or reprisals from either Government officials or private parties."[13]

Without offering a definitive normative analysis of the constitutional limits on the government as facilitator, several aspects of our email option argue strongly in favor of the constitutionality of our proposal. First, courts have already ruled that compelled public disclosure of gun permits can be constitutional. In *CBS v. Block,* the California Supreme Court upheld the right of "press and public" under the California Public Records Act to obtain information about the identity of those licensed to possess concealed weapons, in the face of a dissent that expressly considered the *NAACP v. Alabama* possibility that disclosure might expose licensees to "economic reprisal, loss of employment, threat of physical coercion, and other manifestations of public hostility."[14] The Nevada Supreme Court held similarly in 2010.[15] While now legislatively repealed, a New York State law until 2014 compelled disclosure of the identity of all gun permit holders—thereby identifying all individuals possessing guns.[16] In comparison, our email proposal only discloses the identity of a person who chooses to have the registry send emails to particular addressees. The fact that disclosure under our proposal is voluntary and targeted presents a stronger case for constitutionality than the broad, compelled disclosure regimes that have survived repeated challenges.

Second, our model statute further tailors the scope of the email option and strengthens the case for constitutionality by prohibiting any commercial actor from refusing to contract on the basis of registry status unless the commercial actor has a sufficient self-defense interest in doing so. In *District of Columbia v. Heller*, the Supreme Court held that individual self-defense was "the *central component*" of the Second Amendment right.[17] The right to disassociate from people who possess arms is constitutionally at its strongest when the person disassociating is making a decision about how best to defend their home—where, as *Heller* explained, "the need for defense of self, family, and property is most acute."[18] Thus, our email option does not just make Second Amendment firearm rights contend with First Amendment associational rights—it makes one person's self-defense preferences contend with another person's constitutionally equal self-defense preferences.[19]

In June 2016, Anne Verrill, the owner of two restaurants in Portland, Maine, posted a photo of an AR-15 assault rifle along with the message "If you own this gun, or you condone the ownership of this gun for private use, you may no longer enter either of my restaurants."[20] If our email proposal were adopted, one might imagine that this owner would demand credible evidence that patrons had waived their right to possess firearms as a precondition of service. But our self-defense limitation would prohibit such discrimination. While a restaurant owner has a legitimate basis for prohibiting customers (or others) from carrying firearms onto her property (see Chapter 6), she does not have a sufficient self-defense basis for refusing to serve customers who possess firearms that they have left at home. Thus, our proposal would prohibit most retail sellers from refusing to sell to gun possessors.

With an abundance of caution, our proposal would only allow those who live with or near the potential registrant or those who have an insurance interest in the potential waiver's residence or life to condition their willingness to contract on waiver. Thus, our model statute would allow cotenants, landlords, and homeowners' and condominium associations to condition an individual's residency upon registering to waive his or her Second Amendment rights.[21] Life and property insurers as well as landlords have sufficient property interests in defending the potential waiver's residence and/or continued life to justify conditioning insurance or its terms on an individual's waiver status.

A powerful case could be made for also allowing employers to condition employment on workers' nonpossession of firearms. As mentioned earlier, there were 14,770 workplace homicide victims in the United States between 1992 and 2012.[22] The very term "going postal" derives from "a series of sensational murders at U.S. Postal Service branches" in the late 1980s and early 1990s.[23] A reasonable employer might decide that employee gun possession makes the workplace less safe. Nonetheless, because safety in the workplace does not have the same special constitutional status as safety at home, our model statute prohibits employment discrimination on the basis of waiver status.

While we limit the ability of some commercial contractors to discriminate on the basis of registry status, we place no such limitation on noncommercial associational choices. Private citizens under our proposal would be free to withhold love, affection, and friendship from people who failed to register (as signaled by the email option). Neighbors could refuse to fraternize or allow their kids to have playdates or sleepovers on this basis. While the associational First Amendment rights of commercial actors, like their free-speech First Amendment rights, are subject to constitutional restriction,[24] we are chary to restrict the associational rights of noncommercial individuals and organizations.[25] An individual's choice not to renounce their Second Amendment rights might limit their ability to interact with others in noneconomic spheres, but they remain free to find their own communities of kindred spirits.

In weighing the burdens of the email option on the self-defense choices of potential registrants, it is essential to also take into account the concomitant benefits that the email option produces with regard to the self-defense rights of others. For example, consider a potential registrant who only registers because of the pressure of losing associational opportunities with a neighbor who conditions their association on receiving an email. We can say that the registrant's self-defense choices were burdened by the email option and the possibility of associational pressure that it created. But the email option *furthers* the associational interests and self-defense interests of the neighbor. The neighbor can make more informed associational choices and thereby further her self-defense preference of being less exposed to potentially armed interactions.

A similar analysis applies to those potential registrants who choose not to register even when faced with associational pressure. The non-registrant's self-defense choices were similarly burdened by the email option—because the price of bearing arms is forgoing association with the neighbor. But the email option again empowers the neighbor to make an informed disassociational choice to further her self-defense preference of being less exposed to potentially armed interactions. In both of these cases, there is a symmetry of constitutional interests.

However, there is a final pairing where the email option furthers the associational interests of both the registrant and the (pressuring) neighbor. Without the email option, there may be people who want to register independent of any associational pressure who are still unable to engage in certain forms of association because they are not able to credibly communicate their unarmed status to their neighbor. In this situation, the email option furthers the constitutional interests of both the registrant and the neighbors because the credible signal of registry allows them to achieve association that also comports with their shared self-defense choice that the registrant not be armed. Thus, even if a court were to assess the associational pressure of the neighbor as a constitutional burden, it would need to balance the offsetting benefits regarding the same associational and self-defense interests.

Stepping back, we have proposed a system of limited government intervention to promote informed association by reporting registration only when commercial contractors without sufficient self-defense interests—including employers and virtually all retailers of goods and services—would be prohibited from discriminating against someone for failing to waive the rights to purchase or possess firearms.[26] The email option is a modest form of state action where the state agrees to pass along a registrant message to particular addressees (and by doing so verifies that the registry or revocation has in fact occurred). While the exact contours of any possible constitutional duty on government to refrain from facilitating associational preferences are debatable, given (1) the constitutionality of compelled public disclosure of various gun permits and (2) our prohibition of associational discrimination by commercial contractors without sufficient self-defense interests in the firearm choices of others, we are confident our proposed email option passes constitutional muster.

6

PRIVATIZING GUN-FREE ZONES

The entertainment district of Westport, a small neighborhood in Kansas City, Missouri, was facing a public health and public relations nightmare. The number of gun-related weapons offenses had more than quadrupled, from sixteen in 2016 to sixty-five in 2017. As a result, consumers were starting to shy away from the district's restaurants and bars.[1] To make matters worse, a new Missouri state law allowing anyone to carry concealed weapons without a permit in nearly every public space had gone into effect earlier that year.[2] Westport's restaurants and bars could prohibit patrons from carrying weapons onto their premises, but there was nothing they could do to keep armed pedestrians from carrying concealed weapons on the public sidewalks and streets just outside.

The district's businesses, however, tried something different. They lobbied the city council to sell them a two-block stretch of sidewalks in the core entertainment district.[3] While state law allows pedestrians to carry weapons on public streets and sidewalks, private owners can choose to invite only unarmed citizens to enter their property. Under the proposal, Westport businesses could enforce the weapons ban by requiring visitors to pass through metal detectors between 11 p.m. and 4 a.m. on weekend nights and during special festivals. The gun screening would be contracted out to the same company that handles security for

Major League Baseball, with the costs paid for by the Westport business owners.[4]

The sidewalk privatization proposal was approved by the city council on an 8–5 vote at the end of 2017.[5] Opponents, including the local NAACP chapter,[6] argued that "checking for guns on busy nights opens the door for racial profiling, and that setting up metal detectors at the entrance would make the district look unwelcoming."[7] They advocated instead for increased police presence during certain times.[8] Despite this resistance, plans to move forward with the proposal continued.

Issues with compliance delayed the implementation of the sidewalk privatization by more than nine months. Kim Kimbrough, executive director of the Westport Regional Business League, explained in July 2018 that the league was "still chasing the requirements that the city has placed upon us, the most onerous of which is that we have twenty-two adjoining property owners who have to sign off on this."[9] During the delay, two individuals were shot at 2:45 a.m. on a Sunday morning "in the heart of the area" covered by the privatization.[10] The gun screening measure finally went into effect in September 2018 and is currently being used in the warm weather months of April through October.[11]

The creativity of the Westport merchants is a fitting launching point for the subject of this chapter. While the preceding chapters have focused on letting individual choices guide *who* can bear arms, this chapter focuses instead on *where* arms can be borne.

State and federal laws already include a number of location restrictions. At the federal level, the Gun-Free School Zone Act criminally prohibits any unauthorized individual from knowingly possessing a loaded or unsecured firearm within 1,000 feet of a public, private, or parochial elementary, junior high, or high school.[12] A wide range of states across the political spectrum have also prohibited individuals from carrying guns in a variety of venues, including polling places (Arizona, California, Georgia[13]), courthouses (Alabama, South Dakota, West Virginia[14]), places of worship (Nebraska, Michigan[15]), airports (Illinois, Virginia[16]), government-owned buildings (South Carolina, North Dakota[17]), law enforcement offices (Wisconsin, Arkansas[18]), local government and state legislature meetings (Florida, Alabama[19]), public transit (Colorado, Illinois[20]), zoos, parks, and wildlife preserves (Oklahoma, Minnesota[21]), hospitals, health care, and mental health facilities (Illinois, Michigan, Utah[22]), daycare and childcare facilities (Indiana, Nevada[23]).[24] Some states have also prohibited possession at various private retail establishments, including bars and restaurants that sell alcohol (Alaska, Kentucky[25]), amusement parks (Illinois, Missouri[26]), sport stadiums, arenas, and outdoor music festivals (Michigan, Washington[27]), bingo halls and gaming facilities (North Dakota[28]), and demonstrations and protests (Maryland, North Carolina[29]).

The impressively long list of venues that have been deemed inappropriate for gun possession by such a wide swath of our electorate suggests that there is some political appetite for limiting the places where individuals can bear arms.[30] However, the movement toward placing greater locational limits on gun possession has also met with fierce resistance. In the past decade, several states have repealed statutory prohibitions to once again allow firearms in bars, at universities, and in government buildings.[31] In 2016 alone, six states passed laws that chipped away at gun-free zones, making it easier to bring guns into schools, churches, and workplaces.[32] Gun rights advocates such as John Lott have attacked the idea of gun-free zones, claiming that these areas "actually attract killers who know they will meet only helpless victims rather than anyone able to effectively oppose them."[33] Lott has argued that the 2012 Aurora, Colorado, Cinemark movie theater shooting happened in part because the theater had posted notices that patrons could not bring weapons into the theater.[34]

However, the efforts of the Westport merchants to purchase and thereby privatize their sidewalks stand on a very different footing than legislative locational prohibitions. In keeping with the bottom-up emphasis of this book, Westport's gun-free zone is a case study in giving private citizens more control over whether to invite people bearing arms onto their own property. In contrast to statutory prohibitions that preempt private choice, legislators can do more by giving landowners the ability to exclude people with weapons from entering their property. Part 1's focus on Donna's Law was primarily about "in personam" self-restriction. This chapter is about analogous "in rem" restrictions on real property.[35]

This chapter focuses on how government could facilitate owners' ability to transform their property into gun-free zones both in the present and with regard to successive owners. Nothing in the Constitution gives people a right to bear arms on someone else's property. Leveraging the private choices of property owners can have effects analogous to what we have seen with regard to the declining prevalence of cigarette smoking. State statutes have mandated smoke-free environments at a host of locations, such as restaurants and bars, nursing homes and hospitals, airports, and public transit.[36] In addition to these statutory mandates, the individual choices of private workplaces and retail establishments have greatly reduced the number of areas outside the home where smoking is permitted.[37] Reducing the availability of spaces in which smoking is allowed has made being a smoker more difficult and inconvenient, which has contributed to a decrease in smoking rates.[38] A similar effect is likely with gun ownership. If enlightened policy can lead landowners to ban guns from their property, this can vastly cut down on the geographic areas where individuals can bear arms. This can make bearing guns more inconvenient, which reduces the incentive to possess firearms, just as place restrictions did with smoking.

The remainder of this chapter focuses on two types of tools that government can use to facilitate private choices regarding gun-free environments: defaults and durability.

NO-CARRY DEFAULTS

States can promote gun safety simply by changing two default rules. In most states, if you ask a repair person to fix your washing machine or invite an acquaintance to dinner, your visitor is allowed to carry a weapon onto your land unless you affirmatively condition your invitation on your visitor not being armed.[39] An implied condition of every invitation is that the invitee is welcome to bring a firearm. This right-to-carry default that comes with ordinary invitations to enter private property grows out of an older customary right of individuals not just to carry firearms but also to hunt on land owned by someone else.[40] Indeed, half of states continue to give anyone a default right to carry weapons and discharge them while hunting on rural land owned by another unless the owner posts her land with "no hunting" or "posted" signs at designated intervals.

Thus, in many states there are two wrong-headed defaults: an invitation default in rural areas to enter, carry, and hunt, and a default condition of explicit invitations that an invitee has a right to carry. Both of these defaults should be flipped. A few states have started to change the rural invitation default. Alabama, Maryland, and Ohio have enacted laws requiring hunters to obtain written permission before hunting on any private land.[41] In these states, landowners do not have to go to the hassle of repeatedly posting unsightly signs along the border of their property in order to secure their property from physical invasion.

The right-to-carry default should also be flipped, as it is unlikely, at least in some jurisdictions, to comport with most modern property owners' expectations and preferences. Many people would reasonably be taken aback if their plumber or dinner guest arrived carrying a firearm. Visitors openly carrying a gun can be denied entry, but the current default allows properly licensed invitees to bring concealed weapons onto other people's property in ways that the owner cannot detect. States can and should play a role in better aligning gun policies with people's reasonable expectations.

Instead of requiring property owners to proactively prohibit others from carrying weapons onto their property, the rule could be that people cannot carry weapons onto the private property of others without explicit permission. States might enact a statute saying: "No individual may carry a firearm onto the property of another without first receiving the express consent of the owner or person in legal control or possession." As we discuss below, such a statute would be similar to provisions that already exist in Louisiana and South Carolina.[42]

Some states have adopted no-carry defaults for specific locations. For example, seven states and the District of Columbia have no-carry defaults at places of worship unless the governing body or authority of the place of worship permits the carrying of weapons by otherwise lawful possessors.[43] Georgia's recent Safe Carry Protection Act deploys different defaults for different places: adopting a no-carry default for schools but a carry default for bars unless the owner expressly prohibits patrons from carrying firearms.[44]

Several states combine a right-to-carry default with specific "altering rules" setting out signage requirements for property owners to contract around the default invitation. For example, Arizona's statute requires a sign in "block, capital letters printed in black on white laminated paper at a minimum weight of one hundred ten pound index. The lettering and pictogram shall consume a space at least six inches by nine inches. The letters constituting the words 'no firearms allowed' shall be at least three-fourths of a vertical inch and all other letters shall be at least one-half of a vertical inch."[45] Arkansas has imposed an altering standard which requires "placing at each entrance to the place a written notice clearly readable at a distance of not less than ten feet (10') that 'carrying a handgun is prohibited.'"[46]

Texas has imposed the most onerous impediments to landowners opting out of the right-to-carry default. In Texas, a landowner is required to post two large signs, in contrasting colors, with letters at least one inch in height, both in English and in Spanish with required wording—including "pursuant to Section 30.06, Penal Code (trespass by license holder with a concealed handgun), a person licensed under Subchapter H, Chapter 411, Government Code (handgun licensing law), may not enter this property with a concealed handgun."[47]

Some states have even stripped the right of landowners to restrict their invitation to people without weapons. In 2004, Oklahoma passed a law mandating that employers cannot prevent workers from storing firearms in their locked vehicles on the employer's premises. Since then, more than twenty other states have passed similar "bring your gun to work" laws.[48] Alabama goes further and allows a person possessing a valid concealed weapon permit to carry guns on "private property not his own or under his control" regardless of whether the owner or legal possessor of the premises has consented.[49] Ohio prohibits landlords from restricting a licensed tenant's ability to carry or possess firearms on the premises that the tenant is leasing.[50]

These laws restricting the rights of landowners to limit their invitations to unarmed guests—either through outright prohibitions or onerous altering rules—sacrifice freedom of association and the right to property for the sake of others' right to bear arms. Property owners, in protecting themselves and their possessions, ought to be able to choose whether to exclude people who are carrying weapons from their property. Landlords may have good reasons to not want to rent to armed tenants. Restaurant owners have good reasons to not want to serve alcohol to armed patrons. The idea we present in Chapter 4, of creating an associational marketplace where the preferences of some people to bear arms must contend with the associational preferences of others who do not wish to be around those bearing arms, is particularly strong when it comes to regulating the private spaces owned by others.

Even states that give landowners the right to choose whether invitees are armed mistakenly presume that landowners welcome visitors to carry weapons onto their property. Several solidly blue states that have adopted a host of gun safety policies nonetheless allow concealed carry onto other people's property unless the landowner explicitly prohibits it. Connecticut, for example, disallows firearm permit holders from carrying onto another's land only if possession there "is prohibited by the person who owns or exercises control over such premises."[51] In these right-to-carry default jurisdictions, a landowner can transform her property into a gun-free zone only by posting "no firearms allowed" signs on her land.[52] Many common-interest communities—like homeowners' associations—are already gun-free by covenant.[53] Landlords can similarly restrict gun possession in leases except where this conflicts with state statute.[54]

States would do better to follow the lead of Louisiana and South Carolina, and establish a default rule that third parties may not carry concealed handguns in another's private residence.[55] Such a no-carry default would mean that third-party invitees could not lawfully enter with a gun unless the owner of the premises explicitly invites them to do so. A no-guns default would better comport with homeowner preferences. Many homeowners do not expect or desire dinner guests or repair people to bring concealed weapons onto their property. A substantial majority of Americans live in gun-free homes, and it is natural for these citizens to prefer that their visitors also be unarmed. A large percentage of Democrats in particular want gun-free communities: in a recent poll, 41 percent said it would be harder to get along with a new neighbor who owned a gun.[56] In one nationally representative survey, 50 percent of respondents reported that they would feel less safe if more people in their community owned guns, while only 14 percent said they would feel safer.[57]

Disputes between landlords and tenants would likely be less dangerous if the landlords seeking back rent did not need to encounter armed tenants. A default provision of residential leases might prohibit tenants from possessing firearms. Tenants and landlords would still have the option of contracting around the default and allowing tenant possession. But a no-carry default would give landlords better notice of which tenants would be armed.

A no-carry lease presumption might be justified as a form of majoritarian default rule. Many landowners would likely contract for such a limitation if forced to address the question expressly. But even if only a minority of residential landowners would contract for this right, there is still a "minoritarian" justification for setting a no-carry default based on the negative externalities associated with guns. The iron law of default rules is that more people will adopt a provision if it is set as the default than if some other default is set.[58] The status quo often carries the day.

Thus, we imagine that fewer tenants will possess guns in a no-carry default lease presumption than currently do under the "right to possess" lease default. In fact, fewer tenants might even desire to possess guns in a no-carry default regime.[59] And fewer guns means fewer gun accidents. In Alabama and the other fourteen states with the most guns, eighty-two children aged five to fourteen died from accidental gunshot wounds between 2003 and 2007, as compared with just eight in the six states with the fewest guns (though there were virtually the same number of kids in that age range).[60]

But states should go beyond private residences and establish no-carry defaults for all private land, including places where people go as customers and employees. Extending the no-carry default to cover places of business would preserve property owner rights to permit or exclude guns from their premises while simultaneously nudging those owners toward a public-regarding outcome. A no-carry default for businesses is also likely an example of a majoritarian default setting. Several prominent retailers have banned customers from carrying weapons onto their premises— including Walt Disney World, Costco, Ikea, California Pizza

Kitchen, Whole Foods, AMC Theaters, and Waffle House.[61] Other companies "are reluctant to officially ban guns, for fear of potentially alienating customers, and out of concern that doing so might make employees responsible for confronting armed customers."[62] Many of these businesses—including Chipotle, Levi Strauss, Target, and Trader Joe's[63]—have adopted policies similar to those of Howard Schultz, who as chairman, president, and CEO of Starbucks Coffee Company announced in 2018 that his company was "respectfully requesting that customers no longer bring firearms into our stores or outdoor seating areas—even in states where 'open carry' is permitted."[64] Schultz emphasized that the Starbucks policy was "a request and not an outright ban" in part because "we want to give responsible gun owners the chance to respect our request."[65]

Many of the businesses, such as Kroger, who were reluctant to take a side on the issue used to say that their "longstanding policy on this issue is to follow state and local laws."[66] As a point of legal semantics, it is unclear what it means to follow the law in a jurisdiction that gives landowners the right to either prohibit or allow patrons to carry firearms. The law gives landowners final say over whether or not their properties will be gun-free zones. By stating that they follow state and local laws, these businesses are not offering any specific answer as to what their actual policy is. The law says landowners decide—these landowners say the law decides. Neither of these is a final statement of policy. But in practice, these businesses prefer to stick with the default rule, regardless of what that rule is. Accordingly, there is every reason to believe that only a small minority of businesses and employers would actively contract around a no-carry default and allow patrons to carry concealed weapons onto the premises.

In fact, retailer preference for gun-free zones has recently caused some sellers to change their corporate policy and actively opt out of the local open-carry defaults. For example, in September 2019, both Walmart and Kroger announced policy changes respectfully asking customers not to openly carry firearms into their stores.[67] Walmart in particular has been proactive in its efforts to market firearms responsibly—instituting a number of self-imposed restrictions, including a refusal to sell handguns, military assault rifles, high-capacity magazines, and bump stocks, as well as videotaping firearm sales, "allowing only select associates who have passed a criminal background check to sell firearms," and refusing to sell to people younger than twenty-one.[68]

An important difference between the in personam no-guns registry choice (described above in Part 1) and the in rem no-guns default choice described here is transparency. The no-guns registry keeps registrant identities private unless the registrant chooses to provide an email address to the registry. In contrast, patrons and the public under either a no-guns or guns default can easily learn whether the business has chosen to prohibit patrons from carrying firearms onto the premises. It is as easy as knowing the default rule in a state, and noting whether or not the landowner has contracted around that rule by posting appropriate signage.

Some commentators have suggested that making this information public and easily accessible could be a threat to safety. John Lott has asked gun control supporters whether they would be willing to "post a sign on your home announcing it was a gun-free zone."[69] Lott argues that publicly stating that your home is gun-free will increase the chance that it will be targeted for crime. But there can be safety in numbers. As explained above, making a gun-free default rule means that more premises will be gun-free zones. While a homeowner or business might not want to be the first on their block to announce that their house or business is a gun-free zone, if most of their neighbors are also gun-free, they might feel safer joining the crowd. Where most landowners prohibit arms on their premises, fewer people will find it worthwhile to arm themselves and, notwithstanding Lott's arguments, everyone is safer.

To back up these new no-carry defaults, state law should subject violators to criminal trespass liability or its analog. South

Carolina already does this with regard to its no-carry into private dwellings default. The statute ordains that any "person who violates this provision is guilty of a misdemeanor and, upon conviction, must be fined not less than one thousand dollars or imprisoned for not more than one year, or both, at the discretion of the court and have his permit revoked for five years."[70] The prospect of legal consequences for violators helps level the evidentiary playing field. In many jurisdictions, landlords or condominium associations are free to either mandate or prohibit tenant firearms. But as an evidentiary matter it is much easier for a tenant to prove that she possesses a gun than for her to prove that she does not possess a gun. It is harder to prove a negative. In Chapter 5, we discussed how the associational marketplace extension of Donna's Law helped level the evidentiary playing field. We can now see that subjecting customers, tenants, and employees to the prospect of criminal trespass liability can also help them prove to others that they do not possess firearms. The possibility of criminal liability does not foreordain whether the associational marketplace will lead toward mandated or prohibited possession, but it helps assure that prohibited possession is a more feasible alternative.

It would be useful to level the playing field with regard to potential tort liability as well. Several states have passed legislation immunizing property owners from liability for any harms resulting from guns being allowed on their property.[71] For example, Wisconsin's Concealed Carry Act immunizes a person who "does not prohibit an individual from carrying a concealed weapon on property that the person owns or occupies . . . from any liability arising from [that] decision."[72] If property owners decide to prohibit concealed carry, "they lose this immunity."[73] Opting out of the right to carry default creates the possibility of tort liability for failing to maintain a safe workplace or business. States could level the playing field by removing this one-sided immunity, either by removing the immunity altogether and holding landowners liable for all firearm-related injuries that occur on their property, or by providing the immunity to landowners regardless of whether they opt in or out.

But there is even an argument for states to go further and flip the immunity to favor those property owners who stick with the no-carry default. This might easily be accomplished through an inverse of the Wisconsin provision: A person who prohibits an individual from carrying a concealed weapon on property that the person owns or occupies is immune from any liability arising from their decision. States trying to reduce gun deaths can increase the costs of opting out with the prospect of ex post tort liability while still preserving more property owner choice than would be available under out-and-out government mandates.

Finally, taking a lesson from the Westport entertainment district, it might be possible to give landowners more freedom to control the streets and sidewalks of their neighborhood. A state might pass gun-free streets legislation that would empower property owners of a neighborhood to purchase the streets and sidewalks in their area from the state or municipality, just as Westport merchants did from the city. Under this statute, the acquired land would be privately owned, but the private owners would grant a conditional public easement that allows existing public uses, albeit by unarmed individuals.[74] Crucially, however, the property owners of a neighborhood could opt for gun-free status if more than two-thirds or three-quarters of the owners in the area so voted. The tragic delays in implementing the Westport solution came from the difficulty of securing unanimous support of the businesses in the area. A statute could allow a supermajority of property owners to prohibit gun possession on the streets and mitigate this holdout problem. The feasibility of deciding local land use by majority vote has been extensively analyzed with regard to "land assembly districts," which analogously "avoids holdout problems by requiring the landowners to make their decision through some sort of collective voting procedure."[75]

In sum, by carefully choosing default and altering rules combined with the private owner option to take back streets and sidewalks, state legislatures can radically change the spaces where concealed and open carry can be practiced. None of these proposals would stop people from bearing arms on their own land or in public spaces. Rather, the proposals are focused on facilitating the ability of landowners to stop another person from bearing arms on their land. Legislators have been willing to impose outright bans on gun possession at specific types of venues outlined above. But the proposals outlined here can go much further in tightening the geographic tourniquet while preserving (and even enhancing) the associational rights of property owners.

We think flipping the default hunting invitation and the default right-to-carry term of invitations and leases will lead to gun possession in fewer places and will save lives as a result. But that depends on the choices made by private landowners, landlords, and business owners. As with Donna's Law, private gun-free zones are created by individual decisions, not by government mandate. This is freedom-enhancing gun control.

CREATING DURABLE GUN-FREE ZONES

While the foregoing analysis relates to how property owners can prohibit *others* from bearing arms on the owner's property, there is a separate question of how the law might aid owners' ability to prohibit *themselves* and their successors from bearing arms on the property. Here's the problem: two neighbors can make a binding contract not to bear arms, but if one of them sells their parcel, the buyer (or "successor") is not bound by the contract. While the no-guns registry of Part 1 was about durable waiver of an individual's right to bear arms anywhere, this section focuses on durable waiver of the right to bear arms on particular parcels of land.

Binding successors is not a deviation from our theme of voluntary *self*-restriction. Prospective buyers will be on notice of gun restrictions and may choose to purchase or not purchase accordingly. Donna's Law works by restricting an individual today and for some period in the future. Allowing instant revocation would defeat the intent of the original landowner.

As an initial matter, abutting owners could agree not to a mere contract, but to restrictive covenants that would bind them and future owners to exclude firearms from their land. For example, a 1910 California appeals court upheld as binding on successors a deed that expressly provided that "one of the conditions of this conveyance is that the use of firearms upon said premises is and shall be forever prohibited."[76] Covenants agreed to by neighboring tracts and recorded in public land records are especially likely to be enforceable at common law.[77]

Landowners wishing to make their land gun-free might also be able to take advantage of conservation easement statutes that have been enacted in most jurisdictions.[78] The Uniform Conservation Easement Act defines a conservation easement to be

> a nonpossessory interest of a holder in real property imposing limitations or affirmative obligations, the purposes of which include retaining or protecting natural, scenic, or open-space values of real property; assuring its availability for agricultural, forest, recreational, or open-space use; protecting natural resources; maintaining or enhancing air or water quality; or preserving the historical, architectural, archeological, or cultural aspects of real property.[79]

In *Wooster v. Dept. of Fish and Game,* a state appellate court interpreted a conservation easement, finding that the grant of hunting rights to a state department (so the department could prohibit hunting on the property) was consistent with the statute's easement purpose requirements: "The 'natural' and 'historical,' not to mention 'scenic,' condition of land can easily be understood as land teeming with wildlife—as it was before the advent of men, women, and firearms. Using a conservation easement to ban hunting most certainly does help retain land in this

sort of unspoiled condition."[80] A conservation easement on a particular property that prohibited firearms except those carried by
law enforcement (so the police might more effectively prohibit
firearms on the property) might analogously qualify as having a
"natural," "historical," or "scenic" purpose. Just as governments
provide various financial incentives to stimulate the use of conservation easements,[81] one could imagine states incentivizing the
use of conservation easements to expand the number of gun-free
acres in a jurisdiction.[82]

Alternatively, a landowner who wants the prohibition on guns
to bind subsequent owners could, when selling the property, only
convey a "defeasible fee." This might be accomplished by including what is known as a "fee simple determinable" condition
in the deed: for example, an owner might convey property "to A
so long as A does not knowingly possess or allow others to possess firearms on the premises."[83] The original owner would retain a "possibility of reverter" that would automatically revert
to fee simple absolute ownership if the firearm condition occurs.[84]
In other words, if an owner gives you land on the condition that
you will not possess a firearm on the land, and you violate the
condition, the land goes back to the original owner. Modern title
records would provide notice to potential buyers of these restrictions—as covenants, conservation easements, and defeasibility of
fees would all be recorded and discovered in title searches.[85]

The existing methods provide ample opportunity for owners
to bind themselves and successive owners in interest. However,
to make the land truly gun-free, it is also necessary to constrain
third parties from carrying firearms onto the land and to do so
in a way that durably extends to periods of successive owners.
Durably constraining third parties might be accomplished by including in the covenants, conservation easements, or defeasible
fee grants provisions that impose duties on current and successive owners to post the land with signs notifying third parties
that firearms are not allowed on the property (or to take any

action that would permit third parties to carry firearms on the property).[86]

These in rem gun restrictions on owners, successors in interest, and third parties are constitutional. The Second Amendment restricts state action, not private arrangements like the ones described above.[87] If private gun-free zones became so prevalent that gun owners had difficulty finding places to lawfully possess and store their guns, and the zones were deemed to be "quasi-governmental," the geographic restrictions might conceivably qualify as state action under the "company town" exception.[88] The company town idea is well suited to capture the concern that gun-free zones could burden individuals' right to bear arms in their home by so restricting the set of available residences that there would be no market opportunity to buy or rent a home where guns could be lawfully possessed. But this company town exception is limited to places where a single or small group of private owners constrain contracting options and effectively become the local government.[89] The company town doctrine implicitly facilitates an in rem associational marketplace, because aggregate contracting constraints created by the similar preferences of dispersed private owners do not trigger constitutional scrutiny. Another possible way to meet the state action requirement is criminal prosecution. The police removing a trespasser from a premises pursuant to a criminal trespass statute, without independent investigation, may look like state action, but it does not qualify.[90]

There is another Supreme Court precedent that could be cited in support of the position that judicial enforcement of private covenants amounts to state action: *Shelley v. Kraemer*.[91] Decided in 1948, *Shelley* held that racially restrictive covenants, if enforced by a court, violate the Equal Protection Clause of the Fourteenth Amendment. The argument here would be that judicial enforcement of private no-gun covenants amounts to state action and violates the Second Amendment. This argument has surface appeal, but very few courts in the seventy-plus years since *Shelley* have applied its expansive state action theory.[92] Courts recognize that the *Shelley* rationale has the potential to constitutionalize any private arrangement if enforcement depends on the judicial process.[93] It is unlikely that court enforcement of a gun restriction created by property owners would be deemed to be state action.

State constitutions, unlike the federal constitution, may regulate purely private conduct.[94] Case law on private gun regulation is sparse, but one Connecticut court concluded that the state's broadly worded[95] constitutional right to bear arms "does not prevent a private landowner from prohibiting the otherwise lawful possession of firearms on his land."[96] Even if the federal state action requirement were satisfied or if state constitutional law swept more broadly, place restrictions like these routinely survive constitutional challenge. For example, the Tenth Circuit upheld the United States Postal Service's blanket ban on firearms on postal property.[97] Of particular relevance here is that the court, in rejecting the Second Amendment claim, relied on the fact that the postal service was acting in its proprietary rather than governmental capacity, and its regulation applied "only to discrete parcels of land" and was "directly relevant" to "providing a safe environment for its patrons and employees."[98] Private gun-free zones share these characteristics. The Supreme Court of Virginia similarly upheld a firearm ban covering campus facilities and events against *both* state and federal constitutional challenge.[99] State constitutions are unlikely to stand in the way of property owners making choices about guns on their land.

Courts occasionally extend beyond constitutions to strike down laws on public policy grounds.[100] The right to self-defense overlaps substantially with state and federal constitutional provisions on bearing arms. One court in a state without a constitutional right to bear arms rejected a policy-based challenge to a no-firearms covenant: "We think there is no merit in the contention that the restriction and covenant is void as being either unreasonable or as in violation of the inherent right of the citizen to bear arms."[101] When weighed against the right to property—and specifically the right to exclude—as well as the right to *not* bear arms,[102] it is difficult to see a public policy argument against gun-free zones prevailing,[103] except perhaps if the restrictions leave no genuine options for housing without firearm restrictions.

Possibilities of reverter, rights of entry, conservation easements, and covenants can last more or less indefinitely.[104] An important question is whether the permanence of gun-free zones violates public policy because of standard "dead hand" concerns. This colorful phrase describes the problem of a person making long-lasting decisions without having to experience the consequences that materialize after the person dies. One commentator argues that when covenants are stale, they should be enforceable only by compensatory damages, not specific performance.[105] Limiting parties to compensatory damages, however, would effectively convert gun-free zones to gun-tax zones, and the increased risks and psychological harm would be very difficult to quantify. The same critic of common-interest communities further contends that covenants restricting behavior without externalities (i.e., effects on third parties) are illegitimate.[106] But guns can readily be turned against neighbors, which may explain why so many more people fear more guns in their community than welcome them.[107] Gun-free zones should be just as durable as other restrictions on land.

Traditional gun control interventions have been mandatory rules, limiting the types of people who can bear arms, the types of guns that they can bear, or the types of locations where guns can be borne. But the idea of bottom-up control can deploy default rules that enhance individual liberties while reducing gun violence. Donna's Law and the associational marketplace extension use individual choice to restrict the types of people who can bear arms. The no-carry invitation and various durability options discussed in this chapter use individual choice to reduce the types of locations where guns can be borne. Enhancing property owners' ability to control whether or not their land is gun-free should not substitute for traditional mandatory rules, but choice-enhancing policy can be a powerful and politically attractive complement.

PART III

HARNESSING OTHERS' INFORMATION

7

SYMPTOM-BASED GUN REMOVAL ORDERS

In the early morning of August 7, 2013, two Newport, Rhode Island, police officers responded to a harassment call at a hotel. On arrival they met with Aaron Alexis, who was obviously delusional. The police incident report states that Alexis believed someone had sent three people to follow him and keep him awake by talking to him and sending vibrations into his body with, in Alexis's words, "some sort of microwave machine." Although Alexis reported that he had not personally seen any of these three people, he was nonetheless worried that they were "going to harm him."[1] Less than six weeks later, on September 14, Alexis legally purchased a shotgun in Virginia.[2] He used it two days later to kill twelve people at the Navy Yard in Washington, D.C.[3]

Alexis's paranoid delusions in August should have prevented him from purchasing the shotgun in September. They did not because mental health restrictions on firearm purchases were keyed to diagnosis and treatment, not to symptoms. This is a mistake. Studies suggest that psychotic symptoms are more closely correlated with violence than psychiatric diagnoses. And a symptom-based approach has the potential to prevent gun violence by individuals like Alexis who are never diagnosed with, or treated for, mental illness.

Since 2013, several states have enacted red flag laws in response to mass shootings. A red flag law might not have stopped

Alexis. Red flag laws are designed to remove guns from high-risk individuals. However, currently red flag laws are not automatically triggered by symptoms of dangerousness, but by a discretionary judgment. The Alexis case shows how that distinction can be critical. The police officers who encountered Alexis did not believe he was dangerous enough to arrest or to hospitalize. Rhode Island passed a red flag law in 2018, but officers confronting someone like Alexis may not use it. An objective, symptom-based approach could more effectively mitigate the risk of firearm misuse by individuals displaying evidence-based indicia of dangerousness.

Red flag statutes should allow gun rights revocation triggered by informed lay assessment of risk. We focus on psychotic symptoms as an illustration in this chapter and generalize the insight beyond these symptoms, and beyond mental health, in Chapter 8. For now, we propose that a police officer or health professional who has reason to believe that an individual is suffering from paranoid delusions or threatening hallucinations should be empowered to petition a court to (1) confiscate that person's firearms and (2) add that person's name to the federal background check system, thus preventing firearm purchases until after a successful restoration proceeding. If the court finds sufficient evidence of psychotic symptoms, gun restrictions would be automatic. This is essentially a red flag law with an objective trigger rather than a discretionary judgment of risk. Under our proposal, an individual seeking to regain gun rights would need to submit evidence from a mental health professional showing that symptoms have subsided to the point that the individual has capacity to safely possess a firearm, thereby incentivizing rather than penalizing treatment.[4]

The first section of this chapter elaborates the underdeveloped analogy between driver's license suspension and red flag laws. The second section charts existing mental health firearm restrictions. The traditional state gun control restrictions have generally been premised on proxies for dangerousness such as diagnosis and treatment. This proxy-based approach has left gaps that have allowed dangerous individuals to keep or purchase firearms. Red flag laws represent a major advance by tying gun regulation to dangerousness itself. However, gaps remain, which we endeavor to help fill. The third section surveys the literature on psychosis and violence and concludes that the weight of authority and most applicable studies find a significant positive relationship between the two. The fourth section discusses counterarguments, and the final section discusses validated instruments that laypeople can deploy to identify the presence of risk symptoms.

THE DRIVING ANALOGY

Guns and cars kill more people in the United States than any other devices.[5] Driving is in some ways more heavily regulated. It is therefore not surprising that advocates of stricter gun safety often point to driving regulations. There should be a national license requirement for gun ownership just like the license requirement for driving, they argue. Opponents of stricter regulation instead argue that state gun licenses, like state driver's licenses, should be respected by other states. Indeed, "concealed carry reciprocity" bills have been introduced into Congress requiring states to give full faith and credit to the concealed carry permits issued to residents of other states.[6] Whatever one thinks of these conflicting arguments, we believe that the driving analogy holds with even greater force on the back end: driver's license revocation.

All fifty states and the District of Columbia have review or reexamination processes that can lead to revocation or suspension of driver's licenses.[7] In all of these jurisdictions, a review can be triggered by a referral from a law enforcement officer or a physician. But in forty-six states, a review by licensing authorities can be triggered by an anonymous report from family, friends, or any other citizen. In other words, the vast majority of states permit a broad range of individuals to initiate a review of driving privileges.

In contrast, red flag laws generally limit the petition power to law enforcement officers, close family, and household members.[8] Maryland and the District of Columbia include doctors.[9] As with unsafe driving, strangers can and do observe behavior suggesting danger with firearms: under Connecticut's gun removal statute, about half of reports came anonymously or from strangers.[10] Presumably, the rationale for limiting the petition power under red flag laws to parties with special expertise or a close relationship to the respondent is to avoid harassment and undue interference with the constitutionally protected right to bear arms. Anyone is free to report their concerns to law enforcement or family, even anonymously, but the formal removal process does not begin until an authorized petitioner decides to file a petition. No private citizen should have the power unilaterally to disarm another, but everyone should be empowered to raise a red flag.

States, in fact, do not allow a mere citizen report to immediately revoke another person's driver's license. Rather, citizen reports can start a review process after which revocation may take place, generally if a driver fails the normal driving exam, including vision, knowledge, and road tests. Most states (thirty-nine) do provide for immediate revocation pending medical review, but in narrower circumstances.[11] Typically, for immediate license suspension, a health care provider or law enforcement officer must attest that the driver poses a threat to self or others. We believe the same two categories of specialists should have the power to initiate proceedings to remove guns based on psychotic symptoms.

Also instructive is the restoration process for driving. Most states (forty) give individuals whose driving privileges have been suspended the opportunity to regain their license if they can simply pass the driving test (which, again, includes vision, knowledge, and road components).[12] This could provide a model for firearm rights restoration under red flag laws. Some states require licenses for gun ownership, but more should follow California and Washington and require hands-on firearm training for licensure. Most states have no analog to the road test for driving.

States should at least require safety training and testing after a provisional suspension of gun rights.

The case of immediate suspension of a driver's license provides an almost perfect analogy for our proposal. Law enforcement officers and health care providers do not have to administer a driving test before suspending an individual's license when they deem public safety at risk. This is a discretionary assessment of dangerousness, just like red flag laws. But some states do not rely solely on discretion for driving. Instead, they outline particular disqualifying symptoms. For example, Rhode Island lists unexplained seizures. When this symptom is present, driving privileges are automatically revoked upon report by law enforcement or a health care professional. Red flag laws presently rely on discretionary risk assessment. We will argue that certain symptoms, such as paranoid delusions, should be disqualifying for gun possession and, more broadly, that risk assessment should be guided by actuarial instruments.

CURRENT RESTRICTIONS MISS THE MARK

Mental health gun regulations employ three overlapping criteria: (1) diagnosis, (2) treatment, and (3) dangerousness. Federal law prohibits gun possession by, among other categories, individuals who have "been adjudicated as a mental defective or who ha[ve] been committed to a mental institution."[13] The standard for civil commitment, in turn, is mental disorder and danger to self or others.[14] While someone is in a mental institution, treatment is constitutionally required.[15] Thus, this central federal restriction requires all three criteria to be satisfied and therefore sits in Area B of the Venn diagram in Figure 7.1.

There is empirical support for the federal restriction. Involuntary admission status is a significant risk factor for violence.[16] The risk of self-harm is much higher. Examining many studies, two researchers concluded that individuals released from involuntary hospitalization had a suicide rate thirty-nine times higher than the

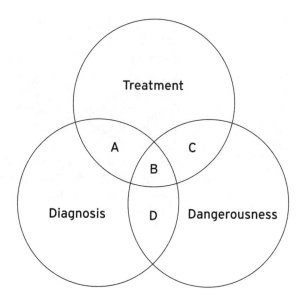

Figure 7.1. Bases for Firearm Restrictions

general population.[17] One problem with the federal restriction, though, is that it misses people like Alexis. Most people with psychotic symptoms are never hospitalized. In 2011, 0.8 percent of adults in the United States received inpatient mental health care.[18] This included both involuntary and voluntary commitments, along with ordinary consensual treatment. By comparison, one study found that 5.1 percent of the general population reported psychotic-like experiences within a twelve-month period.[19] This illustrates that while some people may be voluntarily committed without a diagnosis, many more with severe symptoms are neither diagnosed nor hospitalized.

Several states have concluded that the federal prohibition is too narrow and have expanded the prohibition along one or more dimensions. For example, Hawaii has expanded its prohibition to include essentially the entire diagnosis circle, barring gun possession by anyone with a "significant" mental disorder.[20] The primary criticism of this diagnosis-based approach is overinclusiveness. The vast majority of mentally ill individuals pose no threat to themselves or others.[21]

Other states focus on treatment. For example, Illinois prohibits gun possession by individuals who have been voluntarily admitted to psychiatric facilities,[22] whereas the federal prohibition is limited to involuntary hospitalizations. Of course, hospitalization is only one variety of treatment, but Illinois has expanded its gun restriction into that portion of the treatment circle. As mentioned, a very small fraction of people are hospitalized, either voluntarily or involuntarily, so this treatment-based expansion arguably does not go far enough.

Perhaps the most fundamental shortcoming of diagnosis- and treatment-based restrictions is that they require a diagnosis or treatment. Millions of people with mental illness are not diagnosed and do not receive treatment.[23] In 2011, only 38.2 percent of people with any mental illness and 59.6 percent of those with serious mental illness received mental health treatment.[24] Even where treatment is available and taken advantage of, it may be too late for a person experiencing his first psychotic episode. Troubled individuals like Alexis may interact with law enforcement, and even health care providers, without receiving a diagnosis or inpatient treatment.

All would agree that the real target is dangerousness, so why not aim directly at it? That was the core insight of the Consortium for Risk-Based Firearm Policy in its influential 2013 report.[25] At the time, only three states had targeted dangerousness with gun dispossession statutes keyed to individual assessments of dangerousness. The most limited of these was Texas, which required diagnosis of a mental disorder and finding of dangerousness (Area D in Figure 7.1). Connecticut and Indiana did not require a diagnosis. Since 2013, over a quarter of states and the District of Columbia have adopted red flag laws (also known as emergency risk protection orders or gun violence restraining orders).

These laws all premise gun restrictions on a finding of dangerousness. There are three different approaches as to how mental health should factor into the analysis: (1) consideration of mental health is forbidden; (2) consideration of mental health is permitted or required; and (3) no guidance is offered one way or the other. Oregon is the only state that appears to fall into the first category. The statute does not expressly state that mental health cannot be considered, but rather states that "the court may not include in the findings any mental health diagnosis or any connection between the risk presented by the respondent and mental illness."[26] This provision is no doubt designed to combat stigma—namely, the erroneous view that mental health diagnosis alone makes an individual more dangerous to others. But mental illnesses are often associated with certain symptoms, so taking diagnoses and associated risks off the table completely could lead petitioners and courts to undervalue or ignore dangerous symptoms.

The District of Columbia most clearly requires consideration of mental health. A court shall consider "evidence of the respondent experiencing a mental health crisis, or other dangerous mental health issues."[27] Note that this is not a traditional diagnosis-based provision. The focus instead is on mental health *crises* and other dangerous *issues*. More than a diagnosis is required: real danger, not stigma. Of existing red flag laws, the D.C. approach has the best chance of stopping someone like Alexis, but that outcome is uncertain. A court is instructed only to *consider* a mental health crisis, not required to issue a restraining order when there are psychotic symptoms. Alexis had mental health issues, but were they "dangerous"? The police officers did not think the danger was great enough for an arrest or for civil commitment, so perhaps they (or the court) would not think the danger was great enough for a firearm restraining order.

This recognition motivates the symptom-based approach. Restrictions under red flag laws are triggered by individualized assessments of danger to self or others, not diagnosis or treatment. This approach has worked. One study found reductions in gun suicide associated with the Indiana and Connecticut laws, although there was some suggestion that an increase in non-firearm suicide may have offset the reduction in Connecticut.[28] Another study estimated that the Connecticut law prevented one suicide for every ten to twenty gun confiscation orders.[29] This is much more efficient and targeted than traditional treatment and diagnosis restrictions. However, in the move away from the overly broad proxies for dangerousness of diagnosis and treatment, red flag laws have missed an opportunity to incorporate better proxies, such as paranoid delusions and hallucinations. Supplementing discretionary court assessments with more narrowly focused automatic removal criteria has the potential to make red flag laws even better, as the Alexis case demonstrates.

While medicine focuses on characteristics that are symptoms of disease, here we are focused on evidentiary characteristics that are symptoms of dangerousness. We propose that courts in adjudicating red flag petitions (and public officials in those jurisdictions requiring police or other government officials to file petitions) rely on evidence-based symptoms of dangerousness as central evidentiary criteria. More specifically, we propose that a court finding that an individual has exhibited either paranoid delusions or threatening hallucinations should by itself be sufficient for a court to issue a gun removal order.

EMPIRICAL SUPPORT FOR A SYMPTOM-BASED APPROACH

Current diagnosis- and treatment-based restrictions on gun possession are underinclusive. Discretionary dangerousness approaches are steps in the right direction, but mandatory triggers can helpfully augment coverage. One possible supplement focuses directly on symptoms.

Delusions or hallucinations appear to have been present in those responsible for a string of recent mass shootings, including those in Parkland, Charleston, Littleton, Aurora, Tucson, and the Navy Yard.[30] The data suggest that the relationship between some types of delusions and violence is not merely anecdotal.

Paranoid delusions correlate with violence. One review reported that seventeen of twenty studies found a positive relationship between delusions and violence.[31] A 2006 study using a large dataset representative of the noninstitutionalized U.S. population eighteen years of age or older concluded that people with "psychotic-like experiences" were 5.72 times more likely than others to attack someone with an intent to seriously injure.[32] "Psychotic-like experiences" included seven varieties of hallucinations and delusions.[33] Hearing voices, seeing visions, and paranoid ideations were the most strongly associated with violence.[34] One study found that suspiciousness and fear of persecution, not the delusions per se, were associated with severe violence, and that anger was an important mediator.[35] No predictions of violence come close to perfectly identifying the subset of people who will go on to commit violence. But the evidence of increased risk of dangerousness is sufficient to temporarily restrict the individuals afflicted by psychotic-like symptoms. Indeed, our estimate that one attacker would be correctly disarmed for every 13.5 sufferers who would not attack another[36] is roughly equivalent to Connecticut's experience using a red flag–type law to prevent suicide (1 suicide prevented for every 10–20 gun removals).

The 2006 study reported that 70 percent of the individuals with psychotic-like experiences had not received mental health care in the past year.[37] This strongly suggests that disqualification based on diagnosis or treatment misses many people whose symptoms put them at relatively high risk for violence. And even if treatment had been sought, "it is quite likely that only a minority of these experiences would be identified as clinically significant symptoms and only a small proportion of the individuals with these experiences would be identified as cases of psychotic disorders by a clinician."[38]

A very similar study of Japanese adolescents broadly supports the findings of the 2006 study, although the observed effects were smaller. Overall, those who suffered from psychotic-like experiences were about twice as likely as others to engage in interpersonal violence.[39] The effect remained statistically significant for paranoia and hearing voices even after controlling for other variables.[40]

Paranoia is dangerous. An early comparable study from Israel measured weapon use directly and concluded that "those who score high on threat/control-override symptoms [are] much more likely than those who score low to have engaged in fighting and weapon use."[41] This result held even after controlling for diagnosis and other psychotic symptoms, as well as a host of other variables.[42] Indeed, the study concluded that "the threat/control-override symptoms have primacy over diagnostic distinctions in explaining violence."[43] A more recent study confirmed the significance of threat delusions, but not those involving control-override.[44] One implication is that symptom-based gun control has the potential to prevent more gun violence than diagnosis-based regulation.[45]

It should be noted that other studies question the relationship between delusions and violence.[46] All four of these other studies— including the leading study funded by the MacArthur Foundation— examined highly selected groups as opposed to populations. This is an important distinction. Take, for example, the MacArthur study: it included individuals who were recently released from civil commitment.[47] Because dangerousness is a prerequisite for continued involuntary hospitalization[48] and because there is tremendous pressure to release inpatients as soon as possible,[49] many subjects likely were just below a maximum risk threshold at the time of release. It may well have been an artifact of sample selection, not lack of causation, that those with and without psychotic symptoms were equally safe.[50] The population studies, although far from perfect, are therefore more persuasive for present purposes.

The Consortium for Risk-Based Firearm Policy report that jump-started the red flag law movement itself recognized that risk of violence is higher for "small sub-groups of individuals with serious mental illness, at certain times, such as the period surrounding a . . . first episode of psychosis."[51] The organization perhaps most sensitive to the stigma surrounding mental illness agrees. In written testimony to Congress, the National Alliance on Mental Illness (NAMI) cited "delusions and paranoia, sometimes characteristic of psychosis," as an evidence-based factor that increases the risk of violence.[52] It should be said that NAMI went on to state (accurately) that most people who experience these symptoms will not act violently toward others. When the cost of failing to act is death, of course, some degree of overbreadth should be acceptable.

COUNTERARGUMENTS

Three categories of counterargument are based on the traditional approaches, the discretionary red flag approach, and the symptom-based approach itself. What we have described as the fundamental shortcoming of the diagnosis-based approach—requiring a diagnosis—could be alternatively described as its greatest virtue. Mental health professionals are trained to make accurate diagnoses and thus to ensure that only those who actually have disorders are barred from gun possession. Allowing police officers and family to petition a court and a court to disqualify a respondent based on a psychiatric symptom requires these laypeople to act beyond their expertise.[53]

There are at least two responses. First, it is sometimes relatively easy to identify an active delusion or hallucination, so no formal mental health training is needed. Alexis's fear of a microwave attack demonstrates that there will be easy cases, even if petitioners and courts may sometimes be unsure whether a strange belief is in fact based in reality. On the other hand, an individual might have stockpiled weapons because he believed that President Obama was going to attempt to confiscate all firearms. This belief does not count as a paranoid delusion. The belief, however fanciful, was widely held and supported by any number of Internet sources. Delusions must be *unusual* beliefs.[54]

Second, even if one concedes that less trained police and court officers will not do as well as mental health professionals in identifying delusions and hallucinations, a flawed assessment is better than failing to prevent tragic violence. As mentioned above, vast numbers of people with mental health problems do not receive treatment. To wait for them to get psychiatric care is to roll the dice on what they will do in the meantime. Saving lives justifies a reasonable number of false positives when the cost of the false positive is a merely temporary restriction on the gun rights of a person who would not have misused a firearm.

Another criticism of the symptom-based approach is that it will end up banning gun possession by harmless psychotic individuals without correctly identifying anyone truly dangerous that the discretionary dangerousness approach in existing red flag laws would miss. We have already argued that, by putting out of bounds risks associated with mental illness, the Oregon red flag law is very likely to be underinclusive. The symptom-based approach directly addresses this shortcoming. More generally, an objective symptom-based trigger would capture a high-risk population in every state. Of course, not everyone in that net would misuse a firearm, but no one with paranoid delusions or threatening hallucinations should be trusted with a gun.

A final counterargument is that people will not admit to having delusions or hallucinations. This was not true for Alexis, and it was not true for one of us during two periods of mania with psychosis. A delusion or hallucination seems just as real as any other fact to a person suffering from it. A psychotic individual who genuinely believes something is true often tells others about it when asked—sometimes even when not asked. Concealing psychosis is challenging for a compromised mind. That is why brief screening tests for psychotic symptoms based on self-reporting are effective.[55]

INSTRUMENTALIZING SYMPTOM-BASED CONTROL

It is possible to use statistically validated instruments to determine whether an individual is suffering from paranoid delusions or hallucinations. While it takes considerable training to provide reliable diagnoses of mental illnesses, it is possible for laypeople to administer and score tests to assess symptoms of dangerousness.

Driving again provides a useful analogy. DMV personnel do not need to be optometrists to administer and score eye exams. A finding of impaired vision is not a symptom of a particular disease or illness. The DMV official does not need to know why your vision is impaired. The finding of impairment is a sufficient symptom of dangerousness that the state is justified in denying you permission to drive.

Analogously, it is possible for state officials to administer and score instruments that have been designed and validated to identify paranoid delusions and threatening hallucinations. Dangerousness instruments are already in use with regard to domestic violence. For example, police departments in Connecticut utilize a Lethality Assessment Program instrument that was developed by the Maryland Network Against Domestic Violence. This concise instrument allows police to leverage the knowledge of the potential victim by asking just eleven questions.

1. Has he/she ever used a weapon against you or threatened you with a weapon?
2. Has he/she threatened to kill you or your children?
3. Do you think he/she might try to kill you?
4. Does he/she have a gun or can he/she get one easily?
5. Has he/she ever tried to choke you?

6. Is he/she violently or constantly jealous or does he/she control most of your daily activities?
7. Have you left him/her or separated after living together or being married?
8. Is he/she unemployed?
9. Has he/she ever tried to kill him/herself?
10. Do you have a child that he/she knows is not his/hers?
11. Does he/she follow or spy on you or leave you threatening messages?[56]

These "lethality screening" questions and their precursors have been subjected to validity testing.[57] The use of this instrument shows how experts can design a test that can then be implemented on a decentralized basis by laypeople to provide a decision maker with validated symptoms of dangerousness.

Developing instruments to assess the potential dangerousness of the respondent is potentially more difficult, because respondents may dissemble to avoid negative effects of giving certain responses. It is, for example, more difficult for police to administer an instrument in the field to assess the risk that a person will do harm to herself. A person who is experiencing suicidal ideation may choose not to reveal these thoughts in order to maintain her ability to attempt suicide.[58]

In contrast, people who are harboring paranoid delusions or perceiving threatening hallucinations often feel compelled to speak about them. The very underlying factors that cause these symptoms also can make it harder for these respondents to strategically dissemble about their presence. And as with the domestic violence assessments, concise instruments exist that have already been subject to extensive validation. For example, the Positive and Negative Symptoms Questionnaire (PNS-Q) contains subscales for identifying hallucinations and delusions that consist of just twelve yes/no questions, including "I hear voices inside my head" and "I receive secret messages from the TV or the radio."[59]

In addition, there are validated five-question instruments to assess paranoia in patients experiencing delusions (which ask subjects, e.g., whether they believe they are being followed or laughed
at behind their backs).[60]

The claim here is a limited one. It is not feasible to arm police
with instruments that accurately predict all forms of risk. But
with regard to domestic violence and with regard to paranoid delusions and hallucinations, concise questionnaires exist that can
provide police and ultimately courts with validated symptoms of
dangerousness. With minimal training, these instruments can
be feasibly administered in the field whenever police encounter
someone whose words or actions suggest that they may be experiencing symptoms of dangerousness.[61] Indeed, these instruments
may be valuable for public safety workers more generally. In
Chapter 9, we discuss how enlightened policy might encourage
employers, school officials, and a variety of private citizens to
alert the police about the need for gun removal orders. Public service announcements inundate us with calls to "say something" if
we "see something," but fail to describe what we should be on
lookout for.[62] The use of evidence-based symptoms of dangerousness in our fellow workers, students, and neighbors is a way to
provide more guidance on when it is appropriate to raise a red flag.

Current red flag laws employ dangerousness as the trigger. The
problem with using only dangerousness is that it misses people
like Alexis. Alexis was dangerous, but discretionary assessment
did not see it. Eliminating discretion in a defined set of circumstances can improve decision making. A psychotic individual may
not appear imminently dangerous but is likely still unable to be
objectively reasonable in using a firearm. Take a red flag law and
add the rule that "anyone suffering from paranoid delusions or
threatening hallucinations is dangerous with a firearm."

Identifying such delusions and hallucinations is easier than one
might think. Screening based on short interviews can be effective

and will bring more people suffering from dangerous psychosis to the attention of the police. The police then should be required to petition a court to suspend gun rights. If the court finds paranoid delusions or hallucinations, the court should be required to order gun removal. This proposal would likely have prevented Alexis from purchasing the shotgun used in the Navy Yard shooting. It is grounded in empirical work showing that psychotic symptoms carry an increased risk of violence. Just as a person suffering from unexplained seizures should not be trusted to drive, a person suffering from paranoid delusions or threatening hallucinations should not be trusted to possess a firearm.

8

UNLAWFUL POSSESSION PETITIONS

On June 14, 2019, Joseph Irby was arrested and jailed on domestic violence charges for allegedly trying to hit his estranged wife, Courtney, with a car. Courtney obtained a restraining order against her husband, but she reported to the Lakeland, Florida, police that she was still "in fear for her life" because her husband owned two guns, and she believed "he wasn't going to turn them in."[1] The next day, Courtney allegedly went to her husband's home, took his guns, and brought them to the Lakeland police department. The police department caused a national stir when they responded by arresting Courtney Irby for stealing her husband's property. She was initially charged with two counts of grand theft and one count of armed burglary, which was later reduced to misdemeanor trespassing.[2]

This chapter is about finding a way forward for people like Courtney. Under federal law, Joseph Irby could not legally possess firearms—both because he was subject to a domestic violence restraining order and because he was under indictment for a felony. But as this incident vividly dramatizes, just because Joseph was legally prohibited from possession does *not* mean that the law would take affirmative steps to dispossess him of his weapons. Even after Courtney Irby used the domestic violence petition process to obtain a restraining order against her estranged husband, she could not engage the state's help to disarm him.

Courtney had good reason to be in fear. The Brady Center has estimated on average that between 2006 and 2016 more than 500 women a year were murdered by a partner using a firearm.[3] People like Courtney should not have to prove to a court or the police that Joseph was an imminent risk of harming her. It should be enough for her to establish that he was unlawfully possessing firearms. This chapter proposes that states should give its citizens the right not only to file petitions for domestic violence restraining orders and red flag petitions, but also the right to petition for the removal of unlawfully possessed guns.

The suggestion in Chapter 7 that the existence of particular symptoms should be sufficient evidence of dangerousness to warrant red flag removal orders has a strong empirical warrant. But in addition to strengthening the red flag petition mechanisms, states could go further to harness the power of existing federal statutory prohibitions on purchase and possession. The Gun Control Act of 1968 (as amended by the Firearm Owners Protection Act of 1986 and the Violence Against Women Act of 1994) designates the following eight categories of individuals as ineligible to purchase or possess firearms:

1. Persons under indictment for or convicted in any court of a crime punishable by imprisonment for a term exceeding one year
2. Fugitives from justice
3. Unlawful users or addicts of controlled substances
4. Persons "adjudicated as a mental defective" or involuntarily "committed to any mental institution"
5. Aliens who are "illegally or unlawfully in the United States"
6. Persons dishonorably discharged from the military
7. Persons who have renounced their citizenship
8. Persons convicted of misdemeanor crimes of domestic violence or subject to protective orders restraining them

> from harassing, stalking, or threatening an intimate
> partner or child of such partner[4]

At least some of these eight statutory designations are evidence-based proxies for dangerousness. Empirics show that persons convicted of domestic violence crimes are much more likely to commit other acts of violence.[5] Other categories are less justifiable as an attempt to disarm the dangerous. For example, there is no credible evidence that persons who have renounced their citizenship are more likely to commit violent crimes.[6] These categories might most charitably be explained as excluding groups that Congress found unworthy of bearing arms.

Later in this chapter we will have more to say about how we can modernize these categories to more closely track dangerousness. But to begin, it is important to note how capacious and absolute these existing prohibitions are. We will show below that more than a quarter of the population fits into at least one of these eight prohibited categories (which includes all marijuana users even in states that have legalized medical or recreational marijuana). The NRA and others often call on government to do a better job enforcing existing gun law before passing additional restrictions.[7] This chapter follows that advice and proposes a new way to better enforce the aforementioned federal prohibitions.

Specifically, states could promote gun safety by passing legislation that allows citizens to file unlawful possession (UP) petitions that would give courts the ability to issue gun removal orders akin to red flag orders. While the gun removal order would be the same for both kinds of petitions, the elements required to achieve the remedies would be markedly different. In contrast to red flag proceedings, where courts make discretionary determinations of extreme or imminent risk of causing harm, a court adjudicating an unlawful possession petition would be asked to make a much less discretionary determination of whether the individual falls into an evidence-based prohibited category, either a federally prohibited category or any of the additional "state prohibitor" categories created by the state itself.

UP petitions would form the final piece of our petition trident promoting gun safety. States first gave their citizens the right to petition for temporary restraining orders (TROs) in cases of domestic violence. People found sufficiently dangerous to be subject to protective orders lose the right to bear arms. Many states have followed up by passing red flag statutes that provide for court-ordered disarmament of people who meet various statutory standards of dangerousness. These petition processes call upon courts to consider certain factors in weighing the dangerousness of respondents. Building upon these, the UP petition process would require courts to issue unlawful possession orders whenever they find that a respondent falls into a prohibited category.

In Chapter 7 we called upon courts to automatically issue red flag firearm removal orders upon finding that a respondent was experiencing paranoid delusions or threatening hallucinations, as these symptoms are a kind of *res ipsa loquitur* ("the thing speaks for itself") evidence of dangerousness. Here we are proposing that legislation direct courts to automatically issue removal orders upon a finding that the respondent belongs to a federally prohibited category or any state prohibitor category.

Both federal law and what we are proposing allow for much less judicial discretion than do red flag statutes. This contrast can be seen directly in the language of several red flag statutes. For example, Rhode Island's statute says that a judge *may consider* the "respondent's criminal history, including . . . convictions for felony offenses."[8] But under federal law, being convicted of a felony offense is an absolute bar against gun ownership. Under our proposal, a felony offense punishable by imprisonment for more than a year would constitute a nondiscretionary basis for a gun removal order.

Similarly, the Consortium for Risk-Based Firearm Policy has suggested that courts in assessing the threat of harm to self or others in a red flag proceeding "may consider such factors as the [respondent's] current use of controlled substances, [and prior] involuntary commitment to a psychiatric facility."[9] Current drug use and involuntary commitment, like felony convictions, are automatic disqualifiers for bearing arms. But current red flag enforcement does not seek to disarm individuals who unlawfully possess weapons. The red flag petition process, like the TRO domestic violence petition, is limited to disarming people who the court deems dangerous given the totality of the circumstances. Thus, a respondent may be subject to a red flag removal order even if she is legally allowed to possess firearms under state and federal law if the court finds that she meets the necessary standard of dangerousness. The UP petition usefully complements these two existing petitions by focusing on whether the respondent is in unlawful possession of firearms rather than whether the respondent is dangerous.

Our proposed UP petition process is another example of bottom-up gun control because it helps harness decentralized information from private citizens. We give individuals an enhanced ability to trigger a gun removal order from wrongful possessors. An inference of unlawful possession requires the twofold knowledge that a person both possesses firearms and falls into a prohibited category. Private individuals can be better informed than the state with respect to both pieces of information. The state sometimes knows that a person falls into a prohibited category. The names of such people often appear in the National Instant Criminal Background Check System (NICS) database. But the state may not know if that prohibited person nonetheless possesses a firearm. This is especially true if the gun is acquired illegally or without a NICS background check. In many jurisdictions, the state does not keep a record of who owns firearms and will not have a ready way of determining when a person who originally acquired a gun legally has subsequently become prohibited from possession (for example, because of a subsequent felony conviction). At other times, the state may know that an individual possesses a gun. For example, many states know the identity of individuals who have concealed weapons permits. But the state may not know whether the individual is currently disqualified from possession because, say, she is a habitual user of controlled substances. Unlawful possession petitions can help overcome both of these government information deficits by empowering individuals to inform the state about either unknown firearm possession or unknown prohibited status of the possessor.

The discussion of red flag statutes in Chapter 7 analogously harnessed private information from community members about a respondent's paranoid delusions and threatening hallucinations. But community members might also become aware of a particular person's unlawful possession. Someone might see an Instagram photo of a neighbor with a gun and know that the same neighbor was convicted of a felony. A sibling might know that their sister owns a family rifle and that she has an outstanding arrest warrant from another state. A fellow hunter might know that their hunting partner regularly uses cocaine. A parent might see a gun in the apartment of an adult child recently released from inpatient psychiatric care. And shown through the harrowing ordeal of Courtney Irby, an estranged spouse may know that her husband possesses a gun unlawfully because he is subject to a domestic violence restraining order.

Harnessing this private information network to take fuller advantage of existing law can lead to improved enforcement of both purchase and possession prohibitions. The UP petitions help reduce shortfalls in the NICS database coverage, meaning fewer respondents will fall through enforcement gaps in purchase bans. Every gun removal order under our proposal would result in the FBI updating its databases to include the respondent's name. Making the NICS database more comprehensive will enhance its incapacitation effect, assuring that respondents subject to a gun removal order will not be able to purchase guns from licensed gun dealers anywhere in the country. The UP petition process also sends police officers to physically remove firearms that respondents unlawfully possess, strengthening possession prohibitions.

In addition to harnessing private information, the petition process may strengthen the resolve of police to follow through with dispossession. As we discuss below, federal and state police are currently authorized to seek warrants to seize unlawfully possessed guns. But there is often a reluctance to do so—given the prioritization of other duties, and possible resistance from both the gun possessor and gun rights advocates against police efforts to take guns away from private citizens. Charlton Heston popularized the cry of resistance that gun owners should only surrender their weapons when they are pried from their "cold, dead hands."[10] However, police will have a harder time ignoring or deprioritizing a citizen petition leading to a court's order to search and seize guns unlawfully possessed by a respondent than they do with mere citizen tips.

Finally, we will show how the UP petition process can help modernize the eight federal categories to better reflect the findings of empirical public safety studies. An evidence-based approach can correct for both over- and underinclusion in the federally prohibited purchase and possession categories. First, the UP process can correct for overinclusion by limiting the types of respondents against whom an unlawful petition order can be sought. For example, while the federal prohibition includes those who merely use marijuana, a state might exclude petitions based on marijuana use altogether or only include individuals who have been found to abuse or be addicted to this drug. In this vein, we are attracted to the proposal by the Consortium for Risk-Based Firearm Policy to recommend temporary firearm prohibitions for individuals "convicted of two or more misdemeanor crimes involving a controlled substance in a period of five years."[11]

Second, states can modernize the federal regulations to correct for underinclusive categories by making use of the state prohibitor option currently sanctioned under federal law. As adumbrated above in Part 1, federal law allows states to add to the NICS background check database the names of people who are prohibited from possessing guns under state law. Donna's Law leveraged this opportunity by reporting to NICS the names of any state resident who registered to waive their Second Amendment rights. States can use this same state prohibitor mechanism to add new categories of individuals who have been shown to be at elevated risk of harm to themselves or others. For example, South Carolina prohibits transferring a handgun to anyone who is a "habitual drunkard."[12] While the phrasing of this prohibition is outmoded, the impulse to restrict an alcoholic's gun ownership is supported by an abundance of observational studies.[13] Again, we are drawn to the Consortium's proposal recommending temporary firearm prohibitions for individuals "convicted of two or more DWIs or DUIs in a period of five years."[14] A state that prohibited people with multiple DUIs from possessing guns could (1) report such individuals to the NICS state prohibitor database and (2) include individuals with multiple DUIs as potential respondents in the UP petition process. This state prohibitor option is a vibrant way for states to fill in gaps in the federally prohibited categories. Political gridlock at the federal level need not impede enlightened states from crafting petition processes that disarm citizens whose unlawful gun possession poses the greatest risk and incapacitate them from buying new weapons anywhere in the country.

The remainder of this chapter is divided into four sections. The first two sections describe the size of the problems we aim to address. First, we assess the degree to which the NICS databases are missing the names of people who fall into some of the existing prohibited categories. The second section then assesses the degree to which people in the prohibited categories unlawfully possess firearms (whether or not their names are included in NICS). The third section describes the details of our unlawful petition proposal. And the chapter concludes by responding to two concerns with allowing citizen gun removal petitions without particularized showings of dangerousness: the worry that the petition process will produce unjustified disparities for people of color, and the worry that the process of removing guns from private homes will precipitate violence.

THE CONTINUING PROBLEM OF NICS UNDERINCLUSION

While the aforementioned eight prohibited categories were established as a matter of federal law, the identification of individuals who fall into these categories is predominantly dependent upon state reporting. More than half of all records in the NICS indexes, and more than 85 percent of all nonimmigration records, come from states. Due to this state-centric reporting, underreporting at the state level can lead to significant gaps in the NICS database and allow large numbers of disqualified individuals to purchase firearms. State reporting to NICS is voluntary, and some states choose not to submit information from all relevant state-level databases for a host of reasons, ranging from the desire to preserve the privacy of the mentally ill to the difficulty in assembling compatible electronic data.[15] The problem of state underreporting has been particularly acute for temporary restraining orders, misdemeanors of domestic violence, and mental health adjudications.[16]

We analyzed data from the National Survey on Drug Use and Health (NSDUH) to get a handle on the number of people in the United States who are likely disqualified from purchasing or possessing weapons under the prohibited categories concerning mental health and drug use, shown in Table 8.1. As a proxy for marijuana use, this table relies on the survey's statistics on the number of people who have used marijuana or hashish in the last year. The data show that 9.6 percent of this representative sample of Americans would be prohibited from owning a gun because of recent use of a controlled substance. Federal Form 4473, which gun buyers are required to fill out in order to trigger a NICS background check, makes clear that marijuana use is a disqualifying condition even if "it has been legalized or decriminalized for

Table 8.1. Assessing Potential Mental Health, Controlled Substance, and Undocumented Resident Qualifications

Category	Potential Disqualified	Potential as Share of Population	Actual Disqualified[1]	Actual as Share of Population
Mental Health—Total	8,304,497	3.1%	5,169,853	1.9%
Stayed overnight in a mental institution[2]	2,458,631	0.9%	—	
Serious mental illness[2]	5,845,865	2.2%	—	
Unlawful users of controlled substances—Total	47,573,323	17.6%	29,909	0.0%
Unlawful users of controlled substances other than marijuana[2]	21,705,132	8.0%	—	
Unlawful users of marijuana[2]	25,868,191	9.6%	—	
Total without double counting[2]	55,877,819	20.6%	5,199,762	1.9%
Undocumented resident[3]	9,491,831	3.5%	7,352,511	2.7%
Total	65,369,650	24.1%	12,552,273	4.6%

1. 2017 NICS Operations Report, https://www.fbi.gov/file-repository/active-records-in-the-nics-indices-by-state.pdf.
2. 2017 National Survey on Drug Use and Health (NSDUH). NSDUH includes data on individuals 12 and older, so the potential and actual as a share of population are calculated as the potential or actual divided by the total population age 12 and older.
3. Department of Homeland Security 2015 Estimate, https://www.dhs.gov/sites/default/files/publications/18_1214_PLCY_pops-est-report.pdf.

medicinal or recreational purposes in the state where you reside."[17] The NSDUH analogously provides estimates of the population percentage that has used other controlled substances (specifically, cocaine, heroin, and methamphetamine) during the last year. Based on their calculations, an estimated 8.0 percent of Americans, more than 21 million individuals, have used these other drugs in the past year and thus are prohibited from buying guns.

While there is overlap between the two populations, we have analyzed the proportion of respondents who fall into at least one of these two types of drug users and find that 17.6 percent of surveyed respondents report having used one of the aforementioned substances within the last year. This implies that there are more than 47 million Americans who cannot legally purchase or possess firearms because of recent drug use. But Table 8.1 shows that fewer than 30,000 people are included in the NICS index for reasons of unlawful drug use or addiction.

Certainly this 1,000-fold differential cannot be explained solely by state underreporting, as some drug users who have been arrested or convicted for drug offenses are included in the separate Interstate Identification Index (III), which is queried as part of every background check.[18] But it has long been recognized that many substance users are excluded from both the III and the NICS index. Drug courts and problem-solving courts often fail to report evidence of an individual's admission of drug use or failed drug test to the NICS index.[19] Individuals whose cases are diverted to these courts are often promised that the record of the original case will be dismissed or expunged upon successful completion of the program.[20] Some state agencies are concerned that reporting illegal drug use would violate the Health Insurance Portability and Accountability Act (HIPAA) by disclosing "personal health information." Some states, such as Arizona, have statutes that explicitly prohibit state officials from sharing with any federal agency data about those licensed for use of medical marijuana. For these reasons and more, over a dozen states as of 2017 still had not reported any unlawful drug use entries to the

NICS index. Many more states reported only token numbers that fall far short of the actual population of those who are disqualified from possessing a gun for reasons of drug use.

Table 8.1 tells a somewhat analogous story with regard to the mental health prohibition. Federal law prohibits gun possession by those who have been adjudicated "by a court, board, commission, or other lawful authority" as "a danger to himself or others" or "lacks the mental capacity to contract or manage his own affairs" as "a result of marked subnormal intelligence, or mental illness, incompetency, condition, or disease."[21] To get a handle on the potential size of the population that might fall into this category we use two parts of the NSDUH. As a proxy for those who may have been involuntarily committed, the table shows the proportion of respondents who reported that they had stayed "overnight for mental health treatment in the last 12 months."[22] And as a proxy for serious mental illness we rely on the NSDUH predicted probability that a respondent has a serious mental illness.[23] Almost 1 percent of the population stayed overnight for mental health treatment in the last year, and another 2 percent are more likely than not to have a serious mental illness.[24] This combined estimate of 8.3 million is conservative compared with the 11.2 million individuals estimated by the National Institute of Mental Health to have a serious mental illness.[25]

Overall, the NSDUH analysis suggests that more than 8 million Americans fall into one of these two categories. We again see a shortfall between the potential population of prohibited individuals and those individuals actually identified in the NICS index—although, in contrast with drug use, the number included in NICS for mental health (5.2 million) is more than half of the population suggested by the NSDUH data. Combining our proxies together, we have estimated that more than one in five Americans should be prohibited from purchasing or possessing firearms just on the basis of the mental health and drug prohibitions. If we add to this number the 9.5 million undocumented residents (who are assumed not to overlap with the 50 million

people with drug or mental health prohibitions),[26] we come closer
to an estimate of one in four Americans.[27]

Stepping back, we can estimate that in 2017 approximately 65
million Americans should have been prohibited from purchasing
or possessing guns based on drug use, mental health, or immigration status, but the NICS indexes include only 12.5 million.
The more than 50 million people who are missing from the NICS
indexes represent a kind of white whale for gun safety advocates.
This can give rise to tragic consequences. *Mother Jones* found
that of sixty-two mass shootings between 1982 and 2012, thirty-
eight of the shooters (61 percent) had "displayed outward signs
of mental health problems prior to the killings."[28] And mental
illness is much more strongly associated with suicide than with
violence toward others.[29]

To be sure, some of these 50 million are prohibited from purchasing guns via other characteristics—particularly past felonies.
We crudely estimate that just over half of the approximately 19
million felons currently living in the United States are drug users
or have serious mental illness.[30] But this still leaves a NICS shortfall of about 40 million individuals.[31] And as noted above, the
states' reports of disqualifying convictions to the III database are
themselves often incomplete.

The underinclusiveness of the NICS databases was horrifically
exemplified in 2015 when white supremacist Dylann Roof killed
nine worshipers in South Carolina at Charleston's Emanuel African Methodist Episcopal Church. Even though Roof had recently confessed to drug possession, that confession was not
entered into the background check database, and Roof was able
to buy a Glock two months before the attack.[32]

To date, most of the efforts to improve database coverage have
appropriately been top-down attempts to integrate and automate
information exchange between the states and the FBI's NICS unit.
Connecticut, for example, with the aid of federal funding (NCHIP),
now reports to NICS people cited for possessing less than one-
half ounce of marijuana even though "no information [about the

citation] is recorded in the criminal court computer system or the state criminal history repository."[33]

However, top-down initiatives such as these can be expensive and slow moving, and are liable to run into the same information obstacles as previous efforts. In a world where a person can walk into a gun shop without a license and walk out with a weapon in minutes, we need other ways of filling in the reporting gaps. In keeping with this book's emphasis on choice-expanding reform, we propose integrating the petition processes initiated by private citizens into the NICS system. Some progress has occurred along these lines with regard to TRO petitions, where efforts have been made to report anyone who is subject to protective orders to the NICS index. In 2017, about 68,000 people were entered in this index because of a domestic violence restraining orders (compared with fewer than 2,000 people in 2008).

But bizarrely, many of the newly enacted red flag statutes have no statutory provision for reporting respondents who have been adjudicated as a significant danger to themselves or others. Indeed, we find that eight states—California, Connecticut, Delaware, Illinois, Indiana, Maryland, New Jersey, and Vermont—failed to include NICS reporting requirements in their statutes. Thus, while red flag petitions can lead to gun removal orders, these eight states do nothing to stop the respondent from going out and legally acquiring new weapons in other jurisdictions.[34] These eight states should follow the lead of Colorado and other states that explicitly require law enforcement personnel to report a respondent to NICS as a prohibited purchaser on the same day the extreme-risk protection order is issued.[35] States can prevent any respondent subject to a gun removal order from being able to purchase a weapon from a gun dealer simply by making such individuals subject to a state prohibitor category.

A similar approach should be part of any unlawful possession petition process. Any respondent against whom a gun removal order is issued should also have their name reported to the NICS index under a state prohibitor category. As with the red flag removal orders, the NICS status need not be permanent. As we discuss below, if previously disqualified respondents can subsequently prove to a court that they can now lawfully possess weapons, the national database can be updated to remove their names.

This section has shown that there continues to be a substantial number of individuals—easily in the tens of millions—who are currently disqualified from gun ownership but whose names are not in the NICS databases. UP petitions by themselves are unlikely to rectify this situation. Including successful red flag and UP petitions in NICS is more likely to lead to the kind of coverage that one sees with regard to domestic violence protective orders, measuring merely in the tens of thousands nationally. However, in concert with the other proposals discussed in this book, UP petitions can help fill a crucial gap in the current system.

THE CONTINUING PROBLEM OF UNLAWFUL GUN POSSESSION

While the last section focused on the potential benefit of including UP petitions in the NICS database, the more direct and important benefit of UP petitions is disarming unlawful weapons possessors. People may come to be unlawful possessors of guns for a variety of reasons. They may

- illegally acquire them from a licensed gun dealer because of the just-discussed shortfalls in the NICS background databases;
- illegally acquire them because the NICS system omits private sales (including gun shows);
- illegally acquire them as a gift from family or friends;[36] or
- legally acquire them, but then become prohibited from continued possession by subsequently falling into any one of the eight federal categories or one of the state prohibitor categories for their state of residence.

Lackadaisical federal and state efforts to retrieve this contraband only exacerbate the problem of illegal possession.

There are no currently existing federal programs that identify and retrieve illegally possessed firearms. In recent years, just 8 percent of those illegally attempting to purchase a gun have been arrested.[37] And when individuals are identified as having tried to illegally acquire guns, there is no systematic effort to ascertain whether other firearms are in their possession. This pattern of neglect is not due to a lack of proper authority. When the feds want to retrieve weapons, they are able to do so. Thousands of times a year, the NICS background check process results in a wrongful transfer to a prohibited person.[38] In 2017, for example, guns were sold to almost 5,000 people "who were later flagged in the system after their background checks took longer than three days."[39] Most of these guns are retrieved by federal and state officials. A 2016 audit of the Justice Department's Office of Inspector General determined that ATF field divisions recovered firearms that had been wrongfully transferred 93 percent of the time.[40] Rather, federal inaction is largely due to a lack of reliable information. Outside of retrieval after erroneous background check transfers, federal law enforcement has no system to identify who illegally possesses firearms, much less act to confiscate these weapons.

Efforts to retrieve and remove unlawfully possessed firearms are not much better at the state level. The vast majority of states use a kind of honor system, where people who illegally possess guns are expected to identify themselves and voluntarily relinquish their weapons. These states have no practice of removing firearms from people when they become disqualified from possession. For example, when a resident is convicted of a felony, most states do not inquire whether the person possesses firearms. Even when the state can identify illegal weapons possessors, state officials typically do not seek to remove the illegal firearms.

Only eight states have laws that require people suspected of illegal possession to relinquish their firearms.[41] California, Connecticut, and Nevada expressly require individuals identified as unlawful possessors from permit records "to provide proof of compliance to courts or law enforcement verifying that they relinquished their guns after conviction."[42] Illinois has an analogous relinquishment mechanism for people convicted of serious offenses if the Department of State Police has revoked their firearm owner's identification card as a result of the conviction.[43]

But even states with these more proactive measures often do not require police to seek a court order to confiscate firearms that the state knows are illegally possessed. Giving state police discretion not to act can have tragic consequences. For example, in Illinois, authorities knew for more than four years that Gary Martin, who had previously been convicted of a violent felony, failed to prove that he had surrendered a laser-sighted Smith & Wesson handgun. Martin used this gun to kill five coworkers in Aurora, Illinois.[44] In contrast, California requires police enforcement action if a prohibited possessor fails to provide evidence of relinquishing "his or her firearms in a timely manner."[45]

States have tended to be more proactive with regard to disarming domestic abusers, and with good reason. Studies have estimated that when an abusive partner has access to a firearm, the risk of them killing the other partner (usually a woman) increases more than fivefold. Restricting abusers' access to firearms reduces "domestic violence homicides by as much as 25%."[46] Seven states have a defined process to disarm people who are convicted of domestic violence or subject to domestic violence restraining orders. Three states require that these individuals prove that they have complied with court orders to dispossess themselves of guns.[47] A few states, such as Illinois, require a judge, when issuing an order of protection or an emergency order of protection, to also "issue a warrant for seizure of any firearm in the possession of the respondent, to be kept by the local law enforcement agency for safekeeping."[48]

Even states that succeed in initially removing prohibited firearms often do not confiscate the weapons, but instead allow the illegal possessor to transfer the firearm to a relative. This can also have tragic consequences, as these relatives do not take adequate precautions to keep the prohibited person from reacquiring the firearms. For example, in 2018, Travis Reinking killed four people at a Waffle House in Tennessee using an AR-15 assault rifle that "he had been required to give up under the Illinois law just eight months before."[49] Illinois law had allowed Reinking to surrender the gun to his father, who had subsequently returned the rifle and other weapons to his son even though Reinking was still subject to the prohibition.[50]

Part of states' reluctance to actively confiscate unlawfully possessed weapons stems from a concern that involuntary retrieval will spark violence. Adam Skaggs, chief counsel of the Giffords Law Center to Prevent Gun Violence, admitted to the *New York Times*: "[It's] a challenging situation for law enforcement to knock on a door and say, 'Hey, we're here to take your guns, Mr. Dangerous Criminal.'"[51] Another impediment is the police resources needed to track down and confiscate such weapons. In a world where many unlawful possessors are not an imminent threat of violence, budget-strapped police are rarely inclined to prioritize gun retrieval.

California stands out as a state that has committed substantial resources to identifying and confiscating unlawfully possessed firearms. It is one of the few states that keeps a central database of firearm sale and transfer records, giving it a powerful information advantage. It leverages this information particularly with regard to criminal convictions. Any individual who is convicted of a firearm-prohibiting offense must present receipts to a probation officer that all recorded guns have been relinquished.[52] The state also proactively cross-references its firearm sales records against criminal history records, court mental health orders, and court restraining orders to create a database, the Armed and Prohibited Persons System (APPS), of individuals who are banned from, but likely in possession of, firearms.

Agents from the California Department of Justice have dedicated funding to work with local law enforcement officials to go out and disarm people in the database. "They're like little SWAT teams," Mark Leno, a former California state senator who sponsored a $24 million special appropriation in 2013 to hire thirty-six more state agents and reduce a backlog of suspected illegal gun owners, told the *New York Times*. "It is very labor intensive to do this right, and there is always the risk that someone, especially if they are suffering from a serious mental illness, could become very frightened and might act out," said Mr. Leno, a Democrat from San Francisco.[53]

No-knock SWAT raids have in other settings led to tragic results.[54] Setting incentives in a way to minimize violent police-citizen interactions is essential to implementing a UP Petition proposal. But this potential for tragedy must be weighed against the tragic costs of the current underenforcement of existing gun possession prohibitions. The California program has shown that gun retrieval can be safely accomplished on a large scale. In 2017 alone, the program confiscated almost 4,000 guns.[55] And while the APPS database harnesses the power of big data, individual reports of unlawful possession remain a crucial part of any system of gun retrieval. A recent study of San Mateo found that 55 percent of gun removal respondents were identified by domestic violence petitioners or third-party reports.[56] At this writing, there is some evidence that the State of Washington has been taking action to move in this direction.[57]

Even the more proactive states that have made efforts to identify unlawful possessors and moved to disarm them have tens of thousands of likely prohibited individuals who nonetheless bear arms. A 2019 analysis of Illinois data found that almost 80 percent of residents whose gun possession licenses had been revoked had neither provided evidence of transfer nor had their guns confiscated.[58] And at the end of 2018, the APPS database still identified "more than 20,000 Californians [who] have failed to surrender firearms, despite becoming prohibited possessors."[59]

In sum, there are substantial structural reasons, largely due to state and federal inaction, for why there are many unlawful firearms possessors in America. Most states have failed to identify who is likely to unlawfully possess, and most states fail to proactively disarm individuals they do identify as unlawful possessors.

But how big is the unlawful possession problem? A *New York Times* article published in 2019 concluded that "experts say the number of people who are barred from owning guns but have them anyway may reach into the millions."[60] Somewhat surprisingly, many people responding to our survey admitted they were unlawfully in possession of a firearm. Our results suggest at least hundreds of thousands of illegal possessors nationally. The remainder of this section provides a few indirect statistics to support this conclusion.

To begin, consider underage possessors. In addition to the prohibited possession categories that we focused on above, the federal Youth Handgun Safety Act of 1994 prohibits anyone under the age of eighteen from possessing handguns. Gun dealers are required to verify that transferees are not underage. However, there is a substantial number of youths who possess firearms. The NSDUH asks children ages twelve to seventeen whether they have "carried a handgun" in the last year as a measure of delinquent behavior.[61] About 1.18 million adolescents, or 4.7 percent of this population, answered in the affirmative.

We can also infer something about the prevalence of unlawful possession from surveys of inmates convicted of crimes committed with firearms. A 2016 national survey of inmates who used, carried, or possessed a firearm when their offense occurred found that 40 percent of the inmates were unlawful possessors under federal law at the time of their offense (and nearly 30 percent more could have been unlawful possessors if the state had introduced stricter state prohibitor categories).[62] While there are no reliable estimates of the number of Americans who have committed crimes while possessing firearms, we do know that more than 150,000 people a year are arrested on various weapons charges.[63] This includes people charged not only for unlawful possession, but also for unlawful "concealment or use of firearms," and thus might be overbroad as a measure of unlawful possession.

Underage possessors and crime statistics present only part of the picture of how prevalent unlawful possession is in America. While we cannot estimate exactly how many Americans unlawfully possess weapons, there are good reasons to believe that they number in the millions. These are the people who are the natural and direct targets of UP petitions.

DETAILS OF THE UNLAWFUL POSSESSION PETITION PROPOSAL

In the previous two sections, we have described the extent and severity of the problem of underenforcement in gun control measures. A combination of information gaps, law enforcement deprioritization, and a lack of resources has likely allowed millions of individuals to illegally maintain possession of firearms. In this section, we describe how UP petitions can begin to address this issue.

Our proposed petition would cover illegality based not only on *who* is possessing, but also on *where* and *how* a gun is possessed. A petition might be actionable not only when the firearm possessor falls within a prohibited category, but also if the firearm was taken to a prohibited place, such as within 1,000 feet of a school.[64] Our UP petition statute would also cover possession on any private property that had (by our proposed default or altering rule) prohibited firearms. A court could order seizure of weapons that had been possessed in prohibited places, thus naturally supplementing the gun-free zones we discussed in Chapter 6.

Courts could also order seizure of weapons that had been possessed in unlawful ways. For example, a gun owner who carries a concealed weapon without the required state permit would be subject to a court seizure order. Our proposed petition process would also allow courts to order gun seizure if a petitioner provides probable cause that the gun was unlawfully stored. Unsafe gun storage is a substantial public safety issue—more than half of all gun owners store at least one firearm without any locks or other safe storage measures.[65] The problem is especially acute in families with children who all too often use unlocked weapons to accidently or intentionally kill themselves or others.[66] A 2018 study estimated that roughly 4.6 million minors live in homes with loaded, unlocked firearms.[67] Federal law only requires that gun dealers provide a secure gun storage device at the time of sale.[68] But four states and several municipalities require that guns be stored with locking devices under certain circumstances. Massachusetts is the only state that "generally requires that all firearms be stored with a lock in place."[69] California, Connecticut, and New York require locked storage if the gun owner resides with a minor or a person who "is ineligible to possess a firearm under state or federal law."[70] San Francisco has one of the nation's broadest safe storage requirements because it does not exempt a person from keeping the firearm in a "locked container or disabled with a trigger lock" even if the handgun is in the immediate control of the gun owner.[71] Using the unlawful possession petitions to attack the problem of unsafely stored weapons might substantially reduce unintentional shootings and suicides.

These manner and place seizures would be limited to guns shown to have been possessed improperly (in contrast to the prohibited-person seizures that would apply to any unlawfully possessed guns). But being subject to a manner or place seizure—for example, for failing to safely store a firearm—is also a valid basis for a new state prohibitor category that would prohibit the respondent from purchasing or possessing other firearms for at least a limited period of time (say, five years). Including manner and place violations within the petition process would thus further the goal of enhancing the coverage of the NICS database.

As mentioned above, the UP petition would become the third leg in a triumvirate of decentralized petitions, along with the domestic violence and red flag petition mechanisms adopted by many states. But unlike these other processes, there would be no requirement that the petitioner establish a respondent's dangerousness.[72] And unlike these other processes, any gun removal would require the respondent to permanently forfeit ownership of the illegally possessed weapons. Permanent forfeiture would prevent unlawful possessors from circumventing the law by transferring guns to family members who surreptitiously return the firearms at a later time, often with tragic consequences, as in the case of Travis Reinking.

Our petition process is analogous to existing opportunities for private citizens to bring information of unlawful firearm possession to the police. Many Americans come forward with information of unlawful activity. Based on this information, the FBI and state police agencies could seek search warrants by presenting courts with evidence that there is probable cause[73] that the respondent is in unlawful possession of a firearm or has possessed a firearm in an unlawful place or manner.

As with a search warrant, we recommend that the UP petitions be considered in the first instance on an ex parte basis, without notifying the respondent. The risk is that a respondent who is served and given the opportunity to appear will hide the evidence. But as with ex parte protective orders, the respondent would by statute be given the opportunity to appear after any gun removal search to contest the basis for the order and, when appropriate, have the confiscated gun returned.[74] This subsequent hearing could introduce additional evidence (for example, the results of court-ordered drug testing) that might help more definitively adjudicate whether the respondent falls into a prohibited category.

But our petition mechanism goes beyond the current search warrant option by embracing multiple modes for harnessing private citizens' information. A limitation to the existing search warrants is that police have the option of not acting on private information. Given the hesitation of police departments in many jurisdictions to disarm unlawful possessors, we propose that citizens should have the right to directly bring UP petitions in state court. Citizen-initiated petitions can thus result in nondiscretionary court orders directing police to search and permanently confiscate firearms. But many citizens will not feel comfortable filing direct petitions and may even fear retribution if the respondent learns who triggered a gun removal order. Accordingly, it is appropriate to also allow them to report information to the police in nonpublic and even anonymous ways—as is routinely done in other whistleblower contexts.[75] Bringing information to police can also allow the state to gather evidence of separate elements from different individuals. One neighbor may know that you are a prohibited possessor, while another neighbor may know that you actually possess. Our model statute would accordingly allow either citizens or police to bring UP petitions.

As mentioned above, the petition process can be tailored to mitigate problems of both over- and underinclusion. The eight federal categories that were enacted in 1968 do not all have strong empirical support as being proxies for risk of violence.[76] The concern is that some of the categories were chosen not on the basis of evidence but on stereotypical preconceptions or on a legislative judgment that certain persons do not deserve to own weapons for reasons other than their likelihood of improperly using a firearm. We support tailoring the petition mechanism to apply only to the subset of people who have been empirically shown to be at a heightened risk for gun violence or misuse. As mentioned above, this subset of dangerous individuals would certainly include those individuals who are subject to domestic violence restraining orders. But the authorizing statute for the UP petition process might exclude from the prohibited categories

· undocumented residents[77]
· cannabis users[78]
· citizenship renouncers

· nonviolent offenders and violent offenders twenty years
postconviction[79]

The empirical case for prohibiting these people from owning guns
is weak. As such, an evidenced-based approach would advocate
that they not be included as prohibited individuals.

One possible counterargument for preserving all eight of the
1968 categories is that even if people in these groups do not have
an elevated risk of gun misuse, there is still likely to be a public
health benefit in reducing the aggregate number of people who
own guns. Even arbitrarily increasing the NICS database to include what we estimated above to be 40 million additional people
might well reduce the number of gun fatalities. But while gun prohibitions, as a constitutional matter, need not be narrowly tailored to distinguish higher- versus lower-risk individuals, we, for
reasons of justice as well as political prudence, believe it is wiser
to exclude from the UP petition process categories of individuals
who have not been shown to pose an elevated risk of firearm
misuse.

Trimming the overbreadth of the federal categories has the additional advantage of making a package that simultaneously responds to the underbreadth problems more politically feasible.
Federal law gives states the powerful tool of state prohibitor
status to correct for the substantial underbreadth issues with the
federal categories. By prohibiting additional classes of people
from gun possession as a matter of state law and sending lists of
those individuals to the FBI's NICS unit, the state can incapacitate those individuals from buying guns from gun dealers anywhere in the United States.[80] A state's authorizing statute for UP
petitions could include all of its state prohibitor categories. Many
states have already made substantial progress in utilizing this opportunity to prohibit individuals with elevated risk from owning
weapons.[81] Among those individuals that states should prohibit
from purchase and possession, we would include, for periods of
ten years, the following list of seven categories:

- Anyone convicted of a gun-related or violent misdemeanor.

Prior misdemeanor convictions are a substantial predictor of future violent offenses. Among individuals who legally purchased a gun in California, those with misdemeanor offenses were five times as likely as those with no misdemeanors to be charged with violent crimes in the future.[82] Twenty-six states, including Alabama and California, currently ban individuals convicted of violent or gun-related misdemeanors from possessing or purchasing firearms.[83]

- Anyone held involuntarily for more than twenty-four hours for mental health observation or, by default, anyone who voluntarily commits themselves to a mental health facility.[84]

While the impact of serious mental illness on the likelihood of committing violence is overestimated in the general population, mental illness is still a risk factor for suicide and a weak risk factor for violent crime.[85] Individuals subject to involuntary holds appear to be at even higher risk for both.[86]

- Anyone convicted of a DUI or DWI or alcohol-related offense.

Both alcohol use and alcohol-related convictions are significant predictors of future firearms crimes.[87] Fifteen states and Washington, D.C., bar alcohol abusers from possessing any firearm, and five additional states prevent this group from possessing handguns.[88] The Consortium for Risk-Based Firearm Policy recommends a weapons ban for anyone convicted of two or more DWIs or DUIs in a period of five years.[89]

- Anyone convicted of stalking or subjected to a court order that restrains such person from (1) harassing, stalking, or threatening another person or (2) engaging in other conduct that would place another person in reasonable fear of bodily injury, or (3) from intimidating or dissuading a witness from testifying in court.

Our proposed language is adapted from the Violence Against Women Reauthorization Act of 2019.[90] Both the act and our proposal seek to address the boyfriend and stalker loopholes in federal gun laws. While most female victims of murder or attempted murder by a current or former intimate partner experienced stalking in the year prior to the murder,[91] only partners who were married, lived together, or had children together are covered by current federal law. Only California, Connecticut, Hawaii, and New York currently prohibit possession of a gun by any individual convicted of stalking regardless of their relationship to the victim.

· Anyone on the Terrorist Watch List who has been found by a magistrate to be under "reasonable suspicion" of terrorism.[92]

Despite the fact that several mass shootings were committed by individuals who had previously been placed on the Terrorist Watch List, there is no federal prohibition on allowing these individuals to purchase or possess weapons.[93] Only New Jersey currently bans individuals on the Terrorist Watch List from purchasing firearms.[94]

· Any juvenile convicted of a violent or serious offense.

While an individual's likelihood of committing a crime decreases both with age and with the time since last offense, it is prudent to extend our ten-year prohibition to individuals whose first offense occurred as a juvenile. A study of Chicago youth found that having a juvenile arrest record increased the likelihood of picking up a felony conviction between ages eighteen and twenty-six. This strong connection suggests that juvenile offenders should be banned from possessing firearms into early adulthood.[95]

· Anyone convicted of knowingly violating a firearm place or manner restrictions.

As argued above, someone who is convicted of carrying a firearm into a prohibited area or of unlawfully concealing a firearm or storing the firearm unsafely is reasonably prohibited from purchasing or possessing for a number of years.[96]

To further tailor these state prohibitions, states could allow affected individuals to apply for early reinstatement of their Second Amendment rights by providing a preponderance of evidence that they do not have an elevated risk of gun violence.

In addition to these relatively targeted groups, there is overwhelming evidence that prohibiting young people from purchasing or exercising unsupervised possession of firearms might be an effective method of reducing gun violence. While eighteen-to twenty-year-olds make up just 4 percent of the U.S. population, this group accounted for 17 percent of known homicide offenders and 12 percent of weapons offenders in 2017.[97] Suicide attempts that result in death or hospital treatment are also at the highest rates from ages fourteen through twenty-one.[98]

While federal law prohibits gun dealers from selling handguns to anyone under eighteen and long guns to anyone under twenty-one,[99] several states have prohibited unsupervised possession or purchase of firearms by children and young people, which can reduce the incidence of harm among people under age twenty-one.[100] A 2004 *Journal of the American Medical Association* econometric study of states that had increased their minimum legal age of purchase and unsupervised possession found suggestive evidence that raising the minimum legal age to purchase firearms to twenty-one was "associated with a 9.0% decline in rates of firearm suicides among youth aged 18 through 20 years."[101] These laws would still allow parents to go hunting with their children, but reduce the incidence of youth gun violence toward self and others. UP petitions might be particularly effective in stopping the unsupervised possession of firearms by underaged individuals and hence would represent another manner of possession prohibition.

CAVEATS

The previous section provided details on how UP petitions can help remove guns from people who unlawfully possess weapons *and* belong to categories with elevated risk of gun violence. By relying on ex ante tailoring of these categories, we can relieve the UP petitioner from making the kind of individualized showing of dangerousness that domestic violence and red flag petitioners are required to make. So what's not to like?

As in so many other criminal law contexts, we might worry that UP petitions will create unjustified disparate racial impacts.[102] Even if unlawful possession orders reduced gun violence, one might be leery of our proposal if the petition process also worsens mass incarceration, particularly of minorities.

Unlawful possession orders need not lead to criminal prosecutions. It would be possible to immunize respondents from prosecution unless police uncovered evidence of separate crimes beyond unlawful possession. Immunizing respondents might make some petitioners more willing to come forward with information of unlawful possession. A parent might want her child to be disarmed without the risk that the child will be criminally punished.

To empirically assess the potential racial disparities for four of the forgoing prohibited categories, we return to the data used above in Table 8.1 and ask what proportion of particular racial groups fall within the categories or proxies for those categories.[103] The results are shown in Table 8.2. The table suggests that people of color are not disproportionately overrepresented in some of the prohibited categories. From the NSDUH, we see that African American and Hispanic respondents were less likely than white respondents to report having had an overnight stay for mental health reasons. Similarly, we find that the NSDUH's predicted measure of serious mental illness also shows a lower proportion of African American and Hispanic respondents than it shows for white non-Hispanic respondents. When we aggregate these two measures, we find that 2.6 percent of blacks and 1.9 percent of

Hispanics should likely be prohibited from gun ownership on the basis of mental health issues, while 3.2 percent of whites meet this standard.

The table shows that a higher proportion of African Americans (12.6 percent) than non-Hispanic whites (9.6 percent) report having used cannabis during the last year. This raises concerns that the petition process might disproportionately target African American respondents, but our proposal excludes cannabis use as a basis for UP petitions. If we look instead at the non-cannabis controlled substances or at those people who reported abusing alcohol in the past year (a category we would include in the petition process), we again find that African American and Hispanic respondents would be less likely to qualify for unlawful possession than non-Hispanic whites.

Table 8.2, as expected, shows much starker disparities with regard to immigration and felony status. Undocumented immigrants are a much larger percentage of the Hispanic population (using country of origin as a proxy for race and ethnicity) than of the non-Hispanic white population. But our proposal would exclude immigration status as grounds for bringing an unlawful possession petition. The table also shows, as one can infer from a variety of other sources on mass incarceration, that the felony prohibition category might have disproportionate racial impacts. But we mitigate this disparity by limiting the prohibition for both violent and nonviolent felons to twenty years since they were last incarcerated.

Of course, the lack of disparities in the potential population of prohibited people does not mean that systemic differences in enforcement will not still produce racial disparities in the proportions of minorities who are the targets of UP petitions.[104] Enlightened regulators would scrutinize over time whether the UP petition process produced unjustified racial disparities. An analogous investigation of Marion County, Indiana's experience with red flag petitions found no disproportionate targeting of minority respondents relative to their prevalence in the general population.

Table 8.2. Comparing Potential Percentage Disqualifications of Non-Hispanic Whites, Non-Hispanic Blacks, and Hispanics

Category	Share of Potential Disqualifications for White Non-Hispanic	Share of Potential Disqualifications for Black Non-Hispanic	Share of Potential Disqualifications for Hispanic
Mental health—Total	3.2%	2.6%	1.9%
Committed to a mental institution[1]	0.9%	1.1%	0.7%
Adjudicated as "Mental defectives"[1]	2.3%	1.4%	1.2%
Unlawful users of controlled substances—Total	19.5%	19.8%	17.4%
Unlawful users of controlled substances other than marijuana[1]	8.5%	6.3%	8.1%
Unlawful users of marijuana[1]	9.6%	12.6%	8.4%
Abusers of alcohol[1]	1.3%	1.0%	0.9%
Total without double counting	22.7%	22.4%	19.3%
Undocumented resident[2]	0.3%	0.6%	16.2%
Convicted felon[3]	5.5%	16.3%	
Total	28.4%	39.3%	35.5%

1. 2017 National Survey on Drug Use and Health (NSDUH). NSDUH includes data on individuals 12 and older, so the potential and actual as a share of population are calculated as the potential or actual divided by the total population age 12 and older.
2. Department of Homeland Security 2015 Estimate, https://www.dhs.gov/sites/default/files/publications/18_1214_PLCY_pops-est-report.pdf.
3. Sarah K. S. Shannon et al., "The Growth, Scope, and Spatial Distribution of People with Felony Records in the United States 1948–2010," Demography 54 (2017): 1795–1818.

African Americans comprise 24 percent of the county's population, but from 2006 to 2013 accounted for only 23.3 percent of red flag gun seizures, and "none of the people whose firearms were seized were identified as Hispanic or Asian in court records, although these groups represented 9 percent and 2 percent, respectively, in the 2010 U.S. Census of Marion County."[105] Decentralizing the petition process might mitigate the effects of racially disparate policing. It is possible that disparate policing has disproportionately excluded non-Hispanic whites from the NICS database and, worse, disproportionately allowed prohibited non-Hispanic whites from possessing firearms. Giving a broader, more competitive set of actors, the opportunity to correct for these oversights might tend to remedy these existing disparities.[106] And even if the UP petition process disproportionately removes the firearms of minority people, it may be because petitioners and the people who will be made safer by these gun removals are disproportionately nonwhite.

Beyond the concern with disparate racial impacts and mass incarceration, our UP proposal might cause concern if it led to too many petitions. As mentioned above, police are concerned that disarming unlawful possessors may spark violence. But it is a strained position to say that an unlawful possessor is too dangerous to disarm, so we should allow them to remain in possession of a lethal weapon. And the experiences described above of successful gun retrievals after erroneous NICS approvals or by the California "little SWAT teams" strongly suggest that gun seizures can be accomplished with minimal risk of life.

Alternatively, one might be concerned that delegating this aspect of enforcement to such a large group would inevitably lead to overstepping—with vindictive petitioning motivated by enmity. Our proposal responds to these concerns in a number of ways. First and foremost, gun seizure orders would only be made if a judge determined that there was probable cause to believe that a respondent is in unlawful possession of a firearm. Even petitions that fail to prove probable cause that a respondent is in possession of a gun may produce a social benefit if they establish that a respondent falls within a prohibited category and should have their name added to the NICS database. Second, the respondent would be given an opportunity after the seizure to contest the validity of the seizure in court. And finally, our proposal would subject petitioners to sanctions if a court determined that the petition (or information provided to police) was brought in bad faith. These are the same kinds of mechanisms that are used in other litigation contexts to prevent analogous forms of overstepping.[107]

In contrast to the concern about too many petitions, there is the concern that there may be too few. While this chapter has detailed the substantial size of the NICS missing-names problem and the unlawful possession problem, and shown how UP petitions can respond to both, even the most prudently designed petition mechanism will produce few benefits if no one comes forward. We know from domestic violence and red flag petitions that some people are likely to come forward. The chapter's opening example of Courtney Irby wishing to disarm her estranged husband provides a vivid example. But we can also imagine that parents who are reasonably concerned about the unsafe prevalence of guns at a neighbor's home might be sufficiently motivated to act (at least anonymously). The next chapter puts front and center these issues of motive and incentive.

INCENTIVIZING DISCLOSURE

Our project has sought to identify broad groups of society who have the requisite information and sufficient incentives to take action to reduce the risk of gun violence. We began with self-control. Sometimes it is the person himself who is best placed to choose to disarm—both because he knows if he may become a risk to himself or loved ones and because he is motivated to prevent it.

Sometimes others are best placed to take action. The people who come forward with domestic violence restraining order petitions are aware that they are at risk and have an incentive to protect themselves. We have similarly relied on the self-defense imperative to motivate our associational marketplace. Many property owners do not want their guests to come armed. Many landlords would feel more comfortable collecting late rent if their tenants did not possess guns. Our email option and our proposals to better empower property and business owners to create gun-free zones rely on this fundamental desire for self-preservation.

But sometimes people who have the requisite information about socially deleterious gun possession may not have a sufficient incentive to take action—to come forward to the police or to file red flag or unlawful possession petitions, for example. Individuals and institutions do not have to actively seek out this information; they often learn of it through ordinary interactions with people in their community. An employer may learn that an employee has failed a drug test. A university may learn that a student has been unlawfully bringing a gun to campus. But knowing that someone is dangerous or in unlawful possession of a gun may not be sufficient incentive to come forward and initiate a petition process, especially if the person is not likely to be a danger to you.

This chapter explores how the law can provide supplemental incentives to nudge citizens to make better choices about disclosing this type of information. As in other contexts, a mixture of carrots and sticks can be deployed to motivate action. Here we describe five specific incentives that might be deployed: three carrots and two sticks. We propose using carrots to better incentivize individual disclosure and using sticks to better incentivize institutional disclosure. Penalizing individuals who fail to come forward with red flag or unlawful possession information is often infeasible because it is difficult for the law to identify the individuals who should have come forward. Did relatives of the Orlando shooter or the Las Vegas shooter know enough that the law might hold them responsible?[1] People with relevant information are more likely to self-identify by stepping forward to claim a reward.[2] In contrast, penalties can be more feasibly applied to institutions.[3] Bureaucracies are more likely to keep records of their interactions with individuals in their sphere. Under our proposal, a university that bars a student from campus can be subjected to a stick penalty if it fails to alert authorities about the student's potential dangerousness.

INDIVIDUAL CARROTS

In this section we describe two carrots that might better incentivize individuals to make use of the petition process—gun bounties and gun trusts. We also describe how states can leverage the avoidance of judicial process to noncoercively incentivize no-guns registration.

Gun Bounties

Cash for disclosure is the simplest carrot. Offering monetary rewards for information that leads to arrest and conviction for
various crimes is already commonplace. So a natural extension
of this idea is to pay a bounty for information leading to the removal of unlawfully possessed guns.

Gun bounties are substantially different from gun buyback programs, which offer gun owners the opportunity to sell their guns
to authorities. Gun buyback programs are usually not limited to
unlawfully possessed weapons, and evaluations have found that
such programs do not have any statistically significant impact on
gun crime or injuries.[4] A 2013 study found that the typical gun
buyback program purchased fewer than 1,000 guns.[5] However,
an evaluation of Boston's 2006 buyback program suggests that
program improvements, such as advertising to youth and paying
only for handguns, may help take more high-risk guns out of the
community.[6]

The concept of paying people to provide leads for unlawful
firearm possession has already been implemented in several lo-
calities. A number of Florida cities pay cash rewards for anonymous tips about illegal weapons that lead to an arrest and a
weapons charge, and many of these programs have been successful at more than just removing unlawfully possessed guns.
For example, the Miami gun bounty program, which began in
2007, has not only led to more than 250 arrests and the confiscation of 432 illegally owned guns, but has also recovered $2.2
million in drugs, and has helped to solve several murder and burglary cases.[7] Jacksonville's bounty program has produced more
than 350 arrests and more than 400 gun confiscations.[8] In January 2019, Champaign County, Illinois, began a trial gun bounty
program that in its first three months confiscated ten handguns,
two shotguns, a semiautomatic rifle, and a single-action rifle
(more than quadrupling the number of firearms recovered over

that period the previous year), as well as five kilograms of marijuana and $3,000 in cash.[9]

These existing programs have succeeded with only modest monetary inducements. For example, the Baltimore program pays $500 per illegal firearm and $500 per arrest up to a maximum reward of $2,000 per tip.[10] These programs show that something akin to an incentivized unlawful possession (UP) petition can produce results without threat of government overreach or the instigation of violence. In Chapter 8, we argued that UP petitions could not only correct for shortfalls in the NICS database coverage, but also, and more importantly, disarm unlawful possessors. The experience of gun bounty programs in a number of jurisdictions demonstrates that an additional benefit can be had: the seizure of other forms of contraband uncovered during the execution of a gun confiscation order.

Gun Trusts

Another way to incentivize action is to give the targeted actors more power to tailor their action to their preferences. Allowing gun owners to have this additional measure of control serves as a sort of carrot. You are more likely to sign up for dance lessons if you are able to specify the dances that will be taught. Similarly, by giving individuals the ability to privatize aspects of the red flag petition process, states can incentivize more people to initiate red flag procedures. A gun owner under existing law could create a special gun trust to hold their firearms as trust property under the control (and for the benefit) of the original gun owner. Further, a third person designated in advance by the gun owner could be given the authority to determine if the gun owner lacks capacity or presents a danger, and thereby gain the right to have the guns removed by court order.

While a gun trust can be stylized as a kind of privatized red flag adjudication, it also represents a less intrusive version of the no-guns registry. Instead of registering to immediately dispossess oneself of guns, a person could retain beneficial use of a gun unless her designee determines that she lacks capacity to continue that beneficial use or otherwise presents a threat to herself or others. The gun trust would serve as a private supplement to a state's red flag provision. Any individual might still be subject to the state's determination that she was a danger to herself or others, thus triggering a red flag removal order. But the designee's determination of incapacity or dangerousness would also be sufficient to trigger a court's gun removal order, whether or not the state has a red flag law on the books. Having the designee make such a determination has the added benefit of avoiding what could be a long, costly, and frustrating judicial process if the state were to get involved.

This is a novel use of trust law, so states may want to pass authorizing legislation. Specifically, a gun trust statute would allow gun owners to (1) declare an irrevocable trust with their guns as the trust property, (2) appoint themselves as trustees and lifetime beneficiaries of the trust, (3) name a successor beneficiary after they die, and (4) name a successor trustee in the event of their incapacity. The statute would also authorize the use of arbitration clauses in the trust document, with the designated arbitrator being the same individual empowered to determine the trustee's capacity to responsibly bear arms.

Such an authorizing statute would clarify what is likely already possible under many states' trust laws. One of the traditional purposes of trusts is to protect trust assets from being misused in the event of the settlor's incapacity.[11] It is thus well settled that a settlor may declare a trust with herself as trustee and lifetime beneficiary as long as a successor beneficiary is designated to take the trust property upon the settlor's death.[12] A traditional capacity provision might read:

> For purposes of this agreement, I shall be considered to be unable to manage my affairs if I am under a legal disability or by reason of illness or mental or physical disability am unable to give prompt and intelligent consideration to

financial matters. The determination as to my inability at
any time shall be made by ____ and my physician, or the
survivor of them, and the trustee may rely upon written notice of that determination.[13]

Certainly, the trustee's ability to make good decisions with respect
to "financial matters" is less important in the gun trust context.
We imagine that instead, the statute would include a provision
that at least incorporates the state's red flag standards for when
an individual is deemed unfit to possess a weapon. For example,
drawing on Florida's red flag statute, a gun trust might establish:

> For purposes of this agreement, I shall be considered to be
> unable to manage my affairs if I am under a legal disability
> or by reason of illness or mental or physical disability pose
> a significant danger of causing personal injury. The de-
> termination as to my inability at any time shall be made
> by ____ and my physician, or the survivor of them. Upon
> written notice of a determination by them that I am un-
> able to manage my affairs, the successor trustee will suc-
> ceed me as trustee of this trust with full rights to restrict or
> cease my personal use or access to trust property.[14]

As with traditional capacity-motivated trusts, the relevant
threshold capacity of the trustee/beneficiary would be determined
by predesignated third parties.

Gun trust statutes could further insulate private determinations from judicial oversight by authorizing gun trusts to include
mandatory arbitration clauses. The Uniform Trust Code, which
has been enacted by thirty-four states and the District of Columbia, already includes a provision allowing settlors to use al-
ternate dispute resolution.[15] Some jurisdictions, in what seems to
be the modern trend, expressly allow mandatory arbitration
clauses either by case law or statute.[16] An Arizona statute, for example, provides: "A trust instrument may provide mandatory,

exclusive and reasonable procedures to resolve issues between the trustee and interested persons or among interested persons with regard to the administration or distribution of the trust."[17] However, the status of trust arbitration clauses is unsettled in many jurisdictions,[18] so a gun trust–authorizing statute should make clear that such clauses would be enforceable at least for trusts where the underlying assets are firearms.

Gun trusts themselves already exist and have been tailored to "provide comprehensive estate planning for firearm owners in the event of *incapacity* or at death."[19] However, our use of a gun trust, and our proposal for an authorization statute, are novel. The added value of an authorizing statute is to further tailor trust declarations to adequately address

(1) the federal gun laws concerning proper possession and transfers of the firearms;
(2) the state and regional gun laws where the firearms are located;
(3) the state and regional gun laws where the firearms are going;
(4) the legality in each location;
(5) the proper method for completing any transfer; and
(6) the eligibility of the fiduciary, successor fiduciary, and beneficiaries to possess the firearms.[20]

The authorizing statute might also create a new state prohibitor category so that if gun removal is appropriate under the terms of the trust, the beneficiary's name would be added to the NICS list.

No-Guns Registry Conditions

In Chapter 4, we discussed how private parties can incentivize individuals to enroll in the no-guns registry. A landlord, for example, might only agree to rent property to an individual who is able to reliably verify that they had ceded their right to bear arms.

While that chapter narrowed the set of businesses that could condition their association on an individual's registration, we would let a broader set of individuals and nonprofits offer inducements, including money, for other people's registration. Where the former are "sticks" and could lead to unjustified discrimination, the latter are "carrots" and are less likely to lead to negative prejudicial consequences.

We remain wary, however, of allowing government as a general matter to offer to buy an individual's right to bear arms. In some ways, such an offer would be a natural analog to a government gun buyback program. When buying back firearms from an individual, government might also be willing to pay extra for the assurance that the individual will not rearm themselves. But government inducements to waive Second Amendment rights raise issues of economic coercion. Even if constitutional, such a condition might disproportionately induce poorer Americans to cede their right to bear arms in ways that are problematic.[21]

However, the government might request a gun rights waiver in circumstances where it has a sufficient basis to take other action that would also have caused an individual to cede their ability to carry firearms. For example, more than 300 mental health courts operating in the United States divert offenders with mental illness from incarceration in return for their participation in mental health treatment.[22] There are already efforts to include these diverted individuals in the NICS database so that they would be incapacitated from buying firearms from gun dealers.[23] It would be appropriate for a state with a no-guns registry to also condition diversion to a mental health court upon the individual registering to waive their gun rights (and verifying this registration with an email to the court). The affected group is tailored to individuals who, by taking the benefit of diversion, are acknowledging that they fall in a prohibited category. Thus, conditioning certain state concessions—such as an agreement not to prosecute—on a no-guns registration represents a way to enhance enforcement and is not a curtailment of substantive rights.

An analogous argument applies to drug courts. As a condition of diversion from incarceration, individuals should agree to verified registration, with the court receiving email notification if the individual later attempts to rescind their registration. Again, the diversion functions as a sufficient acknowledgment of the individual's prohibited status that requiring registration, like calling for inclusion in the NICS database, is reasonable.[24]

Of course, one could imagine bad faith threats of prosecution made solely to force innocent citizens to yield their constitutional right to bear arms. But diversion programs with sufficient judicial oversight—including the option to resist diversion and stand trial—reduce the risk of this kind of prosecutorial misconduct. Conditioning diversion on no-guns registration (especially when it is noncoercive) may reduce the willingness of the affected population to take up the diversion opportunity, but we conjecture that framing no-guns registration properly as part of the treatment program would not affect the popularity of these prosecution alternatives. Indeed, prosecutors may be more willing to extend diversion as an option if they are able to negotiate a waiver of gun rights.

With adequate court supervision, prosecutors might also be given discretion to enter into plea agreements that require no-guns registration. States could mandate that such plea agreements may only be sought if, based on the evidence, the prosecution could have brought a charge that with conviction would have placed the individual in a prohibited category. For example, a prosecutor who could have charged an accused individual with a violent felony should have discretion to make registration a part of the plea deal. At least, such discretion is appropriate in jurisdictions where plea agreements receive sufficient judicial scrutiny.[25]

Finally, we imagine situations where law enforcement officials, instead of proceeding with a red flag petition, would give the respondent the option to register to cede her gun rights voluntarily. A police officer or district attorney who has reason to believe that a respondent may be a heightened risk to themselves or others should have discretion to use the no-guns registry as an alternative to the more cumbersome processes of a red flag removal order. To guard against prosecutorial overreach, however, we would again require some judicial supervision by at least a state administrative law judge, charged with determining that the government has a reasonable basis for its safety concern and that registration is knowing and voluntary.

INSTITUTIONAL STICKS

The foregoing carrot incentives might be supplemented by a variety of contingent penalties, or sticks, aimed at encouraging institutions to reveal petition-relevant information to authorities or to take socially beneficial action to reduce the risk of gun violence. Sticks in particular stray a bit from our theme of enhanced freedom. But stick incentives can be less demanding than traditional command-and-control mandates, and can help harness the aid of diverse institutions by making them internalize the social costs of failing to act. Here we organize our discussion around two different types of institutions: community institutions and the states themselves.

Community Institution Sticks

Employers and schools are well placed to learn of red flag–relevant information through the ordinary course of interacting with community members. Just as there is mandatory reporting for certain forms of sexual misconduct, states should mandate reporting for certain categories of red flag—or unlawful possession—related information. First, if an employer has fired an employee or if a university has expelled a student because of a concern that the individual might pose a risk to community members, the institution should be required to report that information to local authorities. While we would not force institutions to bring red flag petitions, mandatory reporting of relevant red flag information can alert authorities and give them the option of investigating whether to initiate a red flag petition.

Second, mandatory reporting might also be appropriate for unlawful possession–related information. An employer, for example, may learn that a worker has failed a drug test for a non-cannabis controlled substance. Even if the employer does not have credible information that the worker possesses a weapon, authorities could still use the reported results of drug tests to enter the employee's name in the NICS database. Finally, mandatory reporting should also be expanded to cover people experiencing paranoid delusions or threatening hallucinations. As we argued in Chapter 7, people with these symptoms pose a sufficient threat of violence such that their ability to acquire weapons should be closely monitored. Many states already require health care and other professionals to report information regarding "threats of harm to self or others."[26] It is not unreasonable that an emergency room physician should be open to malpractice liability for failing to report that a particular patient was exhibiting these kinds of red flag behaviors.[27]

In addition to mandatory reporting obligations, the state could leverage the possibility of tort liability to incentivize community institutions to create private gun-free zones. Chapter 7, for example, proposed inverting Wisconsin's grant of tort immunity to retailers who allow customers to carry concealed weapons in their store. Better to hold retailers liable in tort if their decision to allow concealed carry in their stores causally contributes to gun violence. If a bar decides to allow its patrons to carry guns, and one of its inebriated customers becomes angry and shoots someone, the bar owner should not, as a matter of law, be immune from liability.

State law might also stop insurance companies from de facto immunizing commercial enterprises from such liability. The law traditionally voids as against public policy insurance provisions attempting to reimburse intentional tortfeasors for third-party liability.[28] States might similarly void insurance protection for retailers or other private property owners who have opted to allow others to bear arms on their property if that decision is found to have contributed to a claim. Similarly, state law might prohibit insurance coverage for gun owners who negligently store their gun if that negligence contributed to a subsequent claim. The criminality of a third party should not absolve the gun owner of financial responsibility for negligent storage.

State Sticks

We can also incentivize states themselves to take action. Congress could give or withhold grant money based on whether particular states collaborated with various gun violence initiatives. While these kinds of initiatives may seem infeasible given current partisanship, as recently as 2007, Congress passed just such a bill with the support of President George W. Bush. The NICS Improvement Amendment Act (NIAA) used both carrot and stick incentives to induce states to improve their reporting to the NICS databases. The NIAA was passed with bipartisan support in 2007 after news outlets widely reported that the Commonwealth of Virginia had failed to submit the name of the Virginia Tech shooter to the FBI even though a Virginia court had ruled Seung-Hui Cho a danger to himself.[29]

The NIAA offered states new grant programs to improve their information systems (as well as less burdensome grant requirements if a state reported to the FBI "at least 90 percent of its records identifying the specified prohibited persons").[30] The program also offered the potential stick of losing Byrne Justice Assistance Grants (JAG) for states that fell short of certain reporting completeness goals.[31] The implementation of these incentives has been less than exemplary—in part because the methodology the program uses to calculate completeness is woefully imprecise. Because the FBI gives states credit for reporting the same person more than once, many states are currently listed as reporting more than 100 percent of eligible individuals.[32] To date, no penalties have been imposed.[33]

One might imagine a new NIAA that attempts to rectify these methodological failings and provide more meaningful reporting incentives on a variety of fronts. Here we briefly mention one possibility—giving states better incentives to take action to combat unlawful firearms possession. In Chapter 8, we analyzed data from the NSDUH survey to estimate that more than a million underage Americans are likely to have possessed a handgun in the past year. Table 9.1 reanalyzes the data at the state level to show substantial differences in the per capita prevalence of underage gun possession. More than 10 percent of the underage respondents in Montana and Wyoming reported gun possession. In contrast, Connecticut, New York, and Massachusetts had possession rates of less than 2 percent. Some or all of this discrepancy might be due to the survey's failure to assess whether the possession was lawful notwithstanding the respondent's age because of statutory exceptions for employment, ranching, farming, target practice, and hunting.[34]

While the NSDUH question is at best a rough proxy for unlawful possession, one could design a survey that more directly captures each of the federally prohibited categories. A federal incentive program could withhold federal grants to contingently punish states with the highest per capita levels of unlawful possession on the representative surveys. The federal government has imposed analogous grant penalties based on highway speeding audits.[35] For example, in 1979, if more than 70 percent of surveyed vehicles in a state exceeded fifty-five miles per hour, the federal government withheld 5 percent of the state's highway funds; if less than 60 percent of surveyed vehicles exceeded fifty-five mph, the state received a boost of 10 percent in federal aid highway funds.[36]

As we proceed to our ending, it is fitting that we include ourselves as potential targets of incentives for action. Throughout this book, we have presented ideas that would give individuals power

Table 9.1. Underage Handgun Possession by State

State	Number of 12–17-year-olds reporting having possessed a handgun in last year	Percentage of 12–17-year-olds reporting having possessed a handgun in last year
Montana	12,000	16.2%
Wyoming	5,000	11.4%
Oregon	27,000	9.3%
Idaho	13,000	8.8%
Alaska	5,000	8.6%
New Jersey	16,000	2.3%
Hawaii	2,000	2.1%
Connecticut	4,000	1.5%
New York	20,000	1.4%
Massachusetts	6,000	1.2%

Data source: 2017 National Survey on Drug Use and Health (NSDUH).

over gun control. While the policies we present work from the ground up, they must first be enacted. We hope that the reasons we have laid out incentivize you to join us and engage in the political process to make these proposals a reality.

This book's aim is to activate state lawmakers to carry out our ten proposals:

1. Enact Donna's Law.
2. Create an associational marketplace by giving registrants an email option.
3. Create no-carry default invitations and leases.
4. Allow property owners to durably create gun-free zones.
5. Allow supermajorities to buy back streets and sidewalks to render them gun-free.

6. Create presumptions for red flag removal orders based on validated symptoms of dangerousness.
7. Create an unlawful possession petition process to allow citizen petitions and anonymous, nonpublic reports to police.
8. Require that red flag and unlawful possession removal orders be reported to the FBI's NICS database as state prohibitors.
9. Add the seven validated categories as state prohibitors that are reported to NICS and can trigger unlawful possession petitions, but exclude the four categories of lower-risk individuals.
10. Incentivize disclosure with a combination of carrots (bounties and private trusts) and sticks (mandates and possible tort liability).

To help with the to-do list, we have included model state statutes to implement several of these proposed interventions in Appendix B and as downloadable documents that you can send to your state legislators. Readers interested in helping to bring these proposals to life can find more information about next steps and sign up for email alerts at stopgunsuicide.com.

APPENDIX A: SUPPLEMENTAL TABLES

The three tables in this appendix supplement Chapter 1. Specifically, these tables provide more information regarding the YouGov survey on Donna's Law, including sample and population demographics, key questionnaire language, and complete regression results.

Table A.1. Sample and Population Proportions for Various Demographics

		Nonveteran sample	Nonveteran population[6]	Veteran sample	Veteran population
Gender[1]	Male	48.8%	44.4%	91.9%	90.7%
	Female	51.3%	55.6%	8.1%	9.3%
Race[1]	White	64.2%	62.8%	81.3%	77.5%
	Black	12.0%	12.0%	11.3%	11.4%
	Hispanic	15.5%	16.0%	4.9%	6.5%
	Asian	2.8%	6.0%	0.0%	1.7%
	Native American	0.6%	0.6%	0.4%	0.6%
	Mixed	3.5%	2.3%	0.8%	2.1%
	Other	1.4%	0.4%	1.3%	0.3%

(continued)

Table A.1. (*Continued*)

		Nonveteran sample	Nonveteran population[6]	Veteran sample	Veteran population
Age[1]	18–29	21.6%	22.8%	2.4%	8.1%
	30–44	25.1%	26.1%	11.6%	14.2%
	45–59	22.9%	26.2%	26.8%	22.0%
	60–74	24.7%	17.9%	35.7%	34.2%
	75+	5.8%	6.9%	23.6%	21.6%
Marital status[1]	Married	46.0%	48.6%	65.6%	62.6%
	Divorced	9.7%	11.2%	12.5%	15.2%
	Separated	2.5%	6.0%	1.3%	7.4%
	Widowed	4.2%	2.1%	6.5%	2.0%
	Domestic/civil partnership	5.1%	—	3.9%	—
	Never married	32.5%	32.1%	10.2%	12.8%
Region[1]	Northeast	17.9%	18.2%	11.7%	14.2%
	Midwest	21.1%	21.0%	20.5%	21.1%
	South	37.0%	37.2%	41.8%	42.2%
	West	24.1%	23.7%	26.0%	22.6%
Education[1]	No high school	12.1%	13.3%	2.4%	6.0%
	High school graduate	27.5%	27.6%	30.7%	28.1%
	Some college	20.9%	22.5%	22.5%	27.8%
	2-year	11.9%	7.8%	16.6%	9.8%
	4-year	17.7%	18.3%	16.8%	17.0%
	Post-grad	9.9%	10.5%	10.9%	11.4%
Employment status	Full-time	40.3%	—	33.2%	—
	Part-time	12.0%	—	5.5%	—
	Unemployed	7.5%	—	2.3%	—
	Retired	19.3%	—	45.5%	—
	Student	6.0%	—	2.1%	—

Table A.1. (*Continued*)

		Nonveteran sample	Nonveteran population[6]	Veteran sample	Veteran population
	Temporarily laid off	0.8%	—	0.3%	—
	Permanently disabled	7.3%	—	8.9%	—
	Homemaker	5.7%	—	1.5%	—
	Other	1.1%	—	0.7%	—
Family Income[1]	Less than $29,999	23.9%	22.8%	15.9%	20.4%
	$30,000–$59,999	28.8%	23.4%	28.9%	26.6%
	$60,000–$99,999	19.2%	23.5%	23.7%	25.5%
	At least $100,000	14.0%	30.4%	19.6%	27.6%
	Prefer not to say	14.2%	—	11.9%	—
Any psychiatric condition[2]	Yes	70.5%	46.4%	57.7%	25.0%
	No	29.6%	53.6%	42.3%	75.0%
Firearm in household[3]	Yes	31.3%	30.5%	48.4%	49.0%
	No	63.9%	67.0%	45.9%	43.4%
	Not sure	4.8%	2.5%	5.3%	7.6%
	Not asked	0.0%	—	0.4%	—
3 point party ID[4]	Democrat	34.6%	33.2%	24.6%	23.9%
	Independent	28.7%	41.0%	33.7%	42.9%
	Republican	24.9%	22.0%	33.7%	28.1%
	Other	4.5%	2.7%	6.9%	2.7%
	Not sure	7.3%	1.1%	1.1%	2.4%
2016 Presidential vote post election[5]	Hillary Clinton	34.1%	35.6%	32.2%	27.1%
	Donald Trump	32.0%	31.3%	53.3%	47.8%
	Gary Johnson	1.7%	—	2.6%	—

(*continued*)

Table A.1. (*Continued*)

		Nonveteran sample	Nonveteran population[6]	Veteran sample	Veteran population
	Jill Stein	0.9%	—	0.4%	—
	Evan McMullin	0.6%	—	0.3%	—
	Other	1.2%	4.3%	1.4%	4.8%
	Did not vote for president	29.5%	28.9%	9.9%	20.3%
N		1,000		1,000	

1. *American Community Survey 2016 1-Year PUMS*, U.S. Census Bureau (2016), https://www.census.gov/programs-surveys/acs/data/pums.html.
2. Ronald C. Kessler et al., *Lifetime Prevalence and Age-of-Onset Distributions of DSM-IV Disorders in the National Comorbidity Survey Replication*, 62 Archives of General Psychiatry 593 (2005); Ranak K. Trivedi et al., *Prevalence, Comorbidity, and Prognosis of Mental Health among US Veterans*, 105 Am. J. Public Health 2564 (2015).
3. Firearm presence within a household and party identification are sourced from General Social Survey 2016 data. Tome W. Smith et al., *General Social Surveys, 1972–2018*, NORC (2018), gssdataexplorer.norc.org.
4. Data on voter turnout is sourced from Current Population Survey IPUMS November 2016 data. Sarah Flood et al., *Integrated Public Use Microdata Series, Current Population Survey* (2018), https://cps.ipums.org/cps-action/variables/live_search.
5. Presidential votes are based on 2016 CNN exit polls. *Exit Polls*, CNN (Nov. 23, 2016), https://www.cnn.com/election/2016/results/exit-polls.
6. The proportion of nonveterans with mental illnesses is based on total population estimates, rather than nonveterans. All other statistics presented in the nonveteran population column are specific to nonveterans.

Table A2. Participation Survey Questions (each respondent answered one or the other)

Purchase Restriction

Some people are not allowed to buy firearms. For example, criminals cannot buy firearms. Before selling a firearm, the dealer has to check a list of names. If a person's name is on the list, that person will not be able to buy a firearm. Only firearm dealers can see the list.

Imagine your state lets people put their own names on the list. If you put your name on the list, you will not be able to buy a firearm. If you change your mind, you can ask to have your name taken off the list. Your name will be taken off the list three weeks later, no questions asked.

Some people think letting people put their names on the list will reduce suicide by giving people time to think before using a firearm. Other people think suicide will not go down because people will find another way to kill themselves.

Would you voluntarily put your own name on the list so that you would not be able to buy a firearm?

<1> Yes
<2> No

Purchase and Possession Restriction
Some people are not allowed to buy or keep firearms. For example, criminals cannot have firearms. Before selling a firearm, the dealer has to check a list of names. If a person's name is on the list, that person will not be able to buy a firearm. It is a crime for a person on the list to have a firearm. Only firearm dealers and police officers can see the list.

Imagine your state lets people put their own names on the list. If you put your name on the list, you will not be able to buy or keep a firearm. If you put your name on the list, you will have to give any firearms that you own to someone else. If you change your mind, you can ask to have your name taken off the list. Your name will be taken off the list three weeks later, no questions asked.

Some people think letting people put their names on the list will reduce suicide by giving people time to think before using a firearm. Other people think suicide will not go down because people will find another way to kill themselves.

Would you voluntarily put your own name on the list so that you would not be able to buy or keep a firearm?

<1> Yes
<2> No

Table A.3. Survey Logistic Regressions Results

Variables	Odds ratio of willingness to sign up	
	General population	*Veterans*
Possess option	0.936	0.653*
	(0.169)	(0.143)
Female	1.292	0.871
	(0.247)	(0.378)
Heterosexual	0.747	0.674
	(0.200)	(0.289)
Access to gun	0.590**	0.339***
	(0.122)	(0.082)
Missing gun access question	0.383*	0.092**
	(0.193)	(0.104)
Prohibited from gun purchase	0.724	2.420
	(0.438)	(1.465)
Any psychiatric condition	1.688**	1.343
	(0.343)	(0.316)
7 alcoholic drinks per week	0.707	0.715
	(0.244)	(0.237)
mSBQ score	1.001	1.074*
	(0.029)	(0.044)
Attempted suicide	3.035*	3.918
	(1.990)	(3.397)
2+ suicide attempts	0.512	0.360
	(0.395)	(0.419)
Family member died by suicide	0.948	0.831
	(0.245)	(0.268)
Air Force		1.097
		(0.326)
Navy		1.104
		(0.304)
Marines		2.042*
		(0.797)
Coast Guard/Other		1.574
		(1.322)

Table A.3. (*Continued*)

Variables	Odds ratio of willingness to sign up	
	General population	*Veterans*
Active duty		4.741**
		(3.146)
Deployed		0.587**
		(0.152)
Saw combat		1.427
		(0.412)
Injured in combat		0.668
		(0.218)
Passed over for promotion		0.645
		(0.186)
Demoted		0.978
		(0.390)
Court-martial		1.525
		(0.733)
Age 18–30	1.024	6.307*
	(0.579)	(6.327)
Age 31–45	1.505	2.041
	(0.786)	(1.055)
Age 46–60	0.819	1.005
	(0.416)	(0.391)
Age 61–75	0.461*	1.028
	(0.205)	(0.319)
Black	0.577*	0.996
	(0.190)	(0.350)
Hispanic	1.102	0.660
	(0.338)	(0.358)
Other race	1.210	0.673
	(0.356)	(0.586)
No high school	1.242	0.529
	(0.540)	(0.451)
High school graduate	1.035	0.524*
	(0.336)	(0.189)

(*continued*)

Table A.3. (*Continued*)

Variables	Odds ratio of willingness to sign up	
	General population	*Veterans*
Some college	1.204	0.391**
	(0.387)	(0.155)
2-year degree	0.920	0.782
	(0.331)	(0.289)
4-year degree	1.147	0.574
	(0.351)	(0.221)
Married	0.950	0.892
	(0.222)	(0.337)
Separated/divorced	0.543*	0.775
	(0.201)	(0.342)
Widow	0.607	0.762
	(0.309)	(0.400)
Part-time employee	2.617***	1.002
	(0.834)	(0.509)
Unemployed	0.599	0.285
	(0.248)	(0.244)
Retired	1.691	0.784
	(0.554)	(0.253)
Disabled	1.719	0.459
	(0.692)	(0.221)
Other employment status	1.111	0.422
	(0.337)	(0.263)
Family income < $30K	1.002	1.885
	(0.344)	(0.869)
Family income $30K–$60K	1.270	1.109
	(0.422)	(0.466)
Family income $60K–$100K	1.964*	1.346
	(0.680)	(0.561)
Family income > $100K	1.357	0.976
	(0.509)	(0.427)
Republican	0.621	0.620
	(0.204)	(0.247)

Table A.3. (*Continued*)

Variables	Odds ratio of willingness to sign up	
	General population	*Veterans*
Independent	0.493***	0.638
	(0.127)	(0.209)
Other party	1.011	0.686
	(0.493)	(0.358)
Unknown party	0.568	1.827
	(0.250)	(1.822)
Northeast	1.981**	1.112
	(0.567)	(0.442)
South	1.074	1.418
	(0.271)	(0.458)
West	1.576	0.927
	(0.446)	(0.331)
Donald Trump	0.407***	0.329***
	(0.125)	(0.109)
Gary Johnson	0.544	0.070***
	(0.426)	(0.055)
Other candidate	0.488	0.249*
	(0.232)	(0.183)
Did not vote	0.863	0.323**
	(0.238)	(0.142)
Catholic	1.602*	1.211
	(0.415)	(0.422)
Not religious	1.230	1.113
	(0.289)	(0.319)
Other religion	1.125	1.426
	(0.370)	(0.515)
Constant	0.352	0.447
	(0.238)	(0.474)
Observations	1,000	997

Data source: YouGov survey.
Note: Robust (see form in parentheses). Omitted categories include Army, Democrat, Midwest, Hillary Clinton, and Protestant.
*** p<0.01, ** p<0.05, * p<0.1

VERSION 1: DONNA'S LAW

SYNOPSIS: Under current law, people who fear that they may become a risk to themselves or others are not allowed to restrict their legal ability to purchase firearms.

This bill would authorize people to add their own names into the background check system to protect themselves and others against impulsive gun violence.

BE IT ENACTED BY THE LEGISLATURE OF [STATE]:

Section 1.

(a) [The STATE AGENCY RESPONSIBLE FOR NICS REPORTING] within one year of the passage of this Act shall develop and launch a secure Internet-based platform to allow any person residing in [STATE] to register to add their name to the "[STATE] Do-Not-Sell List."

(b) The [AGENCY] shall ensure that this Internet-based platform credibly (i) verifies the identity of any persons who opt to register, (ii) prevents unauthorized disclosures of any registering persons, and (iii) informs the individual of the legal effects of registration.

(c) The [AGENCY] within six months of the passage of this Act shall develop and widely distribute a hard-copy form to allow any resident to register to add their name to the "[STATE] Do-Not-Sell List" and a form to request removal. The forms may be (i) submitted in person at a county clerk's office with government-issued photo identification, (ii) mailed to the [AGENCY] with a copy of government-issued photo identification, or (iii) texted to the [AGENCY] with a copy of government-issued photo identification and a selfie. (d) In addition, the Internet-based platform and registration form shall provide registrants with an email notification option that shall allow registered individuals to identify at the time of registration or thereafter one or more email addresses. The [AGENCY] shall notify any such email addressees if the individual subsequently seeks to remove his or her name. Providing email contact information constitutes an express authorization of such use of records.

Section 2. Once the Internet-based platform becomes operative and/or forms are made available, any person may request to be added to the "[STATE] Do-Not-Sell List." The [AGENCY] shall on an ongoing basis forward registry information to the Federal Bureau of Investigation to be entered into the NICS Index Denied Persons File, and to any other state that adopts an analogous "Do-Not-Sell List."

Section 3. Registering for the "[STATE] Do-Not-Sell List" or registering in any other state that adopts an analogous "Do-Not-Sell List" renders receipt of a firearm illegal in [STATE]. Transfer of a firearm to a person on the "[STATE] Do-Not-Sell List" by any person or entity required to perform a background check, either knowingly or due to a failure to perform a background check, is punishable by a fine up to $10,000 and/or imprisonment for no more than one year.

Section 4.

(a) A person who has registered with the "[STATE] Do-Not-Sell List" may subsequently request that his or her name be removed from the registry by one of the same methods as provided for registration. The [AGENCY] shall wait twenty-

one days after receipt before notifying the FBI to remove
the requesting person from the NICS Index Denied Persons
File and then the [AGENCY] shall purge any and all records
of the sign-up, transactions, and removal.

(b) A person who has registered with the "[STATE] Do-Not-
Sell List" may deregister by applying for immediate deregistration to [AN APPROPRIATE STATE COURT] and proving
by a preponderance of the evidence that he or she is not likely
to act in a manner dangerous to public safety (including
danger to self) in a proceeding where any public official or
interested party may also present evidence.

Section 5. A person who knowingly makes a false statement
regarding their identity on the Internet-based platform or on any
hard-copy form is guilty of false swearing under [CITE RELE-
VANT SECTION].

Section 6.

(a) In employment, education, government benefits, and
contracting, it shall be illegal to inquire whether an individual under this Section has requested to be added to or
removed from the "[STATE] Do-Not-Sell List" and it shall be
illegal to take action based on such information.

(b) Individuals or organizations who learn, from the "[STATE]
Do-Not-Sell List" or otherwise, the identity of someone who
has requested to be added to or removed from the registry
shall have a duty not to disclose that information to others
unless the individual or organization receives separate nonregistry authorization from the waiving individual to share
that information. Violation of this Section shall be criminally
punishable by a fine of up to $10,000 and/or imprisonment
for no more than one year.

Section 7. A person presenting in an acute-care hospital or a
satellite emergency facility for a probable suicide attempt should,
as a non-binding matter of best practice, be presented with the
opportunity of registering on the Internet-based "[STATE] Do-
Not-Sell List." Any suicide hotline maintained or operated by any

entity funded in whole or part by the state should generally, as a
non-binding matter of best practice, inform callers about the opportunity of registering with the "[STATE] Do-Not-Sell List." All
Department of Motor Vehicle offices serving the public shall offer
individuals the opportunity of registering on the "[STATE] Do-
Not-Sell List." The Board of Counseling, Board of Medicine,
Board of Nursing, and Board of Psychology shall notify all licensees of the existence of the "[STATE] Do-Not-Sell List" created by this act within 60 days after the effective date of this act.

Section 8. The [STATE PUBLIC HEALTH AGENCY] shall
develop and implement a publicity and advertising campaign that,
at a minimum, provides the public with information about the
"[STATE] Do-Not-Sell List," how an individual may register, and
contacts for additional information regarding the list.

VERSION 2: ASSOCIATIONAL MARKETPLACE EXTENSION

SYNOPSIS: Under current law, people who fear that they
may become a risk to themselves or others are not allowed to restrict their legal ability to purchase firearms.

This bill would authorize people to add their own names into
the background check system to protect themselves and others
against impulsive gun violence.

BE IT ENACTED BY THE LEGISLATURE OF [STATE]:

Section 1. [The STATE AGENCY RESPONSIBLE FOR NICS
REPORTING] within one year of the passage of this Act shall
develop and launch a secure Internet-based platform to allow any
person residing in [STATE] to register to add their name to the
"[STATE] No Guns Registry."

(a) The [AGENCY] shall ensure that this Internet-based platform credibly (i) verifies the identity of any persons who opt
to register, (ii) prevents unauthorized disclosures of any registering persons, and (iii) informs the individual of the legal
effects of registration.

[(b) The [AGENCY] within six months of the passage of this Act shall develop and widely distribute a hard-copy form to allow any resident to register to add their name to the "[STATE] No Guns Registry" and a form to request removal. The forms may be (i) submitted in person at a county clerk's office with government-issued photo identification, (ii) mailed to the [AGENCY] with a copy of government-issued photo identification, or (iii) texted to the [AGENCY] with a copy of government-issued photo identification and a selfie.]

(b) In addition, the Internet-based platform and registration form shall provide registrants with an email notification option that shall allow registered individuals to identify at the time of registration or thereafter one or more email addresses. The platform and form will separately ask whether a registrant wishes to provide the email addresses of his or her physician or health care provider. The [AGENCY] shall notify any such email addressees that the individual has registered his or her name with the "[STATE] No Guns Registry" and has thereby waived his or her right to bear arms, and the [AGENCY] shall also notify any such addressees if the individual subsequently seeks to rescind his or her waiver. Providing email contact information constitutes an express authorization of such use of records.

Section 2. Once the Internet-based platform becomes operative and forms are made available, any person may request to be added to the "[STATE] No Guns Registry." The [AGENCY] shall on an ongoing basis forward registry information to the Federal Bureau of Investigation to be entered into the NICS Index Denied Persons File, and to any other state that adopts an analogous "No Guns Registry."

Section 3. Registering for the "[STATE] No Guns Registry" or registering in any other state that adopts an analogous "No Guns Registry" renders possession of a firearm illegal in [STATE]. If a person is in the NICS due to registering in [STATE] or in another state, receipt of a firearm from a person or entity required to perform a background check violates [STATE] law. Knowing possession of a firearm by a person validly registered on the "No Guns Registry" is punishable by a fine of up to $500. Transfer of a firearm to a person on the "[STATE] No Guns Registry" by any person or entity required to perform a background check, either knowingly or due to a failure to perform a background check, is punishable by a fine up to $10,000 and/or imprisonment for no more than one year.

Section 4. A person who has registered with the "[STATE] No Guns Registry" may subsequently request that his or her name be removed from the registry by one of the same methods as provided for registration. [A request for removal must be accompanied by a declaration from a health care provider that the registered person is not an imminent danger to self or others.] The [AGENCY] shall wait twenty-one days after receipt before notifying the FBI to remove the requesting person from the NICS Index Denied Persons File and then the [AGENCY] shall purge any and all records of the sign-up, transactions, and removal. A person who has registered with the "[STATE] No Guns Registry" may deregister by applying for immediate deregistration to a Superior Court and proving by a preponderance of the evidence that he or she is not likely to act in a manner dangerous to public safety (including danger to self) in a proceeding where any public official or interested party may also present evidence.

Section 5. A person who knowingly makes a false statement regarding their identity on the Internet-based platform or on any hard-copy form is guilty of false swearing under [CITE RELEVANT SECTION].

Section 6.

(a) In employment, education, government benefits, and contracting, it shall be illegal to inquire whether an individual under this section has requested to be added to or removed from the "[STATE] No Guns Registry" and it shall be illegal to take action based on such information. However, notwithstanding the foregoing prohibition, it shall not be illegal for an insurer with regard to life, homeowners', or renter's insurance to inquire or base the terms, premia, or issuance of insurance on such information. Nor shall it be illegal for a cotenant, landlord, homeowners' association, or condominium association to condition terms of ownership, tenancy, occupancy, or status as an invitee on such information.

(b) Individuals or organizations who learn, from the "[STATE] No Guns Registry" or otherwise, the identity of someone who has requested to be added to or removed from the registry shall have a duty not to disclose that information to others unless the individual or organization receives separate nonregistry authorization from the waiving individual to share that information. Violation of this section shall be criminally punishable by a fine of up to $10,000 and/or imprisonment for no more than one year.

Section 7. A person presenting in an acute-care hospital or a satellite emergency facility for a probable suicide attempt should, as a non-binding matter of best practice, be presented with the opportunity of registering on the Internet-based "[STATE] No Guns Registry." Any suicide hotline maintained or operated by any entity funded in whole or part by the state should generally, as a non-binding matter of best practice, inform callers about the opportunity of registering with the registry. All Department of Motor Vehicle offices serving the public shall offer individuals the opportunity of registering on the Internet-based "[STATE] No Guns Registry." The Board of Counseling, Board of Medicine, Board of Nursing, and Board of Psychology shall notify all licensees of the existence of the "[STATE] No Guns Registry" created by this act within 60 days after the effective date of this act.

Section 8. The [STATE PUBLIC HEALTH AGENCY] shall develop and implement a publicity and advertising campaign that, at a minimum, provides the public with information about the registry, how an individual may register, and contacts for additional information regarding the list.

No-Carry Default Invitation

No individual may carry a firearm onto the property of another without first receiving the express consent of the owner or person in legal control or possession.

No-Possession Default Lease Provision

No tenant leasing property or person residing in leased property may possess a firearm on that property unless the landlord gives explicit written permission for such possession, nor can a tenant leasing property or a person residing in leased property invite another to bring a firearm onto that property unless the landlord gives explicit written permission for such an invitation.

NOTES

INTRODUCTION

1. CDC, *Deaths: Final Data for 2016* (July 26, 2018), tbl.6, https://www.cdc.gov/nchs/data/nvsr/nvsr67/nvsr67_05.pdf.

2. Global Burden of Disease 2016 Injury Collaborators, *Global Mortality from Firearms, 1990–2016,* 320 JAMA 792 (2018). "Homicide" refers to interpersonal violence and excludes, for example, deaths from war.

3. Everytown, *Gun Violence in America* (Apr. 4, 2019), https://everytownresearch.org/gun-violence-america/#foot_note_21.

4. Maggie Astor and Karl Russell, *After Parkland, a New Surge in State Gun Control Laws,* N.Y. Times (Dec. 14, 2018).

5. Astor and Russell, *After Parkland.*

6. Kenneth D. Kochanek, Sherry L. Murphy, Jiaquan Xu, and Elizabeth Arias, *Deaths: Final Data for 2017,* 68 National Vital Statistics Report, tbl.6, https://www.cdc.gov/nchs/data/nvsr/nvsr68/nvsr68_09-508.pdf.

7. McDonald v. Chicago, 561 U.S. 742, 891 (2010) (Stevens, dissenting).

1. DONNA'S LAW

1. Richard A. Webster, "After Mother's Suicide, Katrina Brees Fights for 'No Guns' Self-Registry," Nola.com (Sept. 27, 2018, 3:10 p.m.), https://expo.nola.com/news/erry-2018/09/39f7db7652102/after-mothers-suicide-katrina.html.

2. Keith Hawton, *Restricting Access to Methods of Suicide: Rationale and Evaluation of This Approach to Suicide Prevention,* 28 Crisis 4, 5 (Supp. 1 2007).

3. Eberhard A. Deseinhammer et al., *The Duration of the Suicidal Process: How Much Time Is Left for Intervention between Consideration and Accomplishment of a Suicide Attempt?*, 70 J. Clinical Psychiatry 19, 21 fig.2 (2009).

4. Linda G. Peterson et al., *Self-Inflicted Gunshot Wounds: Lethality of Method versus Intent*, 142 Am. J. Psychiatry 228 (1985); *see also* Matthew Miller et al., *Suicide Mortality in the United States: The Importance of Attending to Method in Understanding Population-Level Disparities in the Burden of Suicide*, 33 Ann. Rev. Pub. Health 393, 402 (2012) (describing a study in which 70 percent of survivors of near-lethal suicide attempts deliberated less than one hour); Megan Spokas et al., *Characteristics of Individuals Who Make Impulsive Suicide Attempts*, 136 J. Affective Disorders 1125 (2012) (finding that only 36.1 percent contemplated suicide for three or more hours before attempt).

5. Matthew Miller and David Hemenway, *Guns and Suicide in the United States*, 359 New Eng. J. Med. 989, 989 (2008).

6. J. T. O. Cavanagh et al., *Psychological Autopsy Studies of Suicide: A Systematic Review*, 33 Psychol. Med. 395, 399 (2003).

7. E. Clare Harris and Brian Barraclough, *Suicide as an Outcome for Mental Illness: A Meta-Analysis*, 170 Brit. J. Psychiatry 205, 222 (1997).

8. Mark Olfson, Steven C. Marcus, and Jeffrey A. Bridge, *Focusing Suicide Prevention on Periods of High Risk*, 311 JAMA 1107 (2014).

9. C. M. Canuso et al., *Efficacy and Safety of Intranasal Esketamine for the Rapid Reduction of Symptoms of Depression and Suicidality in Patients at Imminent Risk for Suicide: Results of a Double-Blind, Randomized, Placebo-Controlled Study*, 175 Am. J. Psychiatry 620 (2018).

10. U.S. Department of Health and Human Services, Mental Health: A Report of the Surgeon General 64–65 (1999).

11. M. S. Kaplan, B. H. McFarland, and N. Huguet, *Characteristics of Adult Male and Female Firearm Suicide Decedents: Findings from the National Violent Death Reporting System*, 15 Injury Prevention 322, 325 tbl.2 (2009).

12. Kaplan, McFarland, and Huguet, *Characteristics*, at 325.

13. Kaplan, McFarland, and Huguet, *Characteristics*, at 326.

14. Miller et al., *Suicide Mortality in the United States*, at 401.

15. Miller et al., *Suicide Mortality in the United States*, at 397 tbl.1.

16. More broadly, one literature review concluded that "the risk of substitution or displacement towards other methods seems small." Marc S. Daigle, *Suicide Prevention through Means Restriction: Assessing the Risk of Substitution; A Critical Review and Synthesis*, 37 Accident Analysis and Prevention 625, 630 (2005).

17. Miller et al., *Suicide Mortality in the United States*, at 399–400.

18. Miller et al., *Suicide Mortality in the United States*, at 402.

19. Miller et al., *Suicide Mortality in the United States*, at 399–400.

20. Nat'l Res. Council, Firearms and Violence: A Critical Review 181 (Charles F. Wellford, John V. Pepper, and Carol V. Petrie eds., 2004).

21. Peter Cummings et al., *The Association between the Purchase of a Handgun and Homicide or Suicide*, 87 Am. J. Pub. Health 974, 977 (1997).

22. Cummings et al., *Association*, at 976.

23. G. J. Wintemute et al., *Mortality among Recent Purchasers of Handguns*, 341 New Engl. J. Med. 1583 (1999).

24. S. W. Hargarten et al., *Suicide Guns: Why Collect This Information?*, 6 Injury Prevention 245, 246 (2000) (citing *Firearm Fatalities: The Second Annual Report of the Firearm Injury Reporting System (FIRS)*, fig.16 (1999), www.mcw.edu/fic).

25. Arthur Kellerman et al., *Suicide in the Home in Relation to Gun Ownership*, 327 New Eng. J. Med. 467, 470 (1992).

26. Griffin Edwards et al., *Looking Down the Barrel of a Loaded Gun: The Effect of Mandatory Handgun Purchase Delays on Homicide and Suicide*, 128 Econ. J. 3117 (2017).

27. Michael Luca, Deepak Malhotra, and Christopher Poliquin, *Handgun Waiting Periods Reduce Gun Deaths*, 114 Proc. Nat'l Acad. Sci. U.S. 12162 (2017).

28. Nat'l Res. Council, Firearms and Violence.

29. Barbara Stanley and Gregory K. Brown, *Safety Planning Intervention: A Brief Intervention to Mitigate Suicide Risk*, 19 Cognitive and Behav. Prac. 256 (2012).

30. Stanley and Brown, *Safety Planning Intervention*, at 259.

31. Fredrick E. Vars et al., *Willingness of Mentally Ill Individuals to Sign Up for a Novel Proposal to Prevent Firearm Suicide*, 47 Suicide and Life-Threatening Behav. 483 (2017).

32. Ian Ayres and Fredrick E. Vars, *Libertarian Gun Control*, 167 U. Pa. L. Rev. 921 (2019).

33. Doug Rivers, *Pew Research: YouGov Consistently Outperforms Competitors on Accuracy*, YouGov (May 13, 2016, 12:37 p.m.), https://today.yougov.com/topics/finance/articles-reports/2016/05/13/pew-research-yougov.

34. We reproduce the text of the questions in Appendix A, Table A.2.

35. Regression analysis revealed that sign-up rates varied significantly across only a few of the dimensions we assessed. The survey asked and

our model controlled for whether under our proposal possession (in addition to purchase) was barred, age, race, ethnicity, education, gender, sexual orientation, marital status, employment, income, region, political party identification, 2016 presidential vote choice, religion, gun access, whether gun possession was already prohibited, having a mental health diagnosis, high alcohol consumption (more than seven drinks per week), suicide risk score on a modified version of the SBQ-R, prior suicide attempts, and family-member suicide.

36. Full regression results are given in Appendix A, Table A.3.

37. This could save many lives, as discussed above and estimated below.

38. *See, e.g.*, Lulu Garcia-Navarro, *Vermont Governor Vetoes Gun Waiting Period Bill*, Weekend Edition Sunday (June 16, 2019, 8:03 a.m.), https://www.npr.org/2019/06/16/733048204/vermont-governor-vetoes -gun-waiting-period-bill (reporting that Vermont governor vetoed waiting period bill); Steven Shepard, *Gun Control Support Surges in Polls*, Politico (Feb. 28, 2018, 7:27 a.m.), https://www.politico.com /story/2018/02/28/gun-control-polling-parkland-430099 (reporting that 78 percent of respondents favor waiting periods).

39. *See also* Drury D. Stevenson, *Going Gunless*, 85 Brooklyn L. Rev. __ (2020) (forthcoming).

40. Tom Miller, *Austin Veterans Affairs Clinic to Reopen Wednesday after Suicide Shut Down Building*, KXAN (Apr. 10, 2019, 2:02 p.m.), https://www.kxan.com/news/local/austin/suicide-inside-austin-veterans -affairs-clinic-shuts-down-building/1912642256.

41. Jennifer Steinhauer, *V.A. Officials, and the Nation, Battle an Unrelenting Tide of Veteran Suicides*, N.Y. Times, Apr. 14, 2019.

42. U.S. Dep't. of Veterans Affairs, VA National Suicide Data Report 2005–2016 (Sept. 2018), https://www.mentalhealth.va.gov/docs/data -sheets/OMHSP_National_Suicide_Data_Report_2005-2016_508.pdf.

43. U.S. Dep't. of Veterans Affairs, VA National Suicide Data Report 2005–2016.

44. Edwards et al., *Looking Down the Barrel;* Luca, Malhotra, and Poliquin, *Handgun Waiting Periods*.

45. Andrew Anglemyer, Tara Horvath, and George Rutherford, *The Accessibility of Firearms and Risk for Suicide and Homicide Victimization among Household Members: A Systematic Review and Meta-Analysis*, 160 Annals Internal Med. 101 (2014).

46. This estimate is nearly identical to one that can be calculated from the results of a more recent single study using state-level multivariate

regression analysis. Michael Siegel and Emily F. Rothman, *Firearm Owner-ship and Suicide Rates among U.S. Men and Women, 1981–2013*, 106 Am. J. Pub. Health 1316 (2016). That study estimated a 1.9 point re-duction in the overall male suicide rate (per 100,000) associated with a 10 percentage point reduction in gun ownership (Siegel and Rothman, *Firearm Ownership and Suicide Rates*, at 1321 tbl.2), which translates into 1,162 lives saved for a 3.8 percentage point gun ownership reduc-tion. Interestingly, there was no impact on overall female suicide.

2. ANALOGIES, CHOICES, AND CONSTRAINTS

1. Homer, The Odyssey, book 12 (Samuel Butler trans.), http://classics .mit.edu/Homer/odyssey.12.xii.html (last visited May 8, 2014). *See also* Guido Calabresi and A. Douglas Melamed, *Property Rules, Liability Rules, and Inalienability: One View of the Cathedral*, 85 Harv. L. Rev. 1089, 1113 (1972) (describing Ulysses's order as "self paternalism").

2. *See* F. A. Hayek, The Constitution of Liberty 179 (1960) (ex-plaining that the reason for constitutions "is that all men in the pursuit of immediate aims are apt—or, because of the limitation of their intel-lect, in fact bound—to violate rules of conduct which they would never-theless wish to see generally observed. Because of the restricted capacity of our minds, our immediate purposes will always loom large, and we will tend to sacrifice long-term advantages to them").

3. *See* Ian Ayres, Carrots and Sticks: Unlock the Power of Incentives to Get Things Done (2010).

4. Irina Slavina, Note, *Don't Bet on It: Casinos' Contractual Duty to Stop Compulsive Gamblers from Gambling*, 85 Chi.-Kent L. Rev. 369, 369–70 (2010).

5. Nerilee Hing et al., *A Process Evaluation of a Self-Exclusion Pro-gram: A Qualitative Investigation from the Perspective of Excluders and Non-Excluders*, 12 Int'l J. Mental Health and Addiction 509 (2014); Ayres, Carrots and Sticks, at 143.

6. Darren Gelber, *The Reach of New Jersey's Voluntary Self-Exclusion List*, 281 N.J. Law. 50, 51 (2013).

7. Andy Rhea, *Voluntary Self Exclusion Lists: How They Work and Potential Problems*, 9 Gaming L. Rev. 462, 465 (2005).

8. Gelber, *Reach of New Jersey's Voluntary Self-Exclusion List*.

9. Sarah E. Nelson et al., *One Decade of Self Exclusion: Missouri Casino Self-Excluders Four to Ten Years after Enrollment*, 26 J. Gam-bling Stud. 129, 142 (2010).

10. Nelson et al., *One Decade of Self Exclusion*, at 137 tbl.2.

11. Sally M. Gainsbury, *Review of Self-Exclusion from Gambling Venues as an Intervention for Problem Gambling*, 30 J. Gambling Stud. 229, 246 (2014).

12. Gainsbury, *Review of Self-Exclusion*, at 230.

13. *Security Self-Exclusion Form*, Mohegan Sun, Inc., https://mohegansun.com/content/dam/mohegansun/PDF/Misc/self-exclusion.pdf (last visited July 22, 2019).

14. *Listing of Federal Firearms Licensees (FFLs)—2017*, Bureau of Alcohol, Tobacco, Firearms, and Explosives, https://www.atf.gov/firearms/listing-federal-firearms-licensees-ffls-2017.

15. *Listing of Federal Firearms Licensees.*

16. *Living Wills, Health Care Proxies, and Advance Health Care Directives*, A.B.A.: Real Property, Trust and Estate Law, https://www.americanbar.org/groups/real_property_trust_estate/resources/estate_planning/living_wills_health_care_proxies_advance_health_care_directives/.

17. Kuldeep N. Yadav et al., *Approximately One in Three US Adults Completes Any Type of Advance Directive for End-of-Life-Care*, 36 Health Affairs 1244 (2017), https://www.healthaffairs.org/doi/abs/10.1377/hlthaff.2017.0175.

18. Elizabeth M. Gallagher, *Advance Directives for Psychiatric Care: A Theoretical and Practical Overview for Legal Professionals*, 4 Psychol. Pub. Pol'y and L. 746, 746 (1998).

19. Bruce J. Winick, *Advance Directive Instruments for Those with Mental Illness*, 51 U. Miami L. Rev. 57, 83 (1996).

20. Jeffrey W. Swanson et al., *Psychiatric Advance Directives and Reduction of Coercive Crisis Interventions*, 17 J. Mental Health 255, 259–63 (2008).

21. *See* N.C. Gen. Stat. § 122C-72(1) (2018).

22. Eric B. Elbogen et al., *Effectively Implementing Psychiatric Advance Directives to Promote Self-Determination of Treatment among People with Mental Illness*, 13 Psychol. Pub. Pol'y and L. 273, 276 (2007).

23. Elbogen et al., *Effectively Implementing Psychiatric Advance Directives.*

24. Alberto B. Lopez and Fredrick E. Vars, *Wrongful Living*, 104 Iowa L. Rev. 1921 (2019).

25. Lopez and Vars, *Wrongful Living.*

26. David Thun, *The Official 2017 NNA Census: Notaries Are on the Rise Again*, Nat'l Notary Ass'n: Notary Bulletin (Oct. 11, 2017), https://www.nationalnotary.org/notary-bulletin/blog/2017/10/2017-nna-census-notaries.

27. Notarize, https://www.notarize.com/ (last visited July 29, 2019).

28. Jason B. Luoma et al., *Contact with Mental Health and Primary Care Providers before Suicide: A Review of the Evidence,* 159 Am. J. Psychiatry 909, 912 (2002), https://www.ncbi.nlm.nih.gov/pmc/articles /PMC5072576/.

29. Our Donna's Law Model in Appendix B includes in-person, mail-in, text, and online registration options.

30. *See The Identity Protection PIN (IP PIN),* Internal Revenue Serv., https://www.irs.gov/identity-theft-fraud-scams/the-identity-protection -pin-ip-pin (last updated Feb. 4, 2019); *Sign In or Create an Account,* U.S. Soc. Security Admin., https://secure.ssa.gov/RIL/SiView.action (https://perma.cc/R4EF-NDKW) (last visited Oct. 12, 2018).

31. Facebook requires a would-be political advertiser to show a photo ID through a webcam, to provide the last four digits of a Social Security number, and, in an effort to stave off Russian and other foreign influencers, to enter a code delivered by U.S. mail.

32. One commentator recommends an even broader prohibition. *See* Dru Stevenson, *Going Gunless,* 85 Brooklyn L. Rev. __(2020) (forthcoming) (participant must commit not to purchase or possess a firearm, or to live with anyone who possesses a firearm).

33. Compare Stevenson, *Going Gunless* (recommending fines and forfeiture, not criminal conviction).

34. United States v. Howard, 742 F.3d 1334 (11th Cir. 2014).

35. See Chapter 3. One commentator advocates years-long commitments for expressive self-restriction. Stevenson, *Going Gunless.*

36. The American Bar Association agrees with this conclusion and has endorsed Donna's Law. A.B.A. Standing Committee on Gun Violence, 19M106B—NICS Self Reporting Resolution (Apr. 1, 2019), https:// www.americanbar.org/groups/public_interest/gun_violence/policy /19M106B/.

37. District of Columbia v. Heller, 554 U.S. 570 (2008).

38. District of Columbia v. Heller, at 575.

39. Silvester v. Harris, 843 F.3d 816, 821 (9th Cir. 2016), 827–29.

40. *See, e.g.,* Baer v. Lynch, 636 F. App'x 695, 698 (7th Cir. 2016) ("As to violent felons, the statute does survive intermediate scrutiny, we have concluded, because the prohibition on gun possession is substantially related to the government's interest in keeping those most likely to misuse firearms from obtaining them.") (citations omitted); United States v. Chovan, 735 F.3d 1127, 1139–41 (9th Cir. 2013) (persons convicted of domestic violence misdemeanors); United States v. Stegmeier, 701 F.3d 574 (8th Cir. 2012) (fugitive felon); United States v. Carter, 669 F.3d 411

(4th Cir. 2012) (unlawful user of a controlled substance); Hope v. State, 163 Conn. App. 36, 43 (2016) ("[The challenged statute] does not implicate the Second Amendment, as it does not restrict the right of law-abiding, responsible citizens to use arms in defense of their homes. It restricts for up to one year the rights of only those whom a court has adjudged to pose a risk of imminent physical harm to themselves or others after affording due process protection to challenge the seizure of the firearms.").

41. Joseph Blocher, *The Right Not to Keep or Bear Arms,* 64 Stan. L. Rev. 1, 4 (2012).

42. *See* McDonald v. City of Chicago, 561 U.S. 742, 767 (2010) (explaining that "individual self-defense is 'the central component' of the Second Amendment right").

43. Fredrick E. Vars, *Self-Defense against Gun Suicide,* 56 B.C. L. Rev. 1465 (2015), at 1465–99.

44. Brady v. United States, 397 U.S. 742, 748 (1970).

45. Angela Selvaggio and Fredrick E. Vars, *"Bind Me More Tightly Still": Voluntary Restraint against Gun Suicide,* 53 Harv. J. on Legis. 671 (2016).

46. Tyler v. Hillsdale County Sheriff's Department, 837 F.3d 678 (6th Cir. 2016) (en banc).

47. Keyes v. Sessions, 282 F. Supp. 3d 858, 873 (M. D. Pa. 2017).

3. LABORATORIES OF DEMOCRACY

1. New State Ice Co. v. Liebmann, 285 U.S. 262, 310 (1932) (Brandeis, J., dissenting).

2. Copies of all these introduced bills can be found at www.stopgun-suicide.com.

3. Ian Ayres, Fredrick E. Vars, and Nasser Zakariya, *To Insure Prejudice: Racial Disparities in Taxicab Tipping,* 114 Yale L. J. (2005).

4. Email from Lee Harris to Fred Vars (Dec. 16, 2016) (on file with author).

5. The Donna's Law Model bill in Appendix B includes all five features.

6. See Appendix B (Donna's Law Model).

7. Thomas Kral, *2019 Active Witness Slips—Your Action Needed,* Gun Rights 4 Ill. (Feb. 21, 2019), https://www.gunrights4illinois.com /blog/2019-active-witness-slips-your-action-needed/.

8. Richard A. Webster, *After Mother's Suicide, Katrina Brees Fights for "No Guns" Self-Registry,* Nola.com (Sept. 27, 2018), https://expo

.nola.com/news/erry-2018/09/39f7db7652102/after-mothers-suicide
-katrina.html.

9. Mass. Gen. Laws ch. 123, § 8 (West 2019).

10. Mass. Gen. Laws ch. 123, § 36C(b) (West 2019).

11. A number of states have developed programs whereby individuals can complete a form requesting to be excluded from gaming facilities for a set number of years. *See, e.g.,* N.Y. Gaming Comm'n, Request for Voluntary Self-Exclusion from All Gaming Facilities and Entities Licensed, Permitted or Registered by the New York State Gaming Commission, https://www.gaming.ny.gov/pdf/UpdatedSEForm-031418%20 (002).pdf (last visited July 18, 2019).

12. Fredrick Vars, *How Many Lives Could PAS Save? (PAS V),* PrawfsBlawg (Oct. 29, 2015), https://prawfsblawg.blogs.com/praw fsblawg/2015/10/how-many-lives-could-pas-save-pas-v.html; Fredrick Vars, *Would Anyone Voluntarily Give Up Their Right to Buy a Gun? (PAS, Part IV),* PrawfsBlawg (Oct. 21, 2015), https://prawfsblawg.blogs .com/prawfsblawg/2015/10/would-anyone-voluntarily-give-up-their -right-to-buy-a-gun-pas-part-iv.html; Fredrick Vars, *Does PAS Violate the Second Amendment? (PAS, Part III),* PrawfsBlawg (Oct. 19, 2015), https://prawfsblawg.blogs.com/prawfsblawg/2015/10/does-pas -violate-the-second-amendment-pas-part-iii.html.

13. Jennifer Stuber, *My Husband Died by Suicide. Here's What Happened during My Awkward Call with the NRA,* Wash. Post (Apr. 7, 2016).

14. *Washington State Legislative Special Elections* 2017, Ballotpedia, https://ballotpedia.org/Washington_state_legislative_special_elections, _2017 (last visited July 18, 2019).

15. *SB 5553–2017-2018,* Wash. State Legislature, https://app.leg.wa .gov/billsummary?BillNumber=5553&Year=2017 (last visited July 18, 2019).

16. Champe Barton, *An Innovative Tool for Reducing Gun Suicides Is Fizzling in Washington State: Local Officials Say They're Unaware of the "No Buy" List,* https://www.thetrace.org/2019/10/washington-state -gun-suicide-prevention-no-buy-list/ (Oct. 7, 2019).

17. H.R. 3611 § 5, 190th Sess. (Mass. 2017) ("Notwithstanding any general or special law to the contrary, any suicide hotline maintained or operated by any entity funded in whole or part by the commonwealth shall refer callers to the form provided for in section 1 of this act.").

18. The California bill included nearly identical language but described the health provider referrals as a "best practice." A.B. 1927 § 1, 2017–2018 Gen. Assemb., Reg. Sess. (Cal. 2018).

19. *Gun Ownership in Massachusetts,* Mass.gov (2019), https://www
.mass.gov/info-details/gun-ownership-in-massachusetts.

20. Assemb. B. 579, 2017–2018 Leg. (Wis. 2017).

21. *See, e.g.,* Brian Linert, Janis Regnier, Barrett Doyle, and Joseph
Prahlow, *Suicidal Shotgun Wound Employing a Shotgun Barrel, a
Shotgun Shell, and a BB,* 55 Journal of Forensic Sciences 546 (2010)
(giving an overview of suicide cases involving unconventional firearms).

22. H.R. 3611 § 1, 190th Sess. (Mass. 2017).

23. Donald S. Shepard et al., *Suicide and Suicidal Attempts in the
United States: Costs and Policy Implications,* 46 Suicide and Life-
Threatening Behavior 352, 356 tbl.2 (2016).

4. EMAILS AND THE ASSOCIATIONAL MARKETPLACE

1. *See, e.g.,* National Federation of Federal Employees v. U.S., 695 F.
Supp. 1196 (D.D.C. 1988).

2. *See* Joseph Blocher, *The Right Not to Keep or Bear Arms,* 64 Stan.
L. Rev. 1 (2012).

3. For example, if people with a higher risk of suicide are more likely
to register, life insurers may not be economically motivated to give discounts for registering. But insurers would not be likely to increase the
price to registrants, because registrants would then opt not to disclose
that information (via the registry email) to the insurer.

4. Darran Simon, *Virginia Beach Gunman's Resignation Email Hours
before Mass Shooting Offers No Clues,* CNN (June 3, 2019), https://www
.cnn.com/2019/06/03/us/virginia-beach-shooter-resignation-letter
/index.html. *See also* James Queally, *Motive for Calif. Killings a Mys-
tery; Some Think Mix of Extremism, Work Issues Led to Attack,* Chi.
Trib. 1 (Dec. 4, 2015).

5. They account for just 4 percent of mass shootings. Everytown for
Gun Safety, *Analysis of Mass Shootings* (Apr. 11, 2017), https://
everytownresearch.org/reports/mass-shootings-analysis.

6. CDC, *Occupational Violence,* https://www.cdc.gov/niosh/topics
/violence (last visited July 20, 2016).

7. We also would prohibit governments from purchasing waivers—
for example, by requiring waiver as a prerequisite of a gun buyback
program—because government purchasing might constitute an unconstitutional condition. Richard Epstein, *Unconstitutional Conditions,
State Power, and the Limits of Consent,* 102 Harv. L. Rev. 4 (1988).
However, as argued above, we would allow conditioning plea bargaining
(with its independent requirement of wrongdoing) upon waiver.

8. Of course, credible notification could be accomplished using a method other than email. *See* Drury D. Stevenson, *Going Gunless,* 85 Brooklyn L. Rev. __ (2020) (forthcoming) ("certification card"). Because registry status is reversible under our proposal, a certification card may not be feasible. Perhaps a better alternative would be a unique state-issued password that provides real-time access to registry status. This would automatically update and be easier for people who do not currently have Internet access or use email. Traditional mailed notifications would address connectivity concerns, but would arrive with delay.

9. Existing casino self-exclusion programs also subject residents to potential penalties for criminal trespass if they subsequently visit the casino. *See, e.g.,* Missouri Gaming Commission, Voluntary Exclusion Rules, 11 CSR 45.17.010 (2017). John H. Kleschinsky et al., *The Missouri Voluntary Exclusion Program: Participant Experiences across 10 Years* (Phase II Report, Nov. 2008) (detailing prevalence of trespassing prosecutions).

10. Our model statute also notifies email addressees if a registrant should attempt to purchase a firearm or be found with unauthorized possession of a firearm. Like rescission, an unauthorized attempt to purchase or possess is an event that might trigger addressees to make different associational choices or to inquire into the state of the registrant's health.

11. H. 3611, 190th Sess. (Mass. 2017) (introduced by Representative Marjorie C. Decker); S.B. 0617, 109th Gen. Assemb. (Tenn. 2017) (introduced by Senator Lee); Amb. Bill 579 (Wisc. 2017) (announced by Representative Melissa Sargent).

12. S.B. 5553, 65th Leg, Reg. Sess. (Wash 2017).

13. AB 1927 § 1 (Cal. 2018).

14. Discrimination based on waiver status is generally illegal in Washington however one might discover that status: "A voluntary waiver of firearm rights may not be required of an individual as a condition for receiving employment, benefits, or services." Wash. Stat. 9.41.350(5) (2019).

15. Rachel Sereix, *Study Shows Connecticut Temporary Gun Removal Law Lowers Suicide Risk,* The Chronicle (Duke University) (Nov. 29, 2016) (finding that 49 percent of "gun removal cases were initially reported to the police by an acquaintance").

16. Aristophanes, *Lysistrata* (in which Lysistrata persuades the women of Greece to withhold sexual privileges from their husbands and lovers as a means of forcing the men to end the Peloponnesian War).

17. *Colombian Gangsters Face Sex Ban,* BBC News (Sept. 13, 2006), http://news.bbc.co.uk/2/hi/5341574.stm (last visited Aug. 2, 2016). *See also* Oona Hathaway and Scott J. Shapiro, *Outcasting: Enforcement in Domestic and International Law,* 121 Yale L. J. 252, 258 (2011) ("Outcasting involves denying the disobedient the benefits of social cooperation and membership.").

18. More recently, Alyssa Milano called for a #SexStrike to protest anti-abortion laws. *See* Lindsey Bever, *Alyssa Milano Called for a "Sex Strike" to Protest Anti-Abortion Laws,* Wash. Post (May 12, 2019) ("Until women have legal control over our own bodies we just cannot risk pregnancy . . . JOIN ME by not having sex until we get bodily autonomy back.").

19. *See, e.g.,* Derrick Rose, *Witness: Tenant Shot Landlord through Window after Attempt to Collect Rent,* WHAS 11 ABC (June 28, 2016), http://www.whas11.com/news/crime/witness-tenant-shot-landlord-through-window-after-attempt-to collect-rent/258300179.

20. Such a private commitment contract could be created at the commitment contract website cofounded by one of the authors, www.stickk.com.

21. Samuel Hsin-yu Tseng, The Effect of Life Insurance Policy Provisions on Suicide Rates (unpublished manuscript), http://emptormaven.com/img/lifetseng.pdf (thirty-three states "allow for a two-year suicide exclusion, Colorado and North Dakota allow for a one-year exclusion, but Missouri imposes a more stringent regulation, requiring that the insurer cannot use suicide to deny death benefit payments unless it can be shown that the insureds intend to commit suicide when they applied for the policies").

22. Tseng, Effect of Life Insurance Policy Provisions, at 1. *See also* Joe Chen, Yun Jeong Choi, and Yasuyuki Sawada, *Suicide and Life Insurance,* No. CIRJE-F-558, CIRJE F-Series, Center for International Research on the Japanese Economy, Faculty of Economics, University of Tokyo (2008), available at http://www.cirje.e.u-tokyo.ac.jp/research/dp/2008/2008cf558.pdf (using OECD cross-country data from 1980 to 2002 finding analogous exemption period effects).

23. Compare Steven Yaccino, *Schools Seeking to Arm Employees Hit Hurdle on Insurance,* N.Y. Times, A14 (July 7, 2013) (higher insurance premia deterred some from allowing permit holders to bring guns onto public school property).

24. Philip J. Cook and Jens Ludwig, *The Effects of Gun Prevalence on Burglary: Deterrence vs Inducement,* NBER (Working Paper No. 8926, May 2002), http://www.nber.org/papers/w8926.

25. Cook and Ludwig, *Effects of Gun Prevalence,* at 43.

26. *See* Ian Ayres and Steven D. Levitt, *Measuring Positive Externalities from Unobservable Victim Precaution: An Empirical Analysis of LoJack,* 113 Quarterly J. Econ. 43 (1998).

5. LIBERTARIAN CONTRACTING AND ITS LIMITS

1. The constitutionality of self-exclusion with regard to Second Amendment rights has separately been analyzed. See Chapter 2. *See also* Fredrick E. Vars, *Self-Defense against Gun Suicide,* 56 B.C. L. Rev. 1465 (2015); Angela Selvaggio and Fredrick E. Vars, *"Bind Me More Tightly Still": Voluntary Restraint against Gun Suicide,* 53 Harv. J. on Legis. 671 (2016).

2. The constitutionality of the government making private speech more or less credible is also explored in Bruce Ackerman and Ian Ayres, Voting with Dollars: A New Paradigm for Campaign Finance (2004) (arguing that a "donation booth" which makes claims of campaign contributions *less* credible is constitutional).

3. *See* Planned Parenthood v. Casey, 505 U.S. 833 (1992) (stating that state restriction is an undue burden if it has "the purpose or effect of placing a substantial obstacle in the path of a woman seeking an abortion of a nonviable fetus").

4. Alan S. Gerber, Donald P. Green, and Christopher W. Larimer, *Social Pressure and Voter Turnout: Evidence from a Largescale Field Experiment,* 102 Am. Pol. Sci. Rev 33 (2008).

5. NAACP v. Alabama *ex rel.* Patterson, 357 U.S. 449 (1958). *See also* NAACP v. Button, 371 U.S. 415 (1963) (striking down Virginia statute requiring membership list disclosure).

6. Anderson v. Martin, 375 U.S. 399 (1964).

7. Anderson v. Martin, at 433. *See also* Sonu Bedi, *Online Dating Sites as Public Accommodations: Facilitating Racial Discrimination,* in Free Speech in the Digital Age (Susan Brison J. and Katharine Gelber eds., 2019) (arguing that by offering race-filtering options, Roomates .com facilitates private associational discrimination).

8. NAACP v. Alabama *ex rel.* Patterson, 357 U.S. 449, 463 (1958).

9. *See* Washington v. Davis, 426 U.S. 229 (1976) (holding valid laws that have a racially disparate impact but were not enacted with a discriminatory intent).

10. 505 U.S. 833 (1992).

11. *See also* Gonzales v. Carhart, 550 U.S. 124 (2007) ("The State has an interest in ensuring so grave a choice is well informed. . . . It is a reasonable inference that a necessary effect of the regulation and the

knowledge it conveys will be to encourage some women to carry the infant to full term, thus reducing the absolute number of late-term abortions.").

12. Buckley v. Valeo, 424 U.S. 1 (1976).

13. Buckley v. Valeo. Subsequently, the Communist Party provided such evidence and was exempted from disclosing the identity of its contributors. Fed. Election Comm'n v. Hall-Tyner Election Campaign Comm., 678 F.2d 416 (2d Cir. 1982).

14. CBS, Inc. v. Block, 725 P.2d 470, 474 (Cal. 1986) ("Defendants' concern that the release of the information to the press would increase the vulnerability of licensees is conjectural at best."); CBS, Inc. v. Block, at 476 (Mosk, J., dissenting) (quoting NAACP v. Alabama, 357 U.S. 449, 462 (1985)).

15. Reno Newspapers v. Sheriff, 126 Nev. 211, 234 P.3d 922 (2010).

16. NY Secure Ammunition and Firearms Enforcement (SAFE) Act, S. 2230 (N.Y. Jan. 15, 2013); *see also* J. David Goodman, *Newspaper Takes Down Map of Gun Permit Holders,* N.Y. Times, Jan. 18, 2013.

17. District of Columbia v. Heller, 554 U.S. 570, 628 (2008) (stating that the "inherent right of self-defense has been central to the Second Amendment right"). *See also* McDonald v. City of Chicago, 130 S. Ct. 3020 (2010).

18. District of Columbia v. Heller, at 628.

19. First Amendment free exercise rights may also be implicated. *See* Drury D. Stevenson, *Going Gunless,* 85 Brooklyn L. Rev. __ (2020) (forthcoming) (listing religions with commitments to pacifism and nonviolence).

20. Katharine Q. Seelye, *Think AR-15s Are O.K.? You're Not Welcome Here,* N.Y. Times, Aug. 2, 2016, at A10.

21. See Appendix B.

22. CDC, *Occupational Violence,* https://www.cdc.gov/niosh/topics/violence (last visited July 20, 2016).

23. Linda Hamilton Krieger, Backlash against the ADA: Reinterpreting Disability Rights 192 (2010).

24. Roberts v. U.S. Jaycees, 468 U.S. 609, 623 (1984).

25. Boy Scouts of America v. Dale, 530 U.S. 640, 656 (2000).

26. With regard to all of these contractors, an individual's right to possess or to bear arms would be market-inalienable. *See* Margaret Jane Radin, *Market-Inalienability,* 100 Harv. L. Rev. 1849 (1987) ("Something that is market-inalienable is not to be sold, which in our economic system means it is not to be traded in the market.").

6. PRIVATIZING GUN-FREE ZONES

1. Lisa Rodriguez, *Desperate to Stop Gun Violence, Westport Pushes for Private Sidewalks,* KCUR (Dec. 12, 2017), https://www.kcur.org/post /desperate-stop-gun-violence-westport-pushes-private -sidewalks#stream/0.

2. Rodriguez, *Desperate to Stop Gun Violence;* S. 656, 98th Gen. Assemb. (Mo. 2016).

3. The traditional property term for this legal maneuver is "vacation." By vacating streets and sidewalks, the city would be giving the city's public easement interest in those areas to the abutting private landowners. Under the ultimate agreement, the city has the option to reclaim ownership of the sidewalks for three years at a cost of up to $132,784. *Kansas City Entertainment District to Start Weapon Screening,* Wash. Times, Dec. 22, 2017, https://www.washingtontimes.com/news /2017/dec/22/kansas-city-entertainment-district-to-start-weapon/.

4. Shannon O'Brien, *Private Sidewalks in Westport Cause Mixed Emotions for Business Owners, KC Residents,* FOX4kc.com (Dec. 22, 2017), https://fox4kc.com/2017/12/22/private-sidewalks-in-westport -cause-mixed-emotions-for-business-owners-kc-residents/.

5. Lisa Rodriguez and Andrea Tudhope, *Westport Sidewalks a Step Closer to Being Privatized,* KCUR (Dec. 201, 2017), https://www.kcur .org/post/westport-sidewalks-step-closer-being-privatized#stream/0.

6. C. J. Janovy, *Kansas City NAACP Promises to Fight Westport Sidewalk-Privatization Plan,* KCUR (Dec. 29, 2017), https://www.kcur .org/post/kansas-city-naacp-promises-fight-westport-sidewalk -privatization-plan#stream/0.

7. Lisa Rodriguez, *KC Council Makes Two Big Decisions: Keeping Edgemoor for KCI, Shutting Westport Sidewalks,* KCUR (Dec. 21, 2017), https://www.kcur.org/post/kc-council-makes-2-big-decisions-keeping -edgemoor-kci-shutting-westport-sidewalks#stream/0.

8. Janovy, *Kansas City NAACP.*

9. Robert A. Cronkleton and Katy Bergen, "Westport Shooting Leaves Two Injured; Privatization Security Measures Weren't in Place," *Kan. City Star,* July 8, 2018, https://www.kansascity.com/news/local/crime /article214521364.html.

10. Cronkleton and Bergen, "Westport Shooting Leaves Two Injured."

11. David Hudnall, *Westport's Enhanced Weekend Security Starts Back Up Soon. Here's What to Know,* Pitch (Apr. 2, 2019), https://www .thepitchkc.com/news/article/21062336/westport-enhanced-security -starts-soon-in-kc-heres-what-to-know.

12. 18 U.S.C. § 921(a)(25). The act applies if the individual knows, or has reasonable cause to believe, that she is traveling in a school zone, and includes several exemptions including for individuals licensed to carry a firearm. The statute in 1995 was held to be an unconstitutional exercise of congressional authority under the Commerce Clause of the United States Constitution in *United States v. Lopez*, 514 U.S. 549 (1995). The act was amended in 1996 to apply only if a firearm "has moved in or otherwise affects interstate commerce." Omnibus Consolidated Appropriations Act of 1997, Pub. L. No. 104–208, 110 Stat. 3009.

13. Ariz. Rev. Stat. Ann. § 13-3102(A)(11) (2019); Cal. Elec. Code § 18544(a) (West 2019); Ga. Code Ann. § 21-2-413(i) (West 2019).

14. Ala. Code, § 13A-11-61.2(a)(4) (2019); S.D. Codified Laws § 22-14-23 (2019); W. Va. Code § 61-7-11a(g)(1) (2019).

15. Neb. Rev. Stat. Ann. § 69-2441(1)(a) (2019); Mich. Comp. Laws Ann. § 750.234d (West 2019).

16. 430 Ill. Comp. Stat. Ann. 66/65(a)(19) (West 2019); Va. Code Ann. § 18.2-287.01 (2019).

17. S.C. Code Ann. § 16-23-420(A) (2019); N.D. Cent. Code § 62.1-02-05(1) (2019).

18. Wis. Stat. § 175.60(16)(a)(1) (2019); Ark. Code Ann. § 5-73-306 (2019).

19. Fla. Stat. § 790.06(12) (2019); Fla. Stat. § 790.053(1) (2019); Ala. Code § 13A-11-61.2 (2019).

20. Colo. Rev. Stat. § 18-9-118 (2019); 720 Ill. Comp. Stat. 5/24-1(c)(1.5) (2019); 430 Ill. Comp. Stat. 66/65(a)(8) (2019).

21. H.B. 2010, 57th Cong. (Okla. 2019); Minn. Stat. Ann. § 97A.091 (2019).

22. 430 Ill. Comp. Stat. 66/65(a)(7) (2019); Mich. Comp. Laws Ann. § 750.234d (West 2019); Utah Code Ann. § 76-8-311.3(4)(d) (2019).

23. 465 Ind. Admin. Code 2-9-80(b)(3), 2-10-79(b)(3), 2-11-80(b)(3), 2-12-78(b)(3), 2-13-77(b)(3) (2019); Nev. Rev. Stat. Ann. 202.3673(3)(a) (2019).

24. *Location Restrictions*, Giffords Law Ctr. (2018), https://lawcenter.giffords.org/gun-laws/policy-areas/guns-in-public/location-restrictions/#buildings.

25. Alaska Stat. § 11.61.220(a)(2) (2018); Ky. Rev. Stat. Ann. § 244.125(1) (2019).

26. 430 Ill. Comp. Stat. 66/65(a)(20) (2019); Mo. Rev. Stat. § 571.107.1(13) (2019). Open carry is permitted in Missouri.

27. Mich. Comp. Laws Serv. §§ 750.234d(1) (2019); Wash. Rev. Code Ann. § 70.108.150 (2019).

28. N.D. Cent. Code §62.1-02-05(2) (2019).

29. Md. Code Ann., Crim. Law § 4-208 (2019); N.C. Gen. Stat. § 14-277.2 (2018).

30. Public opinion favors a wide array of place restrictions. Julia Wolfson et al., *US Public Opinion on Carrying Firearms in Public Places,* 107 Am. J. Pub. Health 929, 932 fig.1 (2017) (restaurants, retail stores, college campuses, places of worship, government buildings, schools, bars, sports stadiums).

31. Kerry Shaw, *What Is a "Gun-Free Zone," and What's behind the Movement to Get Rid of Them?,* Trace (Mar. 16, 2017), https://www.thetrace.org/2017/03/gun-free-zone-facts/.

32. *2016 Year-End Review: Gun Law Trendwatch,* Giffords Law Ctr. (Dec. 2016), https://lawcenter.giffords.org/wp-content/uploads/2016/12/Trendwatch-Year-End-2016_PAGES.pdf.

33. Don B. Kates, *Gun Free Zones: A Prevalent Delusion,* Indep. Inst. (May 14, 2013), https://www.independent.org/news/article.asp?id=3616.

34. John R. Lott, Jr., *So Are Movie Theaters Near Where the Aurora, Colorado Killer Lived Posted to Prevent Concealed Carry?,* John Lott (Aug. 15, 2012), http://johnrlott.blogspot.com/2012/08/so-are-movie-theaters-in-aurora.html. Lott, an economist and gun rights activist, also claims that since 1950 almost every single mass public shooting in the United States has occurred in a place where guns were banned. John Lott, Jr., *A Look at the Facts on Gun-Free Zones,* Nat'l Rev. (Oct. 20, 2015), https://www.nationalreview.com/2015/10/gun-free-zones-dont-save-lives-right-to-carry-laws-do/. Lott has published a large body of work claiming that crime goes down as states loosen gun laws and allow more people to carry concealed handguns. *An Interview with John R. Lott, Jr.,* U. Chi. Press (1998), https://www.press.uchicago.edu/Misc/Chicago/493636.html. But critics say Lott's work is flawed because he cherry-picks data. Several experts and academics have tested his hypotheses and reached vastly different conclusions. *See generally* Ian Ayres and John J. Donohue III, *Shooting Down the More Guns, Less Crime Hypothesis,* 55 Stan. L. Rev. 1193 (2003) (concluding that the statistical evidence Lott uses to support his argument is "limited, sporadic, and extraordinarily fragile").

35. The two types of restrictions can obviously overlap. In such instances, "in rem" restriction has the advantage of avoiding invidious discrimination directed at disfavored categories of people.

36. *Lists and Maps*, Am. Nonsmokers' Rights Found. (2019), https://no-smoke.org/materials-services/lists-maps/.

37. *See* M. Tynan et al., *State Smoke-Free Laws for Worksites, Restaurants, and Bars—United States, 2000–2010*, Ctr. Disease Control (Apr. 22, 2011), https://www.cdc.gov/mmwr/preview/mmwrhtml/mm6015a2.htm.

38. John P. Pierce, Victoria M. White, and Sherry L. Emery, *What Public Health Strategies Are Needed to Reduce Smoking Initiation?*, 21 Tobacco Control 258, 261 (2012).

39. Christine M. Quinn, Note, *How Businesses Can Ban Guns*, 50 U. Mich. J. L. Reform 955, 959 (2017).

40. As Merrill and Smith note, "If the owner does not make the required notification, then the right to exclude is subordinated to the customary right to hunt on land owned by another." Thomas W. Merrill and Henry E. Smith, Property: Principles and Policies 444 (Found. Press, 2007).

41. *See, e.g.*, Catherine Sharkey, *Trespass Torts and Self-Help for an Electronic Age*, 44 Tulsa L. Rev. 677, 685 (2008–2009); Mark R. Sigmon, *Hunting and Posting on Private Land in America*, 54 Duke L. J. 549, 584 (2004) ("Twenty-nine states currently require private landowners to post their land to exclude hunters, twenty-seven of these states by statute."). These laws impose an affirmative burden of notification on the possessor of land in order to assert the right to exclude. Ala. Code § 9-11-241; Md. Code Ann., Nat. Res. II § 10-411; Ohio Rev. Code Ann. § 1533.17.

42. La. Stat. Ann. § 40:1379.3(O) (2018) ("No individual to whom a concealed handgun permit is issued may carry such concealed handgun into the private residence of another without first receiving the consent of that person."); S. C. Code Ann. § 23-31-225 (2019).

43. *Two States Ban Concealed Carry in Church, Seven Require Permission*, Concealed Nation (Nov. 6, 2017), http://concealednation.org/2017/11/two-states-ban-concealed-carry-in-church-seven-require-permission/.

44. Safe Carry Protection Act, 2014 Ga. Laws 601, §§ 1-5, 1-6, codified at Ga. Code. Ann. §§ 16-11-127 (b)(4), (c); 16-11-127.1(c) (Supp. 2014). *See also* Joseph Blocher and Darrell A. H. Miller, *What Is Gun Control? Direct Burdens, Incidental Burdens, and the Boundaries of the Second Amendment*, 83 U. Chi. L. Rev. 295, 316-17 (2016). Georgia's default with regard to other property owners allows invitee carry unless the owner exercises her "right to exclude or eject a person who is in pos-

session of a weapon or long gun on their private property." Ga. Code. Ann. §§ 16-11-127 (c).

45. Ariz. Rev. Stat. Ann. § 4-229(E) (2019).

46. Ark. Code Ann. § 5-73-306(19)(A) (2019). Arkansas, however, requires any "licensee entering a private home [to] notify the occupant that the licensee is carrying a concealed handgun" (Ark. Code Ann. § 5-73-306(19)(A) (2019), at (19)(D)), which if observed would give the private home occupant the ability to withdraw the invitation to enter.

47. Tex. Penal Code Ann. § 30.06(c) (West 2019). The requirements are substantially similar with regard to prohibiting people from entering a property with an openly carried handgun. Tex. Penal Code Ann. § 30.07 (West 2019).

48. James B. Shrimp, *Employer Firearms Policies in Light of Bring Your Gun to Work Laws,* High Swartz (Oct. 27, 2015), https://www .highswartz.com/blog/employment-law/employer-firearms-policies-in -light-of-bring-your-gun-to-work-laws/.

49. Ala. Code § 13A-11-52 (2019).

50. Ohio Rev. Code Ann. § 2923.126(b) (West 2019) ("A landlord may not prohibit or restrict a tenant who is a licensee and who on or after September 9, 2008, enters into a rental agreement with the landlord for the use of residential premises, and the tenant's guest while the tenant is present, from lawfully carrying or possessing a handgun on those residential premises.").

51. Conn. Gen. Stat. § 29-28 (2019). *See also* 13 AAC 30.110 (b) (Alaska) ("Nothing in this chapter or in AS 18.65.700–18.65.790 precludes a person from posting, to the extent allowed by law, a notice regarding the carrying of a concealed handgun."); Utah Code Ann. § 76-10-530; 430 ILCS 66/65(a-10) ("The owner of private real property of any type may prohibit the carrying of concealed firearms on the property under his or her control."); Mo. Stat. Ann. § 571.107; N.M. Admin. Code § 10.8.2.16(F); N.C.G.S.A. § 14-415.11(c)(8).

52. There is even an argument that the owner of a private residence retains the common law right to exclude firearms even in states that have adopted statutes allowing concealed carry except in specified locations not expressly including private residences. *See* State v. Taylor, 425 P.2d 1014, 1018 (Haw. 1967) ("Statutes in derogation of the common law are strictly construed, and a court should not, merely by application of the maxim expressio unius exclusion alterius, find that the common law has been superseded in the area not mentioned by a statute, where

it does not appear that it was the legislative purpose to supersede the common law."). But compare Blocher and Miller, *What Is Gun Control?*, at 315 (suggesting that "no guns allowed" signs in stores "might not automatically transform all concealed-gun-carrying shoppers into trespassers").

53. Christopher J. Wahl, *Keeping* Heller *Out of the Home: Homeowners Associations and the Right to Keep and Bear Arms,* 15 U. Pa. J. Const. L. 1003, 1003 and n.5 (2013); Blocher and Miller, *What Is Gun Control?*, at 319.

54. Compare Tenn. Op. Atty. Gen. No. 09-170, 2009 WL 3666436 (Oct. 26, 2009) ("A landlord can prohibit tenants, including those who hold handgun carry permits, from possessing firearms within leased premises. Such a prohibition may be imposed through a clause in the lease."), with Ohio Rev. Code R.C. § 2923.126(b) ("A landlord may not prohibit or restrict a tenant who is a licensee and who on or after September 9, 2008, enters into a rental agreement with the landlord for the use of residential premises, and the tenant's guest while the tenant is present, from lawfully carrying or possessing a handgun on those residential premises.").

55. LSA-R. S. 40:1379.3(O) ("No individual to whom a concealed handgun permit is issued may carry such concealed handgun into the private residence of another without first receiving the consent of that person."); S.C. Code 1976 § 23-31-225 ("No person who holds a permit issued pursuant to Article 4, Chapter 31, Title 23 may carry a concealable weapon into the residence or dwelling place of another person without the express permission of the owner or person in legal control or possession, as appropriate.").

56. Hannah Fingerhut, *Partisanship in the U.S. Isn't Just about Politics, but How People See Their Neighbors,* Pew Research Fact Tank (June 27, 2016), http://www.pewresearch.org/fact-tank/2016/06/27/partisanship-in-u-s-isnt-just-about-politics-but-how-people-see-their-neighbors. In contrast, the figure Fingerhut cites for Republicans is only 6 percent.

57. Matthew Miller, Deborah Azrael, and David Hemenway, *Community Firearms, Community Fear,* 11 Epidemiology 709 (2000). A more recent Gallup poll found that 56 percent of Americans believe the country would be safer if more people were allowed to carry concealed weapons, but the poll asked the respondent to suppose that the weapons carriers had "passed a criminal background check and training course." Frank Newport, *Majority Say More Concealed Weapons Would Make U.S.*

Safer, Gallup (Oct. 20, 2015), https://news.gallup.com/poll/186263/majority-say-concealed-weapons-safer.aspx.

58. *See, e.g.,* Richard H. Thaler and Shlomo Benartzi, *Save More Tomorrow: Using Behavioral Economics to Increase Employee Saving,* 112 J. Pol. Econ. S164, S169 (2004) (finding that switching the default retirement plan to auto-enrollment increases rates of retirement contribution).

59. *See generally* Cass R. Sunstein, *Switching the Default Rule,* 777 N.Y.U. L. Rev. 106 (2002) (finding that employees tend to value rights more simply because they are the default rights).

60. David Hemenway, *Risks and Benefits of a Gun in the Home,* 5 Am. J. Lifestyle Med. 502, 503 (2011).

61. Shaw, *What Is a "Gun-Free Zone."*

62. Shaw, *What Is a "Gun-Free Zone."* There is some basis for this fear. At least one gun rights organization, Illinois Carry, maintains on its website a searchable list of "Anti-gun Locations in Illinois." As of July 15, 2019, there were 913 shops listed because they had no-firearm signs. http://www.rightapp.net/input/DisplayIllinois.php.

63. Chipotle: Doug Stanglin, *Chipotle Asks Customers Not to Bring Guns to Its Stores,* USA Today, May 20, 2014; Levi Strauss: Chip Bergh, *An Open Letter to Customers: Our Weapons Policy,* Linkedin (Nov. 30, 2016), https://www.linkedin.com/pulse/open-letter-customers-our-weapons-policy-chip-bergh/?trk=prof-post/; Target: *Target Addresses Firearms in Stores,* Target (July 2, 2014), https://corporate.target.com/article/2014/07/target-addresses-firearms-in-stores; Trader Joe's: *An Update to Our Customers Regarding Guns in Our Stores,* Trader Joe's (Feb. 8, 2016), https://www.traderjoes.com/announcement/an-update-to-our-customers-regarding-guns-in-our-stores.

64. Howard Schultz, *An Open Letter from Howard Schultz, Chairman, President and CEO of Starbucks Coffee Company,* Wall Street J. (Sept. 2018), http://online.wsj.com/public/resources/documents/starbucksletter0918.pdf.

65. Schultz, *Open Letter.*

66. *Policy on Customers Carrying Firearms in Stores,* Kroger (Aug. 2017), https://www.thekrogerco.com/wp-content/uploads/2017/08/Policy-Firearms-In-Stores.pdf; *see also* Schultz, *Open Letter* ("Our company's longstanding approach to 'open carry' has been to follow local laws.").

67. Katie Reilly, *Kroger Joins Walmart in Asking Customers to Stop Openly Carrying Guns in Stores after Mass Shootings,* Time, Sept. 4, 2019.

68. Walmart, Firearms and Ammunition Guidelines, available at https://corporate.walmart.com/policies.

69. Lott, *A Look at the Facts.*

70. S. C. Code Ann. § 23-31-225 (2019).

71. *Location Restrictions,* Giffords Law Ctr.

72. Wis. Stat. § 175.60(21) (2019).

73. *Concealed Carry Laws and Property Management,* Inst. Real Est. Mgmt. (Feb. 2015), https://www.irem.org/File%20Library/Public%20 Policy/ConcealedCarryLaw.pdf.

74. The city would agree to maintain the privately owned roads and sidewalk in return for this conditional public easement. For an example of a "conditional public easement" granted to a city, see *Easement to the City of Walla Walla,* Wallawallawa.gov (2013), https://records.walla wallawa.gov:9443/docs/2013/ccreg/20130327_70/542_542.%20Water-line%20Easement%20CP%20to%20WW%20rev.%20wExhbit%20A.pdf.

75. Michael Heller and Rick Hills, *Land Assembly Districts,* 121 Harv. L. Rev. 1465, 1469 (2008). The statute might allow dissenting landowners to possess guns on their own property and even to transport them along otherwise gun-free paths, if such transport were necessary to access their private property.

76. Guaranty Realty Co. v. Recreation Gun Club, 12 Cal. App. 383, 390 (1910).

77. Thomas W. Merrill and Henry E. Smith, Property: Principles and Policies 1051 (2d ed. 2012).

78. See Restatement (Third) of Property (Servitudes) § 8.5 TD No.7 (1998) (reporting that all but three states had enacted statutes to eliminate questions about the enforceability of conservation servitudes or easements).

79. Uniform Conservation Easement Act (last revised or amended in 2007), https://www.uniformlaws.org/HigherLogic/System/Download DocumentFile.ashx?DocumentFileKey=95e58042-e8d2-2051-1868 -617b5d89a7f9&forceDialog=0.

80. 211 Cal. App. 4th 1020 (2012) at 1034.

81. Christen Linke Young, *Conservation Easement Tax Credits in Environmental Federalism,* 117 Yale L. J. Pocket Part 218 (2008).

82. Conservation easements prohibiting firearms would not, however, qualify for favorable federal tax treatment as having one of the existing "conservation purposes" under the Internal Revenue Code § 170(h)(4)(A) except if the land dedicated was open to the public or was historically important or hosted ecologically significant flora or fauna.

83. A fee simple subject to condition subsequent would also suffice. *See generally* Mountain Brow Lodge No. 82, Independent Order of Odd Fellows v. Toscano, 257 Cal. App.2d 22 (Cal. App. 1967).

84. The possibility of reverter interest is carved out of the original grantor's estate and hence remains vested, thus avoiding the Rule Against Perpetuities concern with remote vesting. Merrill and Smith, Property, 2nd ed., at 510, 516, 574.

85. However, the inclusion of restrictions such as defeasible fees may render the property effectively unmortgageable, as lenders would realize that their security interest or lien was inferior to the defeasance condition and hence the mortgage or lien could be terminated by an action (someone in the future brings a gun on site) over which the lender has no control.

86. An analogous no-hunting provision was included in the conservation easement at issue in Wooster v. Dept. of Fish and Game, 211 Cal. App. 4th 1020 (Cal. Ct. App. 2012), which required a state department to "post the property at all points of entry to inform the public that said property is a State wildlife area and that no trespassing or hunting is allowed."

87. Wahl, *Keeping* Heller *Out of the Home,* at 1024–25.

88. *But see* Yan Sui v. 2176 Pacific Homeowners Ass'n, No. SACV 11–1340 JAK (AJW), 2012 WL 6632758 (C.D. Cal. Aug. 30, 2012). Compare Blocher and Miller, *What Is Gun Control?,* at 343 (outlining a third potential expansion of the state action doctrine derived from First Amendment case law). *But see* John-Patrick Fritz, *Check Your Rights and Your Guns at the Door: Questioning the Validity of Restrictive Covenants against the Right to Bear Arms,* 35 Sw. U. L. Rev. 551 (2007) (arguing for expansion of *Shelley* because the right to bear arms is also fundamental).

89. *See* United Auto Workers, Local No. 5285 v. Gaston Festivals, Inc., 43 F.3d 902, 909 (4th Cir. 1995) ("A private actor must assume plenary control and complete governmental power over the property in question.").

90. Rundus v. City of Dallas, Tex., 634 F.3d 309, 314–15 and n.6 (5th Cir. 2011). Removal, and more so criminal prosecution, could presumably constitute state action if the trespass statute itself were not generally applicable but rather singled out gun possession. Parks v. Ford, 68 F.R.D. 305 (E. D. Pa. 1975).

91. 334 U.S. 1 (1948).

92. Wahl, *Keeping* Heller *Out of the Home,* at 1024–25; Mark D. Rosen, *Was Shelley v. Kraemer Incorrectly Decided? Some New Answers,* 95 Cal. L. Rev. 451, 458–70 (2007).

93. Davis v. Prudential Securities, Inc., 59 F.3d 1186 (11th Cir. 1995).

94. Helen Hershkoff, *State Constitutions: A National Perspective,* 3 Widener J. Pub. L. 7, 20 (1993) ("Some state constitutional provisions, by their express terms, provide protection against private actors").

95. Conn. Const. Art. I, § 15 ("Every citizen has a right to bear arms in defense of himself and the state.")

96. Winters v. Concentra Health Services, Inc., No. CV075012082S, 2008 WL 803134, at *4 (Conn. Super. Mar. 5, 2008).

97. Bonidy v. U.S. Postal Service, 790 F.3d 1121 (10th Cir. 2015).

98. Bonidy v. U.S. Postal Service, at 1126–27. *See* Stephen Kiehl, *In Search of a Standard: Gun Regulations after* Heller *and* McDonald, 70 Md. L. Rev. 1131, 1132–33 (2011) (stating that after *Heller* and *McDonald* "lower courts have easily upheld . . . laws prohibiting the carrying of guns in sensitive places such as airplanes and parks").

99. DiGiacinto v. Rector and Visitors of George Mason University, 704 S.E.2d 365 (Va. 2011). *See also* 79 A.M. Jur. 2d, *Weapons and Firearms* § 30. *See generally* GeorgiaCarry.Org, Inc. v. Georgia, 687 F.3d 1244, 1264 (11th Cir. 2012) ("An individual's right to bear arms as enshrined in the Second Amendment, whatever its full scope, certainly must be limited by the equally fundamental right of a private property owner to exercise exclusive dominion and control over its land.")

100. Nahrstedt v. Lakeside Village Condominium Assn., 878 P.2d 1275 (Cal. 1994); *see also* State v. Shack, 277 A.2d 369 (N.J. 1971).

101. Guaranty Realty Co. v. Recreation Gun Club, 12 Cal. App. 383, 390 (1910).

102. Joseph Blocher, *The Right Not to Keep or Bear Arms,* 64 Stan. L. Rev. 1 (2012).

103. "The right to keep and bear arms is . . . subject to the right of a property owner." 94 C.J.S. Weapons § 18. But compare Wahl, *Keeping* Heller *Out of the Home,* at 1036 (arguing that differences in state constitutional law and public policy make it "likely that a patchwork approach will emerge amongst the states").

104. Andrea J. Boyack, *Common Interest Community Covenants and the Freedom of Contract Myth,* 22 J. L. and Pol'y 767 (2014).

105. Boyack, *Common Interest Community Covenants.*

106. Boyack, *Common Interest Community Covenants.*

107. Matthew Miller, Deborah Azrael, and David Hemenway, *Community Firearms, Community Fear,* 11 Epidemiology 709 (2000).

7. SYMPTOM-BASED GUN REMOVAL ORDERS

1. For a redacted version of the police incident report that followed this encounter, see Newport Police Dep't, Incident Report: #13-17827-OF, at 1 (2013), http://s3.documentcloud.org/documents/793545/new port-r-i-police-report.pdf. Quotes are from p. 2.

2. Michael S. Schmidt, *State Law Prevented Sale of Assault Rifle to Suspect Last Week, Officials Say,* N.Y. Times, Sept. 18, 2013, at A15.

3. Ashley Halsey III et al., *D.C. Navy Yard Rampage Leaves 14 Dead; Alleged Shooter Killed, ID'd as Aaron Alexis,* Wash. Post, Sept. 17, 2013, at A1. This was just the latest in a long string of mass shootings. *See* Halsey et al., *D.C. Navy Yard Rampage* ("The Navy Yard shooting marks the seventh time in the past decade that a gunman has killed 10 or more people in a single incident.").

4. Compare Jeffrey W. Swanson et al., *Implementation and Effectiveness of Connecticut's Risk-Based Gun Removal Law: Does It Prevent Suicide?,* 80 Law and Contemp. Probs. 179, 193 (2017).

5. Jiaquan Xu et al., Nat'l Vital Statistics Reports, Deaths: Final Data for 2016, at 13 (2018), https://www.cdc.gov/nchs/data/nvsr/nvsr67 /nvsr67_05.pdf.

6. *See, e.g.,* Constitutional Concealed Carry Reciprocity Act of 2017, S. 446, 115th Cong. (2017).

7. Kathy H. Lococo et al., Nat'l Highway Traffic Safety Admin., DOT HS 812 402, Medical Review Practices for Driver Licensing, vol. 3, at 484–90 tbl.25 (2017), https://www.nhtsa.gov/sites/nhtsa.dot.gov/files /documents/812402_medicalreviewdriverlicense.pdf.

8. Tara Sklar, *Elderly Gun Ownership and the Wave of State Red Flag Laws: An Unintended Consequence That Could Help Many,* 27 Elder L. J. 35, 44 tbl.1 (2019).

9. Md. Code Ann., Pub. Safety § 5-601 (West 2019); D.C. Code § 7-1201.01 (2019).

10. Swanson et al., *Implementation and Effectiveness of Connecticut's Risk-Based Gun Removal Law,* at 192.

11. Lococo et al., Medical Review Practices for Driver Licensing, vol. 3, at 543–51 tbl.42.

12. Lococo et al., Medical Review Practices for Driver Licensing, vol. 3, at 539–42 tbl.40.

13. 18 U.S.C. § 922(g)(4).

14. *See* Bruce J. Winick, Civil Commitment: A Therapeutic Jurisprudence Model (2005).

15. Wyatt v. Stickney, 325 F. Supp. 781, 785 (M.D. Ala. 1971).

16. Henry J. Steadman et al., *A Classification Tree Approach to the Development of Actuarial Violence Risk Assessment,* 24 L. Hum. Behav. 83, 88 tbl.1 (2000).

17. E. Clare Harris and Brian Barraclough, *Suicide as an Outcome for Mental Illness: A Meta-Analysis,* 170 Brit. J. Psychiatry 205 (1997).

18. U.S. Dep't of Health and Human Servs., Ctr. for Behavioral Health Statistics and Quality, Results from the 2011 National Survey on Drug Use and Health: Mental Health Findings 21 (2012).

19. Ramin Mojtabai, *Psychotic-Like Experiences and Interpersonal Violence in the General Population,* 41 Soc. Psychiatry and Psychiatric Epidemiology 183, 184 (2006).

20. Haw. Rev. Stat. § 134-7(c)(3) (2013).

21. Eric B. Elbogen and Sally C. Johnson, *The Intricate Link between Violence and Mental Disorder: Results from the National Epidemiologic Survey on Alcohol and Related Conditions,* 66 Archives of Gen. Psychiatry 152, 155 (2009).

22. 720 Ill. Comp. Stat. 5/24-3.1(a)(4) (2018).

23. U.S. Dep't of Health and Human Servs., Results from the 2011 National Survey on Drug Use and Health, at 25.

24. U.S. Dep't of Health and Human Servs., Results from the 2011 National Survey on Drug Use and Health, at 23.

25. Consortium for Risk-Based Firearm Policy, Guns, Public Health, and Mental Illness: An Evidence-Based Approach for State Policy (Dec. 2, 2013), https://www.jhsph.edu/research/centers-and-institutes /johns-hopkins-center-for-gun-policy-and-research/_archive-2019/_pdfs /GPHMI-State.pdf [http://perma.cc/9MKL-TDKT].

26. Or. Rev. Stat. Ann. § 166.527(6)(a).

27. D. C. Code § 7-2510.03(e)(7) (2019).

28. Aaron J. Kivisto and Peter Lee Phalen, *Effects of Risk-Based Firearm Seizure Laws in Connecticut and Indiana on Suicide Rates, 1981–2015,* 69 Psychiatric Servs. 855 (2018).

29. Swanson et al., *Implementation and Effectiveness of Connecticut's Risk-Based Gun Removal Law.*

30. Parkland: Megan O'Matz, *Mental Health Provider Had Long History with Parkland Shooter. Was Agency Negligent?,* South Florida Sun-Sentinel, Jan. 16, 2019, 7:30 p.m., https://www.sun-sentinel.com /local/broward/parkland/florida-school-shooting/fl-ne-henderson-cruz -civil-suit-20190116-story.html; Charleston: Kevin Sack, *Trial Documents Show Dylann Roof Had Mental Disorders,* N.Y. Times, Feb. 2, 2017; Littleton: Tony Kovaleski, *Timeline: Concerns about Gunman's Mental State Go Back Years, Increased in Weeks before Shooting,* Denver

Channel: Contact7 Investigates (Jan. 6, 2018, 3:11 p.m.), https://www
.thedenverchannel.com/news/investigations/timeline-concerns-about
-gunmans-mental-state-go-back-years-increased-in-weeks-before
-shooting; Las Vegas: Vanessa Romo, *Police End Las Vegas Shooting Investigation; No Motive Found,* NPR (Aug. 3, 2018, 7:51 p.m.), https://
www.npr.org/2018/08/03/635507299/las-vegas-shooting-investigation
-closed-no-motive-found; Aurora: Erica Goode et al., *Before Gunfire,
Hints of "Bad News,"* N.Y. Times, Aug. 27, 2012, at A1; Tucson: Joseph
Schuman, *Jared Lee Loughner Trial: Judge Grants Doctors More Time
to Restore Accused's Mental Fitness,* Huffington Post (Feb. 6, 2012),
http://www.huffingtonpost.com/2012/02/06/jared-lee-loughner-trial
-mental-competency_n_1258397.html. For the Navy Yard, see discussion and notes at the beginning of this chapter.

31. Stål Bjørkly, *Psychotic Symptoms and Violence toward Others—A
Literature Review of Some Preliminary Findings: Part 1. Delusions,* 7
Aggression and Violent Behav. 617, 622 (2002); compare Stål Bjørkly,
*Psychotic Symptoms and Violence toward Others—A Literature Review
of Some Preliminary Findings: Part 2. Hallucinations,* 7 Aggression and
Violent Behav. 605, 610 (2002) (demonstrating that findings on halluci-
nations are more evenly mixed). Compare Dale E. McNiel et al., *The
Relationship between Command Hallucinations and Violence,* 51 Psychiatric Servs. 1288, 1290 (2000) (finding that patients experiencing
command hallucinations to hurt others were 2.51 times more likely to
be violent), *with* Angela F. Nederlof et al., *Threat / Control-Override
Symptoms and Emotional Reactions to Positive Symptoms as Correlates
of Aggressive Behavior in Psychotic Patients,* 199 J. Nervous and Mental
Disease 342, 346 (2011) (finding that threat but not control-override
symptoms made a significant contribution to aggressive behavior).

32. Mojtabai, *Psychotic-Like Experiences,* at 184, 185; compare
Kevin S. Douglas et al., *Psychosis as a Risk Factor for Violence to Others:
A Meta-Analysis,* 135 Psychol. Bull. 679, 691 (2009) (finding the median odds ratio for hallucinations / delusions to be 2.31, lower than
the 5.72 figure from the population-based study). As will be explained
later in this chapter, there are reasons for present purposes to prefer
the 2006 population-based study to an amalgam of different types of
studies.

33. Mojtabai, *Psychotic-Like Experiences,* at 189.

34. Mojtabai, *Psychotic-Like Experiences,* at 187 tbl.2. More recent
research confirms the role of paranoid ideation. Jeremy W. Coid et al.,
*Paranoid Ideation and Violence: Meta-analysis of Individual Subject
Data of 7 Population Surveys,* 42 Schizophrenia Bulletin 907 (2016).

35. Simone Ullrich et al., *Acting on Delusions: The Role of Negative Affect in the Pathway towards Serious Violence,* 29 Journal of Forensic Psychiatry and Psychology 691, 697 tbl.2, 698 fig.1 (2018).

36. This figure is based on data from the 2006 study. *See* Ullrich et al., *Acting on Delusions,* at 184 ("Psychotic-like experiences were reported by 5.1% of adults in the community.") and at 185 (finding that 1.5 percent of participants reported attacking someone with the intent of hurting that person). The full underlying calculation is on file with the authors of this book.

37. Ullrich et al., *Acting on Delusions,* at 185.

38. Ullrich et al., *Acting on Delusions,* at 187. One might be concerned that, under my proposal, police officers would also miss the symptoms. But the study authors do not question clinicians' ability to identify the symptoms, only that the symptoms would be deemed "clinically significant" or evidence of "psychotic disorders." Ullrich et al., *Acting on Delusions,* at 187. Police officers also should be able to identify symptoms, which is all this proposal requires.

39. Yoshihiro Kinoshita et al., *Psychotic-Like Experiences Are Associated with Violent Behavior in Adolescents,* 126 Schizophrenia Res. 245, 248 tbl.1 (2011).

40. Kinoshita et al., *Psychotic-Like Experiences,* at 249 tbl.3.

41. Bruce G. Link et al., *Real in Their Consequences: A Sociological Approach to Understanding the Association between Psychotic Symptoms and Violence,* 64 Am. Soc. Rev. 316, 325 (1999); *see also* at 330 (stating that the "Threat/Control-Override Symptoms Subscale" asked how often the subject felt that (1) "your mind was dominated by forces beyond your control"; (2) "thoughts were put into your head that were not your own"; and (3) "there were people who wished to do you harm."

42. Link et al., *Real in Their Consequences,* at 326 tbl.3.

43. Link et al., *Real in Their Consequences,* at 329; *see also* Bruce G. Link and Ann Stueve, *Psychotic Symptoms and the Violent/Illegal Behavior of Mental Patients Compared to Community Controls,* in Violence and Mental Disorder: Developments in Risk Assessment 137, 154 tbl.7 (John Monahan and Henry J. Steadman eds., 1996) (reporting that the patient variable lost statistical significance in predicting weapon use when the psychotic symptom variable, which was highly significant, was introduced into a regression model).

44. Jeremy W. Coid et al., *The Relationship between Delusions and Violence: Findings from the East London First Episode Psychosis Study,* 70 JAMA Psychiatry 465, 466 (2013). Delusions of being spied on, per-

secution, and conspiracy were statistically significant in being associated with violence, although the study suggests that the anger produced by such delusions was a mediating cause of violence. Coid et al., *Relationship between Delusions and Violence*, at 468. Note that Alexis experienced precisely these types of delusions.

45. *See* Bruce G. Link et al., *The Violent and Illegal Behavior of Mental Patients Reconsidered*, 57 Am. Soc. Rev. 275, 283tbl.1 (1992) (charting the percentage of patients engaging in violent or illegal behavior based on patient status and type of behavior).

46. *See, e.g.,* Paul S. Appelbaum et al., *Violence and Delusions: Data from the MacArthur Violence Risk Assessment Study*, 157 Am. J. Psychiatry 566, 566 (2000) ("To demonstrate that delusions can precipitate violence, however, is not to say that delusional persons are necessarily more violent than persons with other mental illnesses, or even than their neighbors in the general population."); Olivier F. Colins et al., *Psychotic-Like Symptoms as a Risk Factor of Violent Recidivism in Detained Male Adolescents*, 201 J. Nervous and Mental Disease 478, 482 (2013) (concluding that "by identifying detained youths with delusions in general or [paranoid delusions] or [threat/control override delusions] in particular, clinicians are likely to identify youths with a low risk for committing repetitive violent crimes"); Jeffrey Swanson et al., *Violent Behavior Preceding Hospitalization among Persons with Severe Mental Illness*, 23 L. Hum. Behav. 185, 201 (1999) (finding that paranoid symptoms and psychoticism were not significantly associated with violence, and further suggesting that addressing the problems of substance abuse and poor social environments could best prevent violence by severely mentally ill persons); Eduardo Henrique Teixeira and Paulo Dalgalarrondo, *Violent Crime and Dimensions of Delusion: A Comparative Study of Criminal and Noncriminal Delusional Patients*, 37 J. Am. Acad. Psychiatry L. 225, 225 (2009) ("Contrary to current beliefs, delusional patients who are frightened or who have other negative affects associated with delusional ideas appear to commit fewer violent acts.").

47. Appelbaum et al., *Violence and Delusions*, at 567.

48. O'Connor v. Donaldson, 422 U.S. 563, 575 (1975).

49. *See* Ira D. Glick et al., *Inpatient Psychiatric Care in the 21st Century: The Need for Reform*, 62 Psychiatric Servs. 206, 206 (2011) (lamenting the "current model of ultrashort inpatient hospitalization" and advocating for a new model of psychiatric care).

50. *See* Pamela J. Taylor, *Psychosis and Violence: Stories, Fears, and Reality*, 53 Can. J. Psychiatry 647, 651 (2008) (concluding after reviewing literature that "there is consistent evidence of a general association

between delusions and violence," and dismissing "dissenting studies" on other grounds).

51. Consortium for Risk-Based Firearm Policy, Guns, Public Health, and Mental Illness, at 6.

52. *Red Flag Laws: Examining Guidelines for State Action: Hearing before the S. Jud. Comm.*, 116th Cong. 3 (2019) (statement of Ron Honberg on behalf of the National Alliance on Mental Illness (NAMI)).

53. William Frizzell and Joseph Chien, *Extreme Risk Protection Orders to Reduce Firearm Violence,* 70 Psychiatric Servs. 75, 76 (2019).

54. Am. Psychiatric Ass'n, Diagnostic and Statistical Manual of Mental Disorders 819 (5th ed. 2013).

55. Ian Kelleher et al., *Are Screening Instruments Valid for Psychotic-Like Experiences? A Validation Study of Screening Questions for Psychotic-Like Experiences Using In-Depth Clinical Interview,* 37 Schizophrenia Bulletin 362 (2011) (validating a seven-item instrument).

56. Margaret E. Johnson, *Balancing Liberty, Dignity, and Safety: The Impact of Domestic Violence Lethality Screening,* 32 Cardozo L. Rev. 519, 535 n.73 (2010), https://scholarworks.law.ubalt.edu/cgi/viewcontent.cgi?article=1337&context=all_fac.; Connecticut Coalition against Domestic Violence, Connecticut's Lethality Assessment Program: 2017 Report at 9 (Nov. 2017), http://www.ctcadv.org/files/2515/1084/1466/2017LAP_report_11.17.pdf [https://perma.cc/UM4Y-XHPJ].

57. Johnson, *Balancing Liberty, Dignity, and Safety,* at 530 n.44. A recent study of temporary restraining order hearings suggested three additional questions: Has his/her violence caused someone to require medical assistance? Does he/she use illegal drugs? Has he/she ever sexually assaulted someone else? Ian Ayres, Brendan Costello, and Elizabeth Villarreal, *The Impact of Student Assistance on the Granting and Service of Temporary Restraining Orders,* 53 Connecticut L. Rev. __ (2020) (forthcoming).

58. "Furthermore, multiple scales rely on self-reported current or future suicidal thoughts, which are often denied by individuals with high intent-to-die suicide attempts." Leslie Roos, Jitender Sareen, and James M. Bolton, *Suicide Risk Assessment Tools, Predictive Validity Findings and Utility Today: Time for a Revamp?,* 3 Neuropsychiatry 1, 8 (2013), http://www.jneuropsychiatry.org/peer-review/suicide-risk-assessment-tools-predictive-validity-findings-and-utility-today-time-for-a-revamp-neuropsychiatry.pdf (citing Katie A. Busch, Jan Fawcett, and Douglas G. Jacobs, *Clinical Correlates of Inpatient Suicide,* 64 J. Clinical Psychiatry 14 (2003)); *see also* Bo Runeson et al., *Instruments for the Assessment of Suicide Risk: A Systematic Review Evaluating the Cer-*

tainty of the Evidence, 12 PLoS One e0180292 (2017) (concluding that most suicide risk assessment instruments had too few studies to evaluate accuracy and that the instruments with enough studies failed to meet the standard for diagnostic accuracy).

59. Iulian Iancu et al., *The Positive and Negative Symptoms Questionnaire: A Self-Report Scale in Schizophrenia,* 46 Comprehensive Psychiatry 61, 62 (2005). Compare Kelleher et al., *Are Screening Instruments Valid for Psychotic-Like Experiences?,* at 362 (outlining the seven-item Adolescent Psychotic-Like Symptom Screener (APSS)); Charles L. Scott and Phillip J. Resnick, *Clinical Assessment of Psychotic and Mood Disorder Symptoms for Risk of Future Violence,* 19 CNS Spectrums 468, 470 (2014) (distilling seven factors associated with acting due to command hallucinations and six aspects relevant to increased compliance with violent command hallucinations).

60. Daniel Freeman et al., *Current Paranoid Thinking in Patients with Delusions: The Presence of Cognitive-Affective Biases,* 39 Schizophrenia Bulletin 1281, 1283 (2013).

61. The Lethality Assessment Program explicitly instructs police to initiate a screening when "an intimate relationship is involved AND you believe an assault has occurred; you sense the potential for danger is high; the names of parties or location are repeat names or locations; or you simply believe one should be conducted." Connecticut Coalition against Domestic Violence, Connecticut's Lethality Assessment Program, at 3.

62. *See* Nationwide SAR Initiative (NSI), https://www.dhs.gov/nsi (last visited July 16, 2019).

8. UNLAWFUL POSSESSION PETITIONS

1. Alejandro De La Garza, *Florida Woman Arrested after Giving Husband's Guns to Police,* Time, June 23, 2019, https://time.com/5612834/florida-woman-arrested-guns-police/.

2. Madeleine Marr, *While Her Husband Was in Jail, She Turned In His Guns to Cops. That Got Her Arrested,* Miami Herald, June 21, 2019, https://www.miamiherald.com/news/state/florida/article231826428.html; Shannon Van Sant, *Woman Accused of Turning In Husband's Guns to the Police Will Face Misdemeanor Charge,* NPR (July 3, 2019), https://www.npr.org/2019/07/03/738647670/woman-accused-of-turning-in-husbands-guns-to-the-police-will-face-misdemeanor-ch.

3. Max Samis, Brady Campaign to Prevent Gun Violence, *New Domestic Violence Report Finds More Than 525 Women Shot and Killed Every Year by Intimate Partners,* GlobeNewswire NewsRoom (Oct. 12,

2018), https://www.globenewswire.com/news-release/2018/10/12/1620
737/0/en/New-Domestic-Violence-Report-Finds-More-Than-525
-Women-Shot-and-Killed-Every-Year-By-Intimate-Partners.html.

4. James M. Tien et al., *Cost-Benefit of Point of Contact (POC) versus Non-POC Firearm Eligibility Background Checks* (2008), https://www .ncjrs.gov/pdffiles1/bjs/grants/222674.pdf; Gun Control Act of 1968, Pub. L. No. 90-618, 82 Stat. 1213; Firearm Owners Protection Act of 1986, Pub. L. No. 99-308, 100 Stat. 449; and Violence Against Women Act of 1994, Pub. L. No. 103-322, 108 Stat. 1796. And as emphasized in Part 1 of this book, federal law allows states to add additional categories of its citizens to this catalogue of people who are prohibited from bearing arms. Our no-guns registry took advantage of this option by having states designate anyone who registers as a "state prohibitor."

5. Jacquelyn C. Campbell et al., *Risk Factors for Femicide in Abusive Relationships: Results from a Multisite Case Control Study,* 93 Am. J. Pub. Health 1089 (2003).

6. The Gun Control Act of 1968 banned purchases for individuals under indictment or convicted of a crime with a sentence of at least one year, fugitives from justice, unlawful users of controlled substances, and those with adjudicated mental illness. The Firearm Owners Protection Act of 1986 clarified and expanded these categories, prohibiting gun purchases for undocumented residents and individuals with dishonorable discharges or that have renounced their citizenship. Gun Control Act of 1968, Pub. L. No. 90-618, 82 Stat. 1213; Firearm Owners Protection Act of 1986, Pub. L. No. 99-308, 100 Stat. 449.

7. *Not Enforcing Existing Gun Laws—That's a Crime,* Nat'l Rifle Ass'n–Inst. for Legislative Action (May 1, 2013), https://www.nraila.org /articles/20130501/not-enforcing-existing-gun-laws-thats-a-crime; Charlton Heston, President, Nat'l Rifle Ass'n, Speech Assuming the Presidency of the NRA (Sept. 23, 1998); *Issues: Second Amendment,* U.S. Rep. Phil Roe, M.D., 1st Dist. Tenn., https://roe.house.gov/issues/second -amendment/ (last visited July 30, 2019). Opponents of new gun laws have been making this argument for a very long time. *See* Eltinge F. Warner, *The Anti Anti-Pistol Fight,* Field and Stream, Oct. 1922. at 640 ("Every State in the Union already has a law, every city and town and hamlet an ordinance, which, if enforced, would solve the problem. There is no need whatsoever for additional laws of any kind.").

8. 8 R.I. Gen. Laws § 8-8.3-5 (2018).

9. Consortium for Risk-Based Firearm Policy, Guns, Public Health, and Mental Illness: An Evidence-Based Approach for State Policy (2013).

10. Jeff Johnson, *Heston to Step Down as NRA President*, Nation, Apr. 25, 2003.

11. Jeffrey W. Swanson et al., *Mental Illness and Reduction of Gun Violence and Suicide: Bringing Epidemiologic Research to Policy*, 25 Annals Epidemiology 366 (2015).

12. S.C. Code Ann. § 16-23-30 (2018).

13. Philip H. Smith et al., *Intimate Partner Violence and Specific Substance Use Disorders: Findings from the National Epidemiologic Survey on Alcohol and Related Conditions*, 26 Psychol. Addictive Behav. 236 (2012); Garen J. Wintemute et al., *Firearms, Alcohol and Crime: Convictions for Driving under the Influence (DUI) and Other Alcohol-Related Crimes and Risk for Future Criminal Activity among Authorised Purchasers of Handguns*, 24 Inj. Prevention 68 (2018).

14. *See* Consortium for Risk-Based Firearm Policy, Guns, Public Health, and Mental Illness.

15. In addition to the NICS indexes, background checks for gun purchases utilize data from the Interstate Identification Index (III), the National Crime Information Center (NCIC), and Immigration and Customs Enforcement (ICE). These sources also struggle with underreporting from states, particularly due to a lack of final disposition in criminal cases and nonreporting of active warrants. Even when criminal records are reported, they still could be excluded from the III if they are not submitted with fingerprints. Americans for Responsible Solutions and Giffords L. Ctr. to Prevent Gun Violence, For the Record: NICS and Public Safety: Essential Improvements to the National Instant Criminal Background Check System (2016), https://lawcenter.giffords.org/wp-content/uploads/2016/12/NICS-and-Public-Safety.pdf; Tien et al., *Cost-Benefit of Point of Contact (POC) versus Non-POC Firearm Eligibility Background Checks*.

16. Everytown for Gun Safety, Fatal Gaps: How the Virginia Tech Shooting Prompted Changes in State Mental Health Records Reporting (2018), https://everytownresearch.org/wp-content/uploads/2018/06/FATAL-GAPS-RESEARCH-070218B.pdf; Becki Goggins and Anne Gallegos, National Center for State Courts, State Progress in Record Reporting for Firearm-Related Background Checks: Protection Order Submissions (2016), https://www.ncjrs.gov/pdffiles1/bjs/grants/249864.pdf.

17. *Firearms Transaction Record*, U.S. Dep't of Justice Bureau of Alcohol, Tobacco, Firearms and Explosives (Oct. 2016), https://www.atf.gov/firearms/docs/4473-part-1-firearms-transaction-record-over-counter-atf-form-53009/download; *see also* 27 C.F.R. § 478.11 ("A

drug or other substance, or immediate precursor, as defined in section 102 of the Controlled Substances Act, 21 U.S.C. 802. The term includes, but is not limited to, marijuana, depressants, stimulants, and narcotic drugs.").

18. Becki Goggins and Shauna Strickland, SEARCH and National Center for State Courts, State Progress in Record Reporting for Firearm-Related Background Checks: Unlawful Drug Users (July 2017), https://www.ncjrs.gov/pdffiles1/bjs/grants/250782.pdf.

19. Goggins and Strickland, State Progress.

20. Goggins and Strickland, State Progress.

21. 27 C.F.R. § 478.11.

22. This proxy is admittedly overinclusive because it includes people who voluntarily committed themselves and those who were involuntarily admitted for observation (without a finding of dangerousness).

23. These two proxies are not available at the state level, which is why Figure 8.1 reports cruder estimates.

24. In our nationally representative survey, about 0.4 percent of respondents reported that they had received involuntary mental health treatment. This suggests that the underreporting problem may be somewhat less acute than suggested in the text, but self-reporting may be incomplete, and individuals could be disqualified for other mental health–related reasons.

25. Fed. Bureau Investigation, National Instant Criminal Background Check System (NICS) Operations 2007 (2007), https://www.fbi.gov/file-repository/2007_operations_report.pdf/view. Swanson et al., *Mental Illnesss*.

26. To estimate the number of non-overlapping undocumented residents, we took the Department of Homeland Security's estimate of approximately 12 million undocumented residents and reduced it by 20.6 percent (reported in Table 8.1), applying the assumption that undocumented residents had the same proportion of drug use and mental illness as documented residents. Dep't of Homeland Sec. Office of Strategy, Policy and Plans, Population Estimates: Illegal Alien Population Residing in the United States: January 2015 (2018), https://www.dhs.gov/sites/default/files/publications/18_1214_PLCY_pops-est-report.pdf.

27. Again, we include the number of undocumented immigrants in this section not because we believe that immigration status is an accurate proxy for risk of violence, but to demonstrate that current prohibitions against gun possession are severely underenforced.

28. Mark Follman, *Mass Shootings: Maybe What We Need Is a Better Mental-Health Policy,* Mother Jones (Nov. 9, 2012), http://www.mother jones.com/politics/2012/11/jared-loughner-mass-shootings-mental-illness.

29. Fredrick E. Vars and Amanda Adcock Young, *Do the Mentally Ill Have a Right to Bear Arms?,* 48 Wake Forest L. Rev. 1 (2013).

30. Michael Farrell et al., *Psychosis and Drug Dependence: Results from a National Survey of Prisoners,* 181 Brit. J. Psychiatry 393 (2002); Sarah K. S. Shannon et al., *The Growth, Scope, and Spatial Distribution of People with Felony Records in the United States, 1948–2010,* 54 Demography 1795 (2017); *Offenses,* Federal Bureau of Prisons (last updated July 27, 2019), https://www.bop.gov/about/statistics/statistics_inmate_offenses.jsp.

31. Another way to estimate the total number of individuals who are prohibited from possessing a firearm is simply to ask them. We did just that in the survey described in Chapter 1. Around 3 percent of respondents indicated that they were currently prohibited from buying a firearm, which translates into approximately 6.5 million adults nationwide. Of course, many people who are prohibited may not realize it, and those who do may be hesitant to disclose that even on an anonymous survey.

32. Michael S. Schmidt, *Background Check Flaw Let Dylann Roof Buy Gun, F.B.I. Says,* N.Y. Times, July 10, 2015.

33. Pennsylvania has made the most progress—automating the reporting of misdemeanor drug offenses to the NICS index. Goggins and Strickland, State Progress.

34. While some of the point of contact states may include such individuals in their state database and thereby prevent in-state sales, they would not incapacitate the individuals from buying guns in other states.

35. H. B. 18-1436, 71st Gen. Assemb., 2nd Reg. Sess. (Colo. 2018), https://leg.colorado.gov/sites/default/files/documents/2018A/bills/2018a_1436_ren.pdf.

36. A 1994 study found that 22 percent of gun buyers reported acquiring the weapon without being checked through NICS first. Matthew Miller, Lisa Hepburn, and Deborah Azrael, *Firearm Acquisition without Background Checks: Results of a National Survey,* 166 Annals Internal Med. 233 (2017).

37. Audit Division, U.S. Dep't of Justice, Office of the Inspector General, Audit of the Handling of Firearms Purchase Denials through the National Instant Background Check System (2016), https://oig.justice.gov/reports/2016/a1632.pdf#page=1.

38. Wrongful transfer can occur if the FBI erroneously tells the gun dealer that a transfer may proceed or if the FBI fails to complete a background check within three days but then later discovers that the applicant falls within a prohibited category.

39. Richard A. Oppel, *How So Many Violent Felons Are Allowed to Keep Their Illegal Guns,* N.Y. Times, Feb. 20, 2019.

40. Oppel, *How So Many Violent Felons Are Allowed to Keep Their Illegal Guns.*

41. Oppel, *How So Many Violent Felons Are Allowed to Keep Their Illegal Guns; Disarming Prohibited People,* Giffords L. Ctr. to Prevent Gun Violence, https://lawcenter.giffords.org/gun-laws/policy-areas/who-can-have-a-gun/disarming-prohibited-people/ (last visited Aug. 5, 2019).

42. *Disarming Prohibited People,* Giffords L. Ctr. to Prevent Gun Violence.

43. 430 Ill. Comp. Stat. 65/8 (2015); 430 Ill. Comp. Stat. 65/8.3 (2019).

44. Julie Bosman, *Worker Who Opened Fire inside Factory Had Been Barred from Having Gun,* N.Y. Times, Feb. 16, 2019.

45. *Disarming Prohibited People,* Giffords L. Ctr. to Prevent Gun Violence.

46. Campbell et al., *Risk Factors for Femicide* (quoting Consortium for Risk-Based Firearm Policy, Guns, Public Health, and Mental Illness). *See also* M. Zeoli et al., *Analysis of the Strength of Legal Firearms Restrictions for Perpetrators of Domestic Violence and Their Associations with Intimate Partner Homicide,* 187 Am. J. Epidemiology 1449 (2018) (finding laws requiring abusers to turn in guns linked to a 16 percent reduction in intimate partner gun homicides).

47. *Disarming Prohibited People,* Giffords L. Ctr. to Prevent Gun Violence. States vary on (1) whether court-ordered gun removal is explicitly or implicitly authorized, (2) whether gun removal is required or authorized by state law, and (3) whether notice and hearing with the respondent is required before a gun removal order. Prosecutors against Gun Violence and Consortium for Risk-Based Firearm Policy, Firearm Removal/Retrieval in Cases of Domestic Violence (2016), http://efsgv.org/wp-content/uploads/2016/02/Removal-Report-Updated-2-11-16.pdf.

48. 750 Ill. Comp. Stat. 60/214(b)(14.5) (2019); Prosecutors against Gun Violence and Consortium for Risk-Based Firearm Policy, Firearm Removal/Retrieval.

49. Oppel, *How So Many Violent Felons Are Allowed to Keep Their Illegal Guns;* Alan Blinder, *Waffle House Shooting Suspect Is in Custody, Nashville Police Say,* N.Y. Times, Apr. 23, 2018.

50. Michael Smothers, *Travis Reinking's Father Pleads Not Guilty to Weapons Charge*, J. Star (Apr. 25, 2019), https://www.pjstar.com/news /20190425/travis-reinkings-father-pleads-not-guilty-to-weapons -charge.

51. Oppel, *How So Many Violent Felons Are Allowed to Keep Their Illegal Guns*.

52. *Disarming Prohibited People*, Giffords Law Center to Prevent Gun Violence.

53. Quoted in Oppel, *How So Many Violent Felons Are Allowed to Keep Their Illegal Guns*.

54. Dara Lind, Cops Do 20,000 No-Knock Raids a Year. Civilians Often Pay the Price When They Go Wrong, Vox (May 15, 2015), https://www.vox.com/2014/10/29/7083371/swat-no-knock-raids -police-killed-civilians-dangerous-work-drugs.

55. Lind, Cops Do 20,000 No-Knock Raids a Year.

56. Prosecutors against Gun Violence and the Consortium for Risk-Based Firearm Policy, Firearm Removal/Retrieval.

57. In 2018, Washington State approved a ballot measure that requires the department that controls the database with information on sales and transfers of all pistols and semiautomatic rifles to "verify annually that people who have acquired these weapons remain eligible to possess them, and to take steps to ensure anyone found ineligible does not remain in possession of firearms." *Initiative 1639*, Washington State Office of the Attorney General, https://www.atg.wa.gov/initiative-1639 (last visited Aug. 5, 2019). The "rapid response" team established by King County, Washington, which was tasked with removing guns from alleged domestic abusers subject to restraining orders, quadrupled the number of guns seized. Chris Ingalls, *New Rapid Response Team Disarms Accused Abusers: A New Police Unit Seizes Weapons from Accused Abusers to Make Their Victims Safer*, K5 News (Feb. 7, 2018), https://www.king5.com/article/news/local/new-rapid-response-team -disarms-accused-abusers/281-515919133.

58. Annie Sweeney, Stacy St. Clair, Cecilia Reye, and Sarah Freishtat, *More Than 34,000 Illinoisans Have Lost Their Right to Own a Gun. Nearly 80% May Still Be Armed*, Chi. Trib., May 23, 2019.

59. Office of the Attorney General, California Department of Justice, Armed and Prohibited Persons System 2018: Annual Report to the Legislature (2019), https://oag.ca.gov/system/files/attachments/press-docs /apps-2018.finaldocx.pdf.

60. Oppel, *How So Many Violent Felons Are Allowed to Keep Their Illegal Guns*.

61. Center for Behavioral Health Statistics and Quality, Substance Abuse and Mental Health Services Administration, 2017 National Survey on Drug Use and Health: Methodological Summary and Definitions (2018), https://www.samhsa.gov/data/sites/default/files/cbhsq-reports/NSDUHMethodSummDefs2017/NSDUHMethodSummDefs2017.htm.

62. Katherine A. Vittes et al., *Legal Status and Source of Offenders' Firearms in States with the Least Stringent Criteria for Gun Ownership,* 19 Inj. Prevention 26 (2013); *see also* Philip J. Cook, Susan T. Parker, and Harold A. Pollack, *Sources of Guns to Dangerous People: What We Learn by Asking Them,* 79 Preventive Med. 28 (2015); Anthony Fabio et al., *Gaps Continue in Firearm Surveillance: Evidence from a Large U.S. City Bureau of Police,* 10 Soc. Med. 13 (2016).

63. *Crime in the United States: 2017: Table 29: Estimated Number of Arrests,* Fed. Bureau Investigation Crim. Just. Info. Serv. Division, https://ucr.fbi.gov/crime-in-the-u.s/2017/crime-in-the-u.s.-2017/tables/table-29 (last visited April 13, 2020).

64. See Chapter 6.

65. Cassandra K. Crifasi et al., *Storage Practices of US Gun Owners in 2016,* 108 Am. J. Pub. Health 532 (2018), http://www.ncbi.nlm.nih.gov/pubmed/29470124.

66. David C. Grossman et al., *Gun Storage Practices and Risk of Youth Suicide and Unintentional Firearm Injuries,* 293 JAMA 707 (2005), https://jamanetwork.com/journals/jama/fullarticle/200330.

67. Deborah Azrael et al., *Firearm Storage in Gun-Owning Households with Children: Results of a 2015 National Survey,* 95 J. Urb. Health 295 (2018), http://www.ncbi.nlm.nih.gov/pubmed/29748766.

68. 18 U.S.C. § 922(z)(1) (2015).

69. *Safe Storage,* Giffords L. Ctr. to Prevent Gun Violence, https://lawcenter.giffords.org/gun-laws/policy-areas/child-consumer-safety/safe-storage/ (last visited Aug. 5, 2019).

70. Conn. Gen. Stat. § 29-37i (2013).

71. *Safe Storage,* Giffords L. Ctr. to Prevent Gun Violence; San Francisco Police Code § 4512(a), (c)(2) (2016). *See also* Jackson v. City and Cty. of San Francisco, 746 F.3d 953 (9th Cir. 2014) (finding increased time it takes for a gun owner to access his or her gun did not place an impermissible burden on Second Amendment rights).

72. The Illinois Firearm Seizure Act creates an alternative gun removal petition process that allows any person to bring a complaint but is limited to proof that the respondent has "threatened to use a firearm illegally." 725 Ill. Comp. Stat. 165/1 (2018).

73. U.S. Const. amend. IV.

74. Respondents would be specifically informed about the process, which is more than the Constitution requires for property seizures generally. City of West Covina v. Perkins, 525 U.S. 234 (1999).

75. *Frequently Asked Questions*, U.S. Sec. and Exchange Commission, Off. Whistleblower, https://www.sec.gov/whistleblower/frequently -asked-questions#faq-10 (last modified Aug. 1, 2019).

76. Gun Control Act of 1968, Pub. L. No. 90-618 (Oct. 22, 1968).

77. Several studies have established that undocumented residents are either less or no more likely than citizens to commit violent crime. *See* Brent R. Klein et al., *Immigration and Violence in Rural versus Urban Counties, 1990–2010*, 58 Soc. Q. 229 (2017); Robert Adelman et al., *Urban Crime Rates and the Changing Face of Immigration: Evidence across Four Decades*, 15 J. Ethnicity Crim. Just. 52 (2017); Alex Nowrasteh, *Criminal Immigrants in Texas: Illegal Immigrant Conviction and Arrest Rates for Homicide, Sex Crimes, Larceny, and Other Crimes*, Cato Institute (Feb. 26, 2018), https://www.cato.org/publications /immigration-research-policy-brief/criminal-immigrants-texas-illegal -immigrant.

78. Evidence on the relationship between cannabis use and violence is mixed and inconclusive. Michael K. Ostrowsky, *Does Marijuana Use Lead to Aggression and Violent Behavior?*, 41 J. Drug Educ. 369 (2011).

79. We considered excluding all nonviolent felons, but the evidence suggests that nonviolent property and public-order offenders who serve prison time have substantial likelihood of being arrested for a violent crime within nine years of release. Mariel Alper et al., U.S. Dep't of Just. Off. Just. Programs, Bureau Just. Stat., 2018 Update on Prisoner Recidivism: A 9-Year Follow-Up Period (2005–2014), 10 (2018), https://www .bjs.gov/content/pub/pdf/18upr9yfup0514.pdf.

80. Many states also require background checks for transactions involving unlicensed sellers. *Universal Background Checks*, Giffords L. Ctr. to Prevent Gun Violence, https://lawcenter.giffords.org/gun-laws/policy -areas/background-checks/universal-background-checks/#state (last visited April 13, 2020).

81. *Categories of Prohibited People*, Giffords L. Ctr. to Prevent Gun Violence, https://lawcenter.giffords.org/gun-laws/policy-areas/who-can -have-a-gun/categories-of-prohibited-people/ (last visited April 13, 2020).

82. Garen J. Wintemute, *Prior Misdemeanor Convictions as a Risk Factor for Later Violent and Firearm-Related Criminal Activity among Authorized Purchasers of Handguns*, 280 JAMA 2083 (1998).

83. *Categories of Prohibited People*, Giffords L. Ctr. to Prevent Gun Violence.

84. We are sensitive to the concern that making gun possession illegal for individuals who voluntarily seek inpatient psychiatric treatment may discourage such treatment, particularly with respect to police officers and others who need to carry a weapon as part of their jobs. *See* DeBacker v. City of Moline, 78 F. Supp. 3d 916 (2015) (police officer fired because he was barred from carrying firearm after voluntary hospitalization). States should consider special hardship exceptions to the voluntary admission ban.

85. John S. Rozel and Edward P. Mulvey, *The Link between Mental Illness and Firearm Violence: Implications for Social Policy and Clinical Practice*, 13 Annu. Rev. Clinical Psychol. 445 (2017).

86. Jeffrey W. Swanson et al., *Gun Violence, Mental Illness, and Laws That Prohibit Gun Possession: Evidence from Two Florida Counties*, 35 Health Affairs 1067 (2016).

87. Kelly Kelleher, Mark Chaffin, Janice Hollenberg, and Ellen Fischer, *Alcohol and Drug Disorders among Physically Abusive and Neglectful Parents in a Community-Based Sample*, Am. J. Pub. Health 84, 10 (1994), 1586–90; K. Auerhahn and R. N. Parker, *Drugs, Alcohol, and Homicide*, in Studying and Preventing Homicide: Issues and Challenges 97–114 (1999); Philip J. Cook, Jens Ludwig, and Anthony A. Braga, *Criminal Records of Homicide Offenders*, JAMA 294 (5), 598–601 (2005).

88. *Categories of Prohibited People*, Giffords L. Ctr. to Prevent Gun Violence.

89. Consortium for Risk-Based Firearm Policy, Guns, Public Health, and Mental Illness.

90. Violence Against Women Reauthorization Act of 2019, H.R. 1585, 116th Cong, 1st Sess. § 802 (2019).

91. Judith M. McFarlane et al., *Stalking and Intimate Partner Femicide*, 3 Homicide Stud. 300 (1999).

92. Fredrick Vars, *What Next on Terror and Guns?*, Jurist (Aug. 17, 2016), https://www.jurist.org/commentary/2016/08/fredrick-vars-terror-guns/. Of course, racial or religious stereotypes cannot be grounds for "reasonable" suspicion. Compare Matthew Barakat, *Judge Considers Whether Terror Watchlist Is Unconstitutional*, AP News (Apr. 4, 2019), https://www.apnews.com/6d36e261744b42ec93128edebdc3bcf5.

93. Everytown for Gun Safety, Closing the Terror Gap (2018), https://everytownresearch.org/documents/2015/12/closing-terror-gap.pdf/.

94. N.J. Rev. Stat. § 2C:58-3(c)(9) (2009).

95. Vittes et al., *Legal Status and Source of Offenders' Firearms*.

96. A majority of the public—57.8 percent (including 49 percent of gun owners)—support a ten-year prohibition on anyone found to have carried a concealed gun without a permit. Colleen L. Barry et al., *Perspective: After Newtown—Public Opinion on Gun Policy and Mental Illness*, 368 New Eng. J. Med. 1077 (2013).

97. See *Minimum Age to Purchase and Possess*, Giffords L. Ctr. to Prevent Gun Violence, https://lawcenter.giffords.org/gun-laws/policy-areas/who-can-have-a-gun/minimum-age/ (last visited Aug. 5, 2019).

98. Average of 2013–2017 data. *Web-Based Injury Statistics Query and Reporting System (WISQARS)*, Ctrs. for Disease Control and Prevention, https://www.cdc.gov/injury/wisqars (last reviewed Mar. 21, 2019) (containing fatal and nonfatal injury data).

99. 18 U.S.C. § 922(b)(1)–(c)(1) (2018).

100. See *Categories of Prohibited People*, Giffords L. Ctr. to Prevent Gun Violence.

101. Daniel W. Webster et al., *Association between Youth-Focused Firearm Laws and Youth Suicides*, 292 JAMA 594 (2004).

102. Minorities are subject to excessively high bail, increased charges, and longer sentences than whites arrested for the same crimes. *See, e.g.*, Ian Ayres and Joel Waldfogel, *A Market Test for Race Discrimination in Bail Setting*, 46 Stan. L. Rev. 987 (1993); M. Marit Rehavi and Sonja B. Starr, *Racial Disparity in Federal Criminal Charging and Its Sentencing Consequences*, U. Mich. L. and Econ., Empirical Legal Stud. Ctr. Paper No. 12-002 (2012).

103. In addition to data from the NSDUH and undocumented resident estimates from the Department of Homeland Security, in Table 8.1 we use data from Shannon et al., *Growth, Scope, and Spatial Distribution*, supplementary data table 13524_2017_611_MOESM2_ESM.xlsx, to add a row for the share of convicted felons by race. This data is only broken into black and nonblack categories, so there is no value given for the Hispanic category, and the non-Hispanic white category likely overcounts. Since these estimates are from 2010, the values may underestimate the share of persons in each category that are convicted felons. As above, we scale down the number of undocumented residents and convicted felons by the "total without double-counting" share to limit the possibility for double counting in our total. Shannon et al., *Growth, Scope, and Spatial Distribution*.

104. *Racial Bias in the National Instant Criminal Background Check System*, Data Science W231 | Behind the Data: Humans and Values (Feb. 27, 2018), https://blogs.ischool.berkeley.edu/w231/2018/02/27/racial-bias-in-the-national-instant-criminal-background-check-system/.

105. George F. Parker, *Circumstances and Outcomes of a Firearm Seizure Law: Marion County, Indiana, 2006–2013,* 33 Behav. Sci. L. 308 (2015).

106. Compare Ayres and Waldfogel, *Market Test for Race Discrimination* (finding that competitive bond dealers' pricing of bonds mitigates unjustified disparate racial impacts of judges).

107. Child Welfare Info. Gateway, Child. Bureau, Immunity for Reporters of Child Abuse and Neglect (2018), https://www.childwelfare.gov/pubPDFs/immunity.pdf.

9. INCENTIVIZING DISCLOSURE

1. Colin Dwyer, *Wife of Orlando Nightclub Shooter Cleared of All Charges,* NPR (Mar. 30, 2018), https://www.npr.org/sections/thetwo-way/2018/03/30/598239315/wife-of-orlando-nightclub-shooter-cleared-of-all-charges (last visited July 23, 2019); Keith Coffman and Dan Whitcomb, *Las Vegas Shooter's Girlfriend Won't Face Charges: Sheriff,* Reuters (Jan. 19, 2018), https://www.reuters.com/article/us-lasvegas-shooting/las-vegas-shooters-girlfriend-wont-face-charges-sheriff-idUSKBN1F82EJ (last visited July 23, 2019).

2. *See* Yoshihiro Nakatani et al., *Why the Carrot Is More Effective Than the Stick: Different Dynamics of Punishment Memory and Reward Memory and Its Possible Biological Basis,* 92 Neurobiology of Learning and Memory 370 (2009) (finding that reward memory lasts longer than does punishment memory).

3. A similar logic underlies limiting the use of "innovation sticks" to institutions that can be identified as unreasonably failing to adopt existing technologies. *See* Ian Ayres and Amy Kapczynski, *Innovation Sticks: The Limited Case for Penalizing Failures to Innovate,* 82 Univ. Chi. L. Rev. 1781 (2015).

4. Charles Callahan, Frederick Rivara, and Thomas Koepsell, *Money for Guns: Evaluation of the Seattle Gun Buy-Back Program,* 109 Pub. Health Rep. 472 (1994). Australia's buyback program, which was used to increase compliance with new firearms bans and paid individuals for newly banned guns that were previously licensed, was more successful. It is estimated that the buyback program reduced Australia's stock of firearms by 20 percent. *See* Andrew Leigh and Christine Neill, *Do Gun Buybacks Save Lives? Evidence from Panel Data,* 12 Am. L. Econ. Rev. 509 (2010); Peter Reuter and Jenny Mouzos, *Australia: A Massive Buyback of Low-Risk Guns,* in Evaluating Gun Policy: Effects on Crime and Violence 121 (Jens Ludwig and Philip J. Cook eds., 2004).

5. Anthony A. Braga and Garen J. Wintemute, *Improving the Potential Effectiveness of Gun Buyback Programs,* 45 Am. J. Preventive Med. 668 (2013).

6. Braga and Wintemute, *Improving the Potential Effectiveness of Gun Buyback Programs. See also* Scott W. Phillips, Dae-Young Kim, and James J. Sobol, *An Evaluation of a Multiyear Gun Buy-Back Programme: Re-examining the Impact on Violent Crimes,* 15 International Journal of Police Science and Management 246 (2013) (finding significant decrease in gun robbery when examining program over a longer period than other studies).

7. *Gun Bounty Program Makes Big Bust in South Miami-Dade,* CBS Local Media (Dec. 9, 2010), https://miami.cbslocal.com/2010/12/09/gun -bounty-program-makes-big-bust-in-south-miami-dade/.

8. Courtney Cole, *Gun Bounty Program Helps Get Guns and Criminals Off the Streets,* Action News JAX (Sept. 6, 2018), https:// www.actionnewsjax.com/news/local/gun-bounty-program-helps-get -guns-and-criminals-off-the-streets/828704803 (last visited July 24, 2019).

9. *Champaign Co. Crime Stoppers Extending Gun Bounty Rewards,* WAND (Apr. 30, 2019), https://www.wandtv.com/news/champaign-co -crime-stoppers-extending-gun-bounty-rewards/article_c114e402-6b51 -11e9-88f1-db9fc45ce2ec.html (last visited July 24, 2019); *Crime Stoppers Extends Successful Gun Bounty Reward Program,* WICS / WCCU (Apr. 29, 2019), https://newschannel20.com/news/local/crime-stoppers -extends-successful-gun-bounty-reward-program (last visited July 24, 2019).

10. *Gun Bounty Program,* Metro Crime Stoppers, http://metrocrime stoppers.org/metro-crime-stoppers-partners-with-baltimore-police -concerning-the-gun-bounty-program/ (n.d.) (last visited July 24, 2019).

11. Robert H. Sitkoff and Jesse Dukeminier, Wills, Trusts, and Estates 385 (10th ed. 2017) ("'The purposes for which we can create trusts,' says the leading treatise, 'are as unlimited as our imagination.'") (quoting Scott and Ascher on Trusts sec. 1.1).

12. Sitkoff and Dukeminier, Wills, Trusts, and Estates, at 408.

13. Sitkoff and Dukeminier, Wills, Trusts, and Estates, at 500 (quoting Northern Trust, Will and Trust Forms 200–1 (2004)).

14. *See* Fla. Stat. § 790.401.

15. Uniform Trust Code § 816.23, https://www.uniformlaws.org /committees/community-home?CommunityKey=193ff839-7955-4846 -8f3c-ce74ac23938d.

16. S. I. Strong, *Arbitration of Internal Trust Disputes,* College of Commercial Arbitrators (2017), https://www.ccaarbitration.org/wp-content/uploads/Internal-Trust-Disputes.pdf.

17. Ariz. Rev. Stat. § 14-10205.

18. Sitkoff and Dukminier, Wills, Trusts, and Estates, at 623.

19. Lee-Ford Tritt, *Dispatches from the Trenches of America's Great Gun Trust Wars,* 108 Nw. U. L. Rev. 743, 755 (2014) (emphasis added).

20. Tritt, *Dispatches from the Trenches.*

21. The offer would also likely violate the somewhat nebulous unconstitutional conditions doctrine. *See* Kathleen Sullivan, *Unconstitutional Conditions,* 102 Harv. L. Rev. 1413 (1989); Cass R. Sunstein, *Why the Unconstitutional Conditions Doctrine Is an Anachronism (with Particular Reference to Religion, Speech, and Abortion),* 70 B.U. L. Rev. 593 (1990); Richard A. Epstein, *Foreword: Unconstitutional Conditions, State Power, and the Limits of Consent,* 102 Harv. L. Rev. 4 (1988).

22. Laura N. Honegger, *Does the Evidence Support the Case for Mental Health Courts? A Review of the Literature,* 39 L. Hum. Behav. 478 (2015); *Adult Mental Health Treatment Court Locator,* SAMHSA GAINS Center (last visited July 24, 2019), https://www.samhsa.gov/gains-center/mental-health-treatment-court-locator/adults.

23. Commonsense Gun Laws Partnership, *Commonsense Solutions: How State Laws Can Reduce Gun Deaths Associated with Mental Illness* (2014), https://lawcenter.giffords.org/wp-content/uploads/2015/01/Final-Mental-Health-Toolkit-12.5.14.pdf.

24. Commonsense Gun Laws Partnership, *Commonsense Solutions.*

25. *See* Lowell B. Miller, *Judicial Discretion to Reject Negotiated Pleas,* 63 Geo. L. J. 241 (1974); Nancy J. King, *Judicial Oversight of Negotiated Sentences in a World of Bargained Punishment,* 58 Stan. L. Rev. 293 (2005).

26. MHN Government Services, *Duty to Report: Duty to Warn and Mandated Reporting Guidelines for SPA* (2018), https://www.mhngs.com/static/pdf/MFLC_Duty_to_Warn_Guidelines_for_SPAs.pdf.

27. States may legitimately choose not to subject all doctors to malpractice liability for failing to report potentially dangerous conditions. Fearing liability, doctors who can screen patients may be less willing to treat those in high-risk groups. Compare J. Shahar Dillbary, Griffin Edwards, and Fredrick E. Vars, *Why Exempting Negligent Doctors May Reduce Suicide: An Empirical Analysis,* 93 Ind. L. J. 459 (2018).

28. Sean W. Gallagher, *The Public Policy Exclusion and Insurance for Intentional Employment Discrimination,* 92 Mich. L. Rev. 1264–67 (1994).

29. Alex Yablon, *What Happened to the $1.3 Billion Congress Approved to Improve Federal Gun Background Checks?*, The Trace (July 27, 2015), https://www.thetrace.org/2015/07/nics-background-check-congress-spending/.

30. The Bureau of Justice Statistics explains: "During the 2-year period beginning 3 years after the date of enactment of the Act, up to 3% may be withheld in the case of less than 50% completeness; during the 5-year period beginning 5 years after the date of enactment of the Act, up to 4% may be withheld in the case of less than 70% completeness; thereafter, 5% must be withheld in the case of less than 90% completeness (although the mandatory reduction can be waived if there is substantial evidence of the state making a reasonable effort to comply)." *The NICS Improvement Amendments Act of 2007*, Bureau of Justice Statistics (last visited July 24, 2019), https://www.bjs.gov/index.cfm?ty=tp&tid=49.

31. *NICS Improvement Amendments Act of 2007*.

32. Richard Schauffler et al., *NICS Improvement Amendments Act: State Records Estimates Development and Validation Project, Year Three Report* (2012), https://www.ncjrs.gov/pdffiles1/bjs/grants/240401.pdf. The potential penalties for incomplete reporting are also probably insufficient to sufficiently harness state reporting efforts. For example, in 2019, the maximum (5 percent) penalty New York State might have incurred would amount to less than $500,000. *See Fiscal Year (FY) 2019 State Edward Byrne Memorial Justice Assistance Grant (JAG) Allocations* (2019), https://www.bja.gov/Funding/19JAGStateAllocations.pdf.

33. Bureau of Justice Statistics, *FY 2017 NICS Act Record Improvement Program (NARIP)* 6 (2017), https://www.bjs.gov/content/pub/pdf/FY17NARIPsol.pdf.

34. 18 U.S.C. § 922(x)(3).

35. Federal legislation required states to provide data—such as the percentage of vehicles that exceeded fifty-five mph—to the Federal Highway Administration (FHWA). States collected these data by utilizing monitoring stations that recorded the speeds of passing vehicles during set observation periods. Department of Transportation, Federal Highway Administration, *Speed Monitoring Program Procedural Manual for the National Maximum Speed Limit* I-1 (1980); *see* Nakatani et al., *Why the Carrot Is More Effective*, at 1824–26.

36. Nakatani et al., *Why the Carrot Is More Effective*, at 1824–26; Department of Transportation, Speed Monitoring Program. An even closer analogy was proposed as a manufacturer incentive to reduce youth smoking as part of the multistate tobacco resolution. *See* Michael Givel

and Stanton A. Glantz, *The "Global Settlement" with the Tobacco Industry: 6 Years Later*, Am. J. Pub. Health 220 (2004). Under this proposal, a potential penalty of $2 billion would be contingent on representative surveys of high school students. Jeremy Bulow and Paul Klemperer, *The Tobacco Deal*, Brookings Papers on Economic Activity, Microeconomics 360–64 (1998), https://www.brookings.edu/wp-content/uploads/2016/07/1998_bpeamicro_bulow.pdf.

ACKNOWLEDGMENTS

We have many people to thank. Bruce Ackerman, Joseph Blocher, John Donohue, Heather Elliott, Jack Hitt, Al Klevorick, Mel Kohn, Mike Pardo, David Patton, Allen Rostron, Kristen Underhill, Charles Vars, and seminar participants at Duke, Emory, University of Alabama, and University of Texas law schools provided helpful comments. Griffin Austin, Greg Conyers, Anthony Cozart, Samuel Dong, Amen Jalal, Hope Henson, Tracy Nelson, Zachary Shelley, Amy Underwood, and Susan Wang, as well as Penny Gibson and the rest of the staff in the University of Alabama law library, provided excellent research assistance.

Chapters 1 and 2 build on ideas first discussed in "Self-Defense Against Gun Suicide," *Boston College Law Review* 56:4 (2015): 1465–1499. Chapters 4 and 5 expand on research presented in "Libertarian Gun Control," *University of Pennsylvania Law Review* 167 (2019): 921–974. Chapter 7 traces its origin to "Symptom-Based Gun Control," *Connecticut Law Review* 46 (2014): 1633–1650.

INDEX

abortion jurisprudence, 74–75
access, gun: likelihood of signing up for self-restriction and, 23; popularity of self-restriction and, 21; suicide and, 17, 24
accidents, gun, 88
advance directives, 29–31
Alabama, self-restriction proposal in, 40–41
Alabama Law Institute (ALI), 40
alcohol, 15, 127, 145
Alexis, Aaron, 103, 108, 111, 114, 115, 118–119
Alliance for Gun Responsibility, 55
analogies to self-restriction, 26; advance directives, 29–31; gambling self-exclusion programs, 27–29
Anderson v. Martin, 73
Armed and Prohibited Persons System (APPS), 137, 138
associational choices, 3–5, 61–71, 86; constitutional concerns and, 72–79; email option and, 8, 78–79; First Amendment and, 78; gun-free zones and, 98; libertarianism, 62–63; mandated disclosure of, 73, 74, 75–76; negotiated exclusion and, 69–70; noncommercial, 77–78; rescission and, 66; waiving free-speech rights and, 61. *See also* communication about self-restriction;

constitutional concerns; email option; gun-free zones; insurance; landlords / property owners
associational discrimination, 51–52, 64, 79
associational marketplace extension, 182–186
Aurora (Colorado) shooting, 82
Australia, 228n4
Ayres, Ian, 26, 39, 44, 48

back-end notification, 33, 34, 41, 49, 51, 52, 67–68. *See also* email option
background checks: databases for, 31, 130, 219n15; drug use and, 128, 130–131. *See also* National Instant Criminal Background Check System (NICS)
bills. *See* gun policy; state proposals for self-restriction
Bonta, Rob, 41, 42
bottom-up / choice-enhancing gun control, 1–2, 63, 93, 98, 99, 124. *See also* libertarianism
bounties, 155–156, 160
Brady Campaign, 55
Brandeis, Louis, 39
Brees, Katrina, 13, 44, 55
Brown, Jerry, 42
Buckley v. Valeo, 75

burglary rates, 70
Bush, George W., 164
buyback programs, 155–156, 160,
    228n4

California, 67; gun policy in, 52;
    gun removal and, 137–139, 151;
    self-restriction proposal in, 41–42,
    55
campaign contributions, mandated
    disclosures of, 75
CBS v. Block, 75
certification card, 197n8
choice-enhancing/bottom-up gun
    control, 1–2, 63, 93, 98, 99, 124
Clinton, Hillary, 21
coercive treatment, 30, 37–38,
    107–108
commodified marketplace, 69
communication about self-restriction,
    61, 197n8. See also associational
    choices; email option
company town exception, 96
confidentiality, 32, 33–34, 50
conservation easements, 94–95,
    208n82
Consortium for Risk-Based Firearm
    Policy, 109, 114, 123–124, 126,
    127, 145
constitutional concerns: association and,
    72–79; email option and, 75–79;
    government purchase of waivers,
    196n7; government's underlying
    purpose and, 74; mandatory
    disclosure and, 79; private gun-
    free zones and, 96–98; self-defense
    limitation, 76–77. See also associa-
    tional choices; First Amendment; gun
    policy; gun rights advocates; Second
    Amendment
Cook, Philip, 70
cooling-off period. See waiting periods
covenants, 94, 95, 98
crime statistics, unlawful possession
    and, 139–140

dangerousness, 5–6, 36–37, 107;
    incentives to report, 154–162;
    penalties for failure to report, 154,
    162–165; proxies for, 122. See also
    diagnosis- and treatment-based
    restrictions; prohibited possession
    categories; red flag statutes; symptom-
    based restrictions
"dead hand" concerns, 98
decentralization, 2, 8. See also
    bottom-up/choice-enhancing gun
    control
Decker, Marjorie, 46, 52
defeasible fees, 95, 209n85
delay period. See waiting periods
delusions, 111–114, 117–118,
    214–215n44, 215n46. See also
    symptom-based restrictions
diagnosis- and treatment-based
    restrictions, 107–111, 112, 114.
    See also prohibited possession
    categories; red flag statutes
Dick's Sporting Goods, 29
disarmament. See Donna's Law; gun
    removal petitions; removal of unlawfully
    possessed guns; self-restriction,
    voluntary; unlawful possession (UP)
    petitions
disclosure: incentivizing, 154–165;
    mandatory, 79, 162–164
discrimination: associational, 51–52,
    64, 79; based on waiver status,
    197n14; employment, 77
District of Columbia v. Heller, 76
diversion programs, 160–161
domestic violence, 116–117, 120–121,
    122, 134, 136, 146
Donna's Law, 3, 98; adoption of,
    57–58; associational marketplace
    extension of, 91, 182–186 (see also
    associational choices); background
    of, 13–14; gauging popularity
    of, 18–25, 169–177; gun rights
    advocates and, 8; implementation
    schemes, 17–18; indirect mechanisms

of, 17–18; model statute for,
179–182; potential impact
of, 23–25; reporting to NICS
and, 127; Second Amendment
and, 26, 36–38; sign-up options
for (see sign-up options for self-
restriction); state proposals for,
39–58 (see also state proposals
for self-restriction; individual
states); versions of, 19; voluntariness
of, 38. See also self-restriction,
voluntary
Do-Not-Sell List, 13. See also Donna's
Law; purchase bans; self-restriction,
voluntary
driver's license suspension,
105–107
drug courts, 161
drug use, 128, 130–131. See also
prohibited possession categories
DUIs/DWIs, 127, 145. See also
prohibited possession categories

economic associational discrimination,
64
economic coercion, 160
email option, 4, 61–71; associational
choices and, 8, 78–79; back-end
notification, 33, 34, 41, 49, 51,
52, 67–68 (see also reinstatement
of gun rights); constitutional
concerns, 75–79; controversy
over, 67; disclosure and, 75–76;
front-end notification, 33–34, 66,
67, 68; government facilitation
of, 73–79; interim emails, 67, 68;
negotiated exclusion and, 68–70;
self-defense interests and, 78;
in state proposals, 51, 67, 68;
unauthorized purchase attempts
and, 197n10; as updatable across
time, 66. See also registration
options for self-restriction
emergency risk protection orders.
See red flag statutes

employers: discrimination by, 64, 77;
mandatory reporting of red flag
information for, 163
Equal Protection Clause, 96
esketamine, 15
exclusion, negotiated, 68–70
Extreme Risk Protection Order (ERPO),
46. See also red flag statutes

Facebook, 33
Farley, Allen, 40, 41
federalism, 68
felony status, 36, 149. See also
prohibited possession categories
Firearm Owners Protection Act of
1986, 121, 218n6
firearms. See guns
First Amendment, 4–5, 61, 76. See also
associational choices; constitutional
concerns
Florida, gun bounties in, 155
Forefront Suicide Prevention, 55
Fourteenth Amendment, 96
free-speech rights, 61, 65. See also First
Amendment
front-end notification, 33–34, 66, 67,
68. See also email option

gambling self-exclusion programs,
27
Garden, Charlotte, 47
Giffords Law Center, 55, 137
gun accidents, 88
gun control, 132–133; choice-
enhancing/bottom-up, 1–2, 63, 93,
98, 99, 124 (see also self-restriction,
voluntary); top-down/traditional,
1–2, 98, 132–133 (see also National
Instant Criminal Background Check
System [NICS])
Gun Control Act of 1968, 121, 218n6
gun control advocates, state proposals
and, 55
gun deaths, 1. See also suicide, gun
Gun-Free School Zone Act, 81

gun-free zones, 5, 83; binding successors and, 93–95; as choice-enhancing gun control, 99; constitutional concerns, 96–98; defaults and, 84–93; durable, 93–98; individual decisions and, 93; legal consequences for violators, 91; liability and, 91–92; privatizing, 93; resistance to, 82; retailers and, 88–90; signage requirements, 85–86, 95; UP petitions and, 140, 146–147; Westport (Missouri) entertainment district, 80–81, 82–83, 92. *See also* Associational choices; landlords/property owners; property, private

gun policy: constraints on, 1 (*see also* constitutional concerns); enforcing, 122 (*see also* unlawful possession (UP) petitions); political expression and, 21–22; state proposals and, 52. *See also* red flag statutes

gun removal orders. *See* removal of unlawfully possessed guns

gun removal petitions, 6–7, 69. *See also* prohibited possession categories; red flag statutes; unlawful possession (UP) petitions

gun rights advocates, 8, 43, 49–50. *See also* constitutional concerns; National Rifle Association (NRA)

Gun Rights 4 Illinois, 43

gun storage, 141

gun suicide. *See* suicide, gun

gun trusts, 156–159

gun violence, 1. *See also* mass shootings; suicide, gun

Gun Violence Restraining Orders (GVROs), 69. *See also* red flag statutes

Guzzardi, Will, 43

Habib, Cyrus, 47, 50

hallucinations, 111–114, 117–118. *See also* symptom-based restrictions

Harris, Jimmy, 44

Harris, Lee, 39, 40

health care advance directive, 29–31

Health Insurance Portability and Accountability Act (HIPAA), 130

Heston, Charlton, 126

Heyrman, Mark, 42

homicides, gun, 1. *See also* mass shootings

hospitalization, involuntary, 30, 37–38, 107–108

hunting, x, 84, 94–95

identity verification, 32–33

Illinois: gun bounties in, 155–156; gun removal in, 136, 137, 224n72; self-restriction proposal, 42–43, 53

Immigration and Customs Enforcement (ICE), 219n15

immigration status, 131–132, 149, 220n26

immunity, tort, 163

implementation of self-restriction, 31–35; duration/durability of, 35 (*see also* reinstatement of gun rights); privacy/confidentiality and, 33–34; registration in, 32–33 (*see also* sign-up options for self-restriction); scope of restriction in, 34–35 (*see also* possession bans; purchase bans); voluntariness of self-restriction and, 31–33

incarceration, mass, 148, 151

incentives to report dangerousness, 154–165

Indiana, red flag petitions in, 149, 151

ineligibility to purchase or possess firearms. *See* possession bans; prohibited possession categories; purchase bans; unlawful possession

in personam no-guns registry choice, 90

in rem restrictions, 83, 90. *See also* gun-free zones

Inslee, Jay, 50

institutions, mandatory reporting of red flag information for, 162–164

insurance, 62, 63, 70, 77, 163–164,
    196n3. *See also* associational
    choices
interim emails, 67, 68
Interstate Identification Index (III), 130,
    219n15
invitations, 84, 186
involuntary treatment, 30, 37–38,
    107–108, 145
Irby, Courtney, 120, 125, 152
Irby, Joseph, 120–121
Israel Defense Forces, 15

juvenile offenders, 146

Kagan, Elena, x
Kansas City (Missouri). *See* Westport
    (Missouri) Entertainment District
Kimbrough, Kim, 81
Kroger, 89

landlords / property owners, 63, 77;
    demand for self-exclusion and, 69;
    email notifications and, 68; liability
    and, 91–92; in model statute, 186;
    no-carry lease presumption, 87–88;
    private choices of, 83; prohibition of
    firearms and, 205–206n52; right-to-
    carry defaults and, 86, 87; signage
    requirements, 85–86, 95; in state
    proposals, 51, 67. *See also* associa-
    tional choices; gun-free zones;
    property, private; retailers
Latham, Othni, 40
laws. *See* gun policy; red flag
    statutes
legislation. *See* Donna's Law;
    model statutes; self-restriction,
    voluntary; state proposals for
    self-restriction
legislators, relationships with, 46, 54
Leno, Mark, 138
Lethality Assessment Program,
    217n61
liability, 91, 163

libertarianism, 2, 62–63, 72. *See also*
    bottom-up / choice-enhancing gun
    control
license, gun, 52, 105, 106–107
life crises, 15
location restrictions, 81–82. *See also*
    gun-free zones
Lott, John, 82, 90
Louisiana: no-carry default in, 87;
    self-restriction proposal in, 44, 54, 56
Ludwig, Jens, 70

MacArthur Foundation, 113
mandatory reporting of relevant red
    flag information, 162–164
manner and place seizures, 140–144
marijuana, 122. *See also* drug use
Martin, Gary, 136
Martini, Danny, 44
Massachusetts, self-restriction
    proposal in, 45–47, 51, 52–53, 55
mass shootings: Aurora, Colorado, 82;
    gun removal and, 136, 137; Gary
    Martin and, 136; mental health and,
    111–112, 132; Navy Yard, 103–104,
    108, 111, 118–119; Parkland,
    Florida, 1; Travis Reinking and, 137,
    142; Dylann Roof and, 132; Virginia
    Tech, 164. *See also* workplace violence
McDonald v. Chicago, 4
mental health: disclosure about, 46;
    eligibility for self-restriction and,
    46; gun ownership prohibition and,
    131–132; involuntary treatment
    and, 30, 37–38, 107–108; mass
    shootings and, 111–112, 132;
    suicide and, 132; treatment and,
    109; violence and, 112–114, 145
mental health gun regulations: criteria in,
    107–111; diagnosis- and treatment-
    based restrictions, 107–111, 112, 114;
    federal restriction, 107–108; finding
    of dangerousness and, 110–111; states
    and, 108–111. *See also* red flag statutes;
    symptom-based restrictions

misdemeanors, 145
model statutes, 3, 65, 167, 179–186,
    197n10. *See also* email option;
    registry, proposed; state proposals
    for self-restriction
Mother Jones, 132

NAACP, 81
NAACP v. Alabama, 73, 74, 76
Nathan, Donna, 13, 25, 44. *See also*
    Donna's Law
National Alliance on Mental Illness
    (NAMI), 114
National Crime Information Center
    (NCIC), 219n15
National Instant Criminal Back-
    ground Check System (NICS),
    39–40; awareness of unlawful
    possession and, 124; drug use
    and, 128, 130–131; gun trusts and,
    159; incentivizing states to improve
    reporting to, 164–165; integrating
    gun removal petitions with, 7;
    reporting requirements, 133, 134;
    in self-restriction proposals, 50,
    53; states' supplementation of,
    127, 144–147; underinclusion in,
    128–134, 231n30, 231n32; UP
    petitions and, 125–126, 133–134,
    141, 143, 152. *See also* reporting,
    mandatory
National Institute of Mental Health,
    131
National Research Council (NRC), 16
National Rifle Association (NRA),
    8, 48, 122. *See also* gun rights
    advocates
National Survey on Drug Use and
    Health (NSDUH), 128, 131, 139,
    148, 165
Navy Yard shooting, 103–104, 108,
    111, 118–119
NCHIP, 132
NIAA (NICS Improvement Amend-
    ment Act), 164–165

NICS (National Instant Criminal
    Background Check System). *See*
    National Instant Criminal Back-
    ground Check System (NICS)
no-carry defaults, 84–93, 186
no-knock SWAT raids, 138
notarization, 32, 53. *See also* sign-up
    options for self-restriction

Oregon, self-restriction proposal in,
    43–44
Ostas, Joseph, 45, 55
owners of real property. *See* landlords/
    property owners

paranoia, 111–113, 117–118
Parkland (Florida) shooting, 1. *See
    also* mass shootings
Pedersen, Jamie, 48, 50, 67, 68
penalties, for failure to report
    dangerousness, 154, 162–165
Pittman, Trip, 40–41
Planned Parenthood v. Casey, 74–75
police, gun removal and, 126
policy, gun. *See* gun policy
political affiliation/expression: gun-free
    zones and, 87; gun policy and,
    21–22; likelihood of signing up for
    self-restriction and, 23
Positive and Negative Symptoms
    Questionnaire (PNS-Q), 117
possession: interpretation of, 34;
    self-defense imperative and, 37
possession bans, 34–35, 44; enforce-
    ment of, 125–126; scope of, 37; in
    state proposals, 54. *See also* gun
    removal petitions; prohibited posses-
    sion categories; removal of unlawfully
    possessed guns; unlawful possession;
    unlawful possession (UP) petitions
privacy/confidentiality, 32, 33–34, 50
prohibited possession categories, 7,
    121–122, 218n6; gun removal
    petitions and, 7; immigration status
    and, 131–132; mental health and,

131–132; potential racial disparities in, 148–151; state prohibitors, 7; underage possessors, 139, 146, 147, 165; UP petitions and, 126, 143–147. *See also* National Instant Criminal Background Check System (NICS)
prohibitor option, 126–127
property, private, 5, 80. *See also* associational choices; gun-free zones; landlords/property owners
prosecution, threats of, 160–161
psychiatric advance directive (PAD), 30
public space, 80–81. *See also* gun-free zones
purchase bans, 35, 39–40, 44, 54, 125

race/ethnicity, UP petitions and, 148–151
racial profiling, 81
Rayfield, Dan, 43
red flag petitions, 149. *See also* unlawful possession (UP) petitions
red flag statutes, 5–7, 46, 123; analogies for, 105–107; disclosure of risk and, 8; discretionary dangerousness approach, 107, 110–111, 115, 123–124; gaps in, 104–105, 115; gun removal orders and, 122–123, 124; incentives to report dangerousness and, 154–162; limited petition power in, 106; mass shootings and, 103; NICS and, 7, 133, 134; penalties for failure to report dangerousness, 162–165; race/ethnicity and, 149, 151; suicide prevention and, 111, 112. *See also* dangerousness; gun policy; mental health gun regulations; symptom-based restrictions
registration options for self-restriction. *See* sign-up options for self-restriction
registry, national, 30. *See also* National Instant Criminal Background Check System (NICS)

registry, proposed, 62–71. *See also* email option
Reinking, Travis, 137, 142
reinstatement of gun rights: approval for, 28; associational choices and, 66; notification of, 67, 68 (*see also* back-end notification); in state proposals, 42, 47, 48, 52, 68; waiting period for, 53
religion, 65
removal of unlawfully possessed guns, 121–152; at federal level, 135; mass shootings and, 137; red flag statutes and, 122–123 (*see also* red flag statutes); resistance to, 126; at state level, 135–139; violence and, 151. *See also* gun removal petitions; unlawful possession (UP) petitions
reporting, mandatory, 133–134, 162–164. *See also* National Instant Criminal Background Check System (NICS)
rescission. *See* back-end notification; reinstatement of gun rights
res ipsa loquitur, 123
restraining orders, 69, 123, 133
retailers: gun policies of, 88–90; liability of, 163; self-restriction and, 29. *See also* landlords/property owners
revocation of self-restriction. *See* reinstatement of gun rights
right-to-carry default, 84–93
risk categories. *See* prohibited possession categories
Roof, Dylann, 132

safety plans, 17–18
sales, gun, 90. *See also* purchase bans
Sargent, Melissa, 47
Scalia, Antonin, x
schools, no-carry default for, 85
school shootings. *See* mass shootings
Schultz, Howard, 89

Scopelitis, Andrea, 46
Second Amendment, 1; associational discrimination and, 64; Donna's Law/self-restriction and, 26, 36–38; email option and, 76; private gun-free zones and, 96–98; reinstatement of rights of, 147; self-defense imperative and, 37, 76–77; *Silvester v. Harris*, 36; waiting period and, 36; waivers of rights of, 3, 37 (*see also* Donna's Law; self-restriction, voluntary)
self-defense, 37, 64, 76–77, 78, 79
self-restriction, voluntary: communication about, 197n8 (*see also* email option); described, 2–3; duration/durability of, 28, 35 (*see also* reinstatement of gun rights); effectiveness of, 28; eligibility for, 46, 52–53; enforcement of, 28; gauging popularity of, 18–25, 169–177; implementation of, 31–35; model statutes for, 179–186 (*see also* model statutes); opposition to, 43, 49–50 (*see also* constitutional concerns; gun rights advocates); privatization of, 28–29; promotion of, 47; retailers and, 29; revocation of (*see* reinstatement of gun rights); sign-up options for (*see* sign-up options for self-restriction); versions of, 19, 23, 179–186; veterans and, 23. *See also* Donna's Law; gun control: choice-enhancing/bottom-up; state proposals for self-restriction
Shafer-Ray, Reed, 46, 54–55
Shelley v. Kraemer, 96–97
sidewalks, privatizing, 80. *See also* gun-free zones
signage requirements for landlords/property owners, 85–86, 95
sign-up options for self-restriction, 30, 37; in adopted bills, 57; costs of, 56; demand for, 63; ease of, 32; online registration, 32–33, 39, 41, 44,

56; in state proposals, 41, 44, 48, 49, 53, 56
Silvester v. Harris, 36
Skaggs, Adam, 137
smoke-free environments, 83
South Carolina, no-carry default in, 87, 91
stalking, 145–146
Starbucks, 89
state action, 73–79
state proposals for self-restriction, 39–58; associational discrimination and, 51–52; confidentiality in, 50; email option in, 51, 67, 68; existing gun laws and, 52; funding and, 56–57; lobbying strategy for, 54–57; NICS in, 50, 53; opposition to, 43, 49–50; purchase vs. possession bans in, 54; reinstatement in, 42, 47, 48, 52, 68; scope of restriction in, 53. *See also individual states*
states/District of Columbia: concealed carry reciprocity bills, 105; incentivizing to improve reporting, 164–165; as laboratories of democracy, 39, 51, 68; location restrictions in, 81–82; mental health gun regulations and, 108–111; model statutes for, 167, 179–186; NICS enhancement and, 127, 144–147; no-carry defaults in, 87, 91; private gun-free zones and, 97; prohibition by, 133; prohibitor option, 126–127; removal and, 135–139; right-to-carry defaults in, 85–88; underreporting from, 128, 130–131, 133, 219n15, 231n32; UP petitions and, 144–147. *See also individual states*
Stevens, John Paul, 4
stickK.com, 26
storage, gun, 141
streets, privatizing, 80. *See also* gun-free zones
Stuber, Jennifer, 48–49, 55
successors, binding, 93–95

suicidal impulse, 14–15
suicide: assessing potential for, 117; mental health and, 132; motivations for, 14–15; safety plans and, 17–18; substitution of methods, 15
suicide, gun: among youth, 147; delay period and, 15–17; rate of, 1, 3; success of attempts, 15; types of guns used, 53–54. *See also* self-restriction, voluntary
suicide rate/risk, 1, 3; among veterans, 22–23; gun access and, 14, 17, 24; of individuals released from involuntary hospitalization, 107–108
Surovell, Scott, 58
survivor-advocates, 54–55
symptom-based restrictions, 5–6, 103–119; assessing symptoms, 116–118; counterarguments to, 114–116; empirical support for, 111–114. *See also* mental health gun regulations; prohibited possession categories; red flag statutes

temporary restraining orders (TROs), 123, 133
tenants. *See* landlords/property owners
Tennessee, self-restriction proposal in, 39–40
Tennessee Bureau of Investigation (TBI), 40
Terrorist Watch List, 146
top-down/traditional gun control, 1–2, 98, 132–133. *See also* National Instant Criminal Background Check System (NICS)
transfer-in-crisis paradigm, 48, 49
transparency, default rules and, 90
treatment, coercive, 30, 37–38, 107–108, 145
treatment-based restrictions, 107–111, 112, 114. *See also* prohibited possession categories; red flag statutes

Trump, Donald, 21, 23
trusts, 156–159
Tseng, Samuel Hsin-yu, 70
Tyler, Clifford Charles, 37–38

underage possessors, 139, 146, 147, 165
Uniform Conservation Easement Act, 94
Uniform Trust Code, 158
United States Postal Service, 97
unlawful possession: awareness/reporting of, 124–125, 138 (*see also* removal of unlawfully possessed guns; unlawful possession (UP) petitions); crime statistics and, 139–140; extent of, 139–140. *See also* possession bans; prohibited possession categories
unlawful possession (UP) petitions, 121–152; awareness of unlawful possession and, 124–125, 142–143; as bottom-up gun control, 124; caveats, 148–152; enforcement of, 125; gun-free zones and, 140, 146–147; gun removal and, 122–123, 126, 134–140; immigration status and, 149; incentives for reporting, 153–165; manner and place seizures, 140–144; NICS and, 125–126, 133–134, 141, 143; potential racial disparities, 148–151; preventing overstepping, 152; prohibited categories and, 126, 143–147; proposal, 140–147; states and, 144–147; underage individuals and, 147. *See also* gun removal petitions; possession bans; prohibited possession categories; removal of unlawfully possessed guns
UP (unlawful possession) petitions. *See* unlawful possession (UP) petitions
Utah, self-restriction proposal in, 58

Vars, Fredrick, 30, 39–41, 43, 44, 47, 48
verification, 65. *See also* email
    option
Verrill, Anne, 76
veterans, 22–23, 169–172, 174–177
violence: mental health and, 145;
    predictions of, 112–114 (*see also*
    red flag statutes)
violence, domestic, 153
Violence Against Women Act of
    1994, 121
Violence Against Women Reauthoriza-
    tion Act of 2019, 146
Virginia, adoption of Donna's Law in,
    57–58
Virginia Tech shooting, 164
voluntary restriction. *See* self-restriction,
    voluntary
voting, disclosure of, 72–73

Waffle House shooting, 137, 142
waiting periods: effects of, 23–24;
    gun suicide and, 15–17; Second
Amendment and, 36; in state
    proposals, 41–42, 49, 50, 53
Walmart, 29, 89–90
warning signs, 6. *See also* red flag
    statutes
Washington State: gun removal in,
    223n57; proposals in, 47–50, 51–52,
    53, 55, 56, 67, 68
Westport (Missouri) entertainment
    district, 80–81, 82–83, 92
Wisconsin, 47; self-restriction
    proposal in, 52, 53–54; tort
    immunity in, 163
witness slips, 43
Wooster v. Dept. of Fish and Game, 94
workplace violence, 64, 77, 136.
    See also mass shootings

YouGov, 20, 169
youth: suicide among, 147. *See also*
    underage possessors
Youth Handgun Safety Act of 1994,
    139